DECOMPOSITION METHODOLOGY FOR KNOWLEDGE DISCOVERY AND DATA MINING

THEORY AND APPLICATIONS

SERIES IN MACHINE PERCEPTION AND ARTIFICIAL INTELLIGENCE*

Editors: **H. Bunke** (Univ. Bern, Switzerland)
P. S. P. Wang (Northeastern Univ., USA)

*For the complete list of titles in this series, please write to the Publisher.

eries in Machine Perception and Artificial Intelligence – Vol. 61

DECOMPOSITION METHODOLOGY FOR KNOWLEDGE DISCOVERY AND DATA MINING

THEORY AND APPLICATIONS

Oded Maimon
Lior Rokach
Tel-Aviv University, Israel

 World Scientific

NEW JERSEY • LONDON • SINGAPORE • BEIJING • SHANGHAI • HONG KONG • TAIPEI • CHENNAI

Published by

World Scientific Publishing Co. Pte. Ltd.

5 Toh Tuck Link, Singapore 596224

USA office: 27 Warren Street, Suite 401-402, Hackensack, NJ 07601

UK office: 57 Shelton Street, Covent Garden, London WC2H 9HE

British Library Cataloguing-in-Publication Data
A catalogue record for this book is available from the British Library.

DECOMPOSITION METHODOLOGY FOR KNOWLEDGE DISCOVERY AND
DATA MINING: THEORY AND APPLICATIONS
Series in Machine Perception and Artificial Intelligence — Vol. 61

ISBN-13 978-981-256-079-7
ISBN-10 981-256-079-3

Printed in Singapore

To our families

Oded Maimon and Lior Rokach

Preface

Data mining is the science and technology of exploring data in order to discover previously unknown patterns. It is a part of the overall process of knowledge discovery in databases (KDD). The accessibility and abundance of information today makes data mining a matter of considerable importance and necessity.

One of the most practical approaches in data mining is to use induction algorithms for constructing a model by generalizing from given data. The induced model describes and explains phenomena which are hidden in the data. Given the recent growth of the field as well as its long history, it is not surprising that several mature approaches to induction are now available to the practitioner. However according to the "no free lunch" theorem, there is no single approach that outperforms all others in all possible domains. Evidently, in the presence of a vast repertoire of techniques and the complexity and diversity of the explored domains, the main challenge today in data mining is to know how to utilize this repertoire in order to achieve maximum reliability, comprehensibility and complexity.

Multiple classifiers methodology is considered an effective way of overcoming this challenge. The basic idea is to build a model by integrating multiple models. Researchers distinguish between two multiple classifier methodologies: ensemble methodology and decomposition methodology. Ensemble methodology combines a set of models, each of which solves the same original task. Decomposition methodology breaks down the classification task into several manageable classification tasks, enabling each inducer to solve a different task

This book focuses on decomposition in general data mining tasks and for classification tasks in particular. The book presents a complete methodology for decomposing classification problems into smaller and more manageable sub-problems that are solvable by using existing tools. The various elements are then joined together to solve the initial problem.

The benefits of decomposition methodology in data mining include: increased performance (classification accuracy); conceptual simplification of the problem; enhanced feasibility for huge databases; clearer and more comprehensible results; reduced runtime by solving smaller problems and by using parallel/distributed computation; and the opportunity of using different solution techniques for individual sub-problems. These features are discussed in the book.

Obviously the most essential question that decomposition methodology should be able to answer is whether a given classification problem should be decomposed and in what manner. The main theory presented in this book is that the decomposition can be achieved by recursively performing a sequence of single, elementary decompositions. The book introduces several fundamental and elementary decomposition methods, namely: Attribute Decomposition, Space Decomposition, Sample Decomposition, Function Decomposition, and Concept Decomposition. We propose a unifying framework for using these methods in real applications.

The book shows that the decomposition methods developed here extend the envelope of problems that data mining can efficiently solve. These methods also enhance the comprehensibility of the results that emerge and suggest more efficient implementation of knowledge discovery conclusions.

In this comprehensive study of decomposition methodology, we try to answer several vital questions:

- What types of elementary decomposition methods exist in concept learning?
- Which elementary decomposition type performs best for which problem? What factors should one take into account when choosing the appropriate decomposition type?
- Given an elementary type, how should we infer the best decomposition structure automatically?
- How should the sub-problems be re-composed to represent the original concept learning?

The decomposition idea shares properties with other fields mainly ensemble methods, structured induction and distributed data mining. Numerous researches have been performed in these areas and the methodology described in this book exploits the fruits of these insightful studies. However, the book introduces a broader methodology, which results from a rather different motivation: the desire to decompose data mining tasks and gain the benefit mentioned above.

This book was written to provide investigators in the fields of information systems, engineering, computer science, statistics and management, with a comprehensive source for decomposition techniques. In addition, those engaged in the social sciences, psychology, medicine, genetics, and other data-rich fields can very much benefit from this book.

Much of the material in this book has been developed and taught in undergraduate and graduate courses at Tel Aviv University. In particular we would like to acknowledge four distinguished graduate students that contributed to this book: Omri Arad, Lital Keshet, Inbal Lavi and Anat Okon. Therefore, the book can also serve as a text or reference book for graduate/advanced undergraduate level courses in data mining and machine learning. Practitioners among the readers may be particularly interested in the descriptions of real-world data mining projects performed with decomposition methodology.

Oded Maimon
Lior Rokach

Contents

Chapter 1

Knowledge Discovery and Data Mining: Concepts and Fundamental Aspects

1.1 Overview

The goal of this chapter is to summarize the preliminary background required for this book. The chapter provides an overview of concepts from various interrelated fields used in the subsequent chapters. It starts by defining basic arguments from data mining and supervised machine learning. Next, there is a review on some common induction algorithms and a discussion on their advantages and drawbacks. Performance evaluation techniques are then presented and finally, open challenges in the field are discussed.

1.2 Data Mining and Knowledge Discovery

Data mining is the science and technology of exploring data in order to discover previously unknown patterns. Data Mining is a part of the overall process of Knowledge Discovery in databases (KDD). The accessibility and abundance of information today makes data mining a matter of considerable importance and necessity.

Most data mining techniques are based on inductive learning (see [Mitchell (1997)]), where a model is constructed explicitly or implicitly by generalizing from a sufficient number of training examples. The underlying assumption of the inductive approach is that the trained model is applicable to future, unseen examples. Strictly speaking, any form of inference in which the conclusions are not deductively implied by the premises can be thought of as induction.

Traditionally *data collection* is considered to be one of the most important stages in data analysis. An analyst (e.g., a statistician) used the available domain knowledge to select the variables to be collected. The number of variables selected was usually small and the collection of their values could be done manually (e.g., utilizing hand-written records or oral interviews). In the case of computer-aided analysis, the analyst had to enter the collected data into a statistical computer package or an electronic spreadsheet. Due to the high cost of data collection, people learned to make decisions based on limited information.

However, since the information-age, the accumulation of data become easier and storing it inexpensive. It has been estimated that the amount of stored information doubles every twenty months [Frawley *et al.* (1991)]. Unfortunately, as the amount of machine readable information increases, the ability to understand and make use of it does not keep pace with its growth. Data mining is a term coined to describe the process of sifting through large databases in search of interesting patterns and relationships. Practically, Data Mining provides tools by which large quantities of data can be automatically analyzed. Some of the researchers consider the term "Data Mining" as misleading and prefer the term "Knowledge Mining" as it provides a better analogy to gold mining [Klosgen and Zytkow (2002)].

The Knowledge Discovery in Databases (KDD) process was defined my many, for instance [Fayyad *et al.* (1996)] define it as "the nontrivial process of identifying valid, novel, potentially useful, and ultimately understandable patterns in data". [Friedman (1997a)] considers the KDD process as an automatic exploratory data analysis of large databases. [Hand (1998)] views it as a secondary data analysis of large databases. The term "Secondary" emphasizes the fact that the primary purpose of the database was not data analysis. Data Mining can be considered as a central step of the overall process of the Knowledge Discovery in Databases (KDD) process. Due to the centrality of data mining in the KDD process, there are some researchers and practitioners that use the term "data mining" as synonymous to the complete KDD process.

Several researchers, such as [Brachman and Anand (1994)], [Fayyad *et al.* (1996)], [Maimon and Last (2000)] and [Reinartz (2002)] have proposed different ways to divide the KDD process into phases. This book adopts a hybridization of these proposals and suggests breaking the KDD process into the following eight phases. Note that the process is iterative and moving back to previous phases may be required.

(1) Developing an understanding of the application domain, the relevant prior knowledge and the goals of the end-user.

(2) Selecting a data set on which discovery is to be performed.

(3) Data Preprocessing: This stage includes operations for Dimension Reduction (such as Feature Selection and Sampling), Data Cleansing (such as Handling Missing Values, Removal of Noise or Outliers), and Data Transformation (such as Discretization of Numerical Attributes and Attribute Extraction)

(4) Choosing the appropriate Data Mining task such as: classification, regression, clustering and summarization.

(5) Choosing the Data Mining algorithm: This stage includes selecting the specific method to be used for searching patterns.

(6) Employing The Data mining Algorithm.

(7) Evaluating and interpreting the mined patterns.

(8) Deployment: Using the knowledge directly, incorporating the knowledge into another system for further action or simply documenting the discovered knowledge.

1.3   Taxonomy of Data Mining Methods

It is useful to distinguish between two main types of data mining: verification-oriented (the system verifies the user's hypothesis) and discovery-oriented (the system finds new rules and patterns autonomously) [Fayyad *et al.* (1996)]. Figure 1.1 illustrates this taxonomy.

Discovery methods are methods that automatically identify patterns in the data. The discovery method branch consists of prediction methods versus description methods. Description-oriented Data Mining methods focus on (the part of) understanding the way the underlying data operates, where prediction-oriented methods aim to build a behavioral model that can get newly and unseen samples and is able to predict values of one or more variables related to the sample.

However, some prediction-oriented methods can also help provide understanding of the data.

Most of the discovery-oriented techniques are based on inductive learning [Mitchell (1997)], where a model is constructed explicitly or implicitly by generalizing from a sufficient number of training examples . The underlying assumption of the inductive approach is that the trained model is applicable to future unseen examples. Strictly speaking, any form of inference in which the conclusions are not deductively implied by the premises can be thought of as induction.

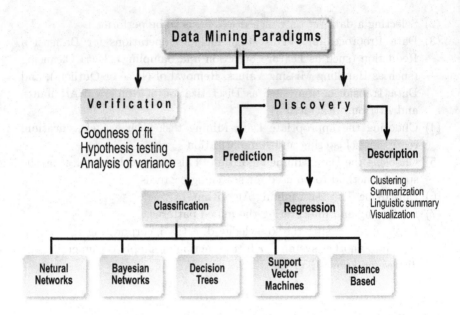

Fig. 1.1   Taxonomy of Data Mining Methods.

Verification methods, on the other hand, deal with evaluation of a hypothesis proposed by an external source (like an expert etc.). These methods include the most common methods of traditional statistics, like goodness-of-fit test, t-test of means, and analysis of variance. These methods are less associated with data mining than their discovery-oriented counterparts because most data mining problems are concerned with selecting a hypothesis (out of a set of hypotheses) rather than testing a known one. The focus of traditional statistical methods is usually on model estimation as opposed to one of the main objectives of data mining: model identification [Elder and Pregibon (1996)].

1.4   Supervised Methods

1.4.1   *Overview*

Another common terminology used by the machine-learning community refers to the prediction methods as supervised learning as opposed to unsupervised learning. Unsupervised learning refers to modeling the distribution of instances in a typical, high-dimensional input space.

According to [Kohavi and Provost (1998)] the term "Unsupervised learning" refers to "learning techniques that group instances without a prespecified dependent attribute". Thus the term unsurprised learning covers only a portion of the description methods presented in Figure 1.1, for instance it does cover clustering methods but it does not cover visualization methods.

Supervised methods are methods that attempt to discover the relationship between input attributes (sometimes called independent variables) and a target attribute (sometimes referred to as a dependent variable). The relationship discovered is represented in a structure referred to as a *Model*. Usually models describe and explain phenomena, which are hidden in the dataset and can be used for predicting the value of the target attribute knowing the values of the input attributes. The supervised methods can be implemented on a variety of domains such as marketing, finance and manufacturing.

It is useful to distinguish between two main supervised models: *Classification Models (Classifiers)* and *Regression Models*. Regression models map the input space into a real-valued domain. For instance, a regressor can predict the demand for a certain product given it characteristics. On the other hand classifiers map the input space into predefined classes. For instance classifiers can be used to classify mortgage consumers to good (fully payback the mortgage on time) and bad (delayed payback). There are many alternatives to represent classifiers, for example: Support Vector Machines, decision trees, probabilistic summaries, algebraic function, etc.

This book deals mainly in classification problems. Along with regression and probability estimation, classification is one of the most studied approaches, possibly one with the greatest practical relevance. The potential benefits of progress in classification are immense since the technique has great impact on other areas, both within data mining and in its applications.

1.4.2 *Training Set*

In a typical supervised learning scenario, a training set is given and the goal is to form a description that can be used to predict previously unseen examples.

The training set can be described in a variety of languages. Most frequently, it is described as a *Bag Instance* of a certain *Bag Schema*. A *Bag Instance* is a collection of tuples (also known as records, rows or instances) that may contain duplicates. Each tuple is described by a vector of attribute values. The bag schema provides the description of the attributes and their domains. For the purpose of this book, a bag schema is denoted as $B(A \cup y)$ where A denotes the set of input attributes containing n attributes: $A = \{a_1, \ldots, a_i, \ldots, a_n\}$ and y represents the class variable or the target attribute.

Attributes (sometimes called field, variable or feature) are typically one of two types: nominal (values are members of an unordered set), or numeric (values are real numbers). When the attribute a_i is nominal it is useful to denote by $dom(a_i) = \{v_{i,1}, v_{i,2}, \ldots, v_{i,|dom(a_i)|}\}$ its domain values, where $|dom(a_i)|$ stands for its finite cardinality. In a similar way, $dom(y) = \{c_1, \ldots, c_{|dom(y)|}\}$ represents the domain of the target attribute. Numeric attributes have infinite cardinalities.

The instance space (the set of all possible examples) is defined as a Cartesian product of all the input attributes domains: $X = dom(a_1) \times dom(a_2) \times \ldots \times dom(a_n)$. The Universal Instance Space (or the *Labeled Instance Space*) U is defined as a Cartesian product of all input attribute domains and the target attribute domain, i.e.: $U = X \times dom(y)$.

The training set is a Bag Instance consisting of a set of m tuples. Formally the training set is denoted as $S(B) = (\langle x_1, y_1 \rangle, \ldots, \langle x_m, y_m \rangle)$ where $x_q \in X$ and $y_q \in dom(y)$.

Usually, it is assumed that the training set tuples are generated randomly and independently according to some fixed and unknown joint probability distribution D over U. Note that this is a generalization of the deterministic case when a supervisor classifies a tuple using a function $y = f(x)$.

This book uses the common notation of bag algebra to present projection (π) and selection (σ) of tuples ([Grumbach and Milo (1996)]. For example given the dataset S presented in Table 1.1, the expression $\pi_{a_2,a_3} \sigma_{a_1 = "Yes" \ AND \ a_4 > 6} S$ result with the dataset presented in Table 1.2.

1.4.3 *Definition of the Classification Problem*

This section defines the classification problem. Originally the machine learning community has introduced the problem of *concept learning*. Concepts are mental categories for objects, events, or ideas that have a common set of features. According to [Mitchell (1997)]: "each concept can be viewed as describing some subset of objects or events defined over a larger set" (e.g., the subset of a vehicle that constitues trucks). To learn a concept is to infer its general definition from a set of examples. This definition may be either explicitly formulated or left implicit, but either way it

Table 1.1   Illustration of a Dataset S having five attributes.

a_1	a_2	a_3	a_4	y
Yes	17	4	7	0
No	81	1	9	1
Yes	17	4	9	0
No	671	5	2	0
Yes	1	123	2	0
Yes	1	5	22	1
No	6	62	1	1
No	6	58	54	0
No	16	6	3	0

Table 1.2   The Result of the Expression $\pi_{a_2,a_3} \sigma_{a_1="Yes"AND_{a_4>6}} S$ Based on the Table 1.1.

a_2	a_3
17	4
17	4
1	5

assigns each possible example to the concept or not. Thus, a concept can be regarded as a function from the Instance space to the Boolean set, namely: $c : X \rightarrow \{-1, 1\}$. Alternatively one can refer a concept c as a subset of X, namely: $\{x \in X : c(x) = 1\}$. A *concept class* C is a set of concepts.

To learn a concept is to infer its general definition from a set of examples. This definition may be either explicitly formulated or left implicit, but either way it assigns each possible example to the concept or not. Thus, a concept can be formally regarded as a function from the set of all possible examples to the Boolean set {True, False}.

Other communities, such as the KDD community prefer to deal with a straightforward extension of *Concept Learning*, known as The *Classification Problem*. In this case we search for a function that maps the set of all possible examples into a predefined set of class labels which are not limited to the Boolean set. Most frequently the goal of the Classifiers Inducers is formally defined as:

Given a training set S with input attributes set $A = \{a_1, a_2, \ldots, a_n\}$ and a nominal target attribute y from an unknown fixed distribution D over the labeled instance space, the goal is to induce an optimal classifier with minimum generalization error.

The Generalization error is defined as the misclassification rate over the distribution D. In case of the nominal attributes it can be expressed as:

$$\varepsilon(I(S), D) = \sum_{\langle x,y \rangle \in U} D(x, y) \cdot L(y, I(S)(x))$$

where $L(y, I(S)(x)$ is the zero one loss function defined as:

$$L(y, I(S)(x)) = \begin{cases} 0 \; if \, y = I(S)(x) \\ 1 \; if \, y \neq I(S)(x) \end{cases} \tag{1.1}$$

In case of numeric attributes the sum operator is replaced with the integration operator.

Consider the training set in Table 1.3 containing data concerning about ten customers. Each customer is characterized by three attributes: Age, Gender and "Last Reaction" (an indication whether the customer has positively responded to the last previous direct mailing campaign). The last attribute ("Buy") describes whether that customer was willing to purchase a product in the current campaign. The goal is to induce a classifier that most accurately classifies a potential customer to "Buyers" and "Non-Buyers" in the current campaign, given the attributes: Age, Gender, Last Reaction.

Table 1.3   An Illustration of Direct Mailing Dataset.

Age	Gender	Last Reaction	Buy
35	Male	Yes	No
26	Female	No	No
22	Male	Yes	Yes
63	Male	No	Yes
47	Female	No	No
54	Male	No	No
27	Female	Yes	Yes
38	Female	No	Yes
42	Female	Yes	Yes
19	Male	No	No

1.4.4   *Induction Algorithms*

An *Induction algorithm*, or more concisely an *Inducer* (also known as learner), is an entity that obtains a training set and forms a model that generalizes the relationship between the input attributes and the target attribute. For example, an inducer may take as an input specific training tuples with the corresponding class label, and produce a *classifier*.

The notation I represents an inducer and $I(S)$ represents a model which was induced by performing I on a training set S. Using $I(S)$ it is possible to predict the target value of a tuple x_q. This prediction is denoted as $I(S)(x_q)$.

Given the long history and recent growth of the field, it is not surprising that several mature approaches to induction are now available to the practitioner.

Classifiers may be represented differently from one inducer to another. For example, C4.5 [Quinlan (1993)] represents model as a decision tree while Naïve Bayes [Duda and Hart (1973)] represents a model in the form of probabilistic summaries. Furthermore, inducers can be deterministic (as in the case of C4.5) or stochastic (as in the case of back propagation)

The classifier generated by the inducer can be used to classify an unseen tuple either by explicitly assigning it to a certain class (Crisp Classifier) or by providing a vector of probabilities representing the conditional probability of the given instance to belong to each class (Probabilistic Classifier). Inducers that can construct Probabilistic Classifiers are known as Probabilistic Inducers. In this case it is possible to estimate the conditional probability $\hat{P}_{I(S)}(y = c_j \,|a_i = x_{q,i} \; ; i = 1, \ldots, n)$ of an observation x_q. Note the addition of the "hat" — ˆ — to the conditional probability estimation is used for distinguishing it from the actual conditional probability.

The following sections briefly review some of the major approaches to concept learning: Decision tree induction, Neural Networks, Genetic Algorithms, instance-based learning, statistical methods, Bayesian methods and Support Vector Machines. This review focuses more on methods that have the greatest attention in this book.

1.5 Rule Induction

Rule induction algorithms generate a set of if-then rules that jointly represent the target function. The main advantage that rule induction offers is its high comprehensibility. Most of the Rule induction algorithms are based on the separate and conquer paradigm [Michalski (1983)]. For that reason these algorithms are capable of finding simple axis parallel frontiers, are well suited to symbolic domains, and can often dispose easily of irrelevant attributes; but they can have difficulty with nonaxisparallel frontiers, and suffer from the fragmentation problem (i.e., the available data dwindles as induction progresses [Pagallo and Huassler (1990)] and the small disjuncts problem i.e., rules covering few training examples have a high error rate [Holte *et al.* (1989)].

1.6   Decision Trees

A Decision tree is a classifier expressed as a recursive partition of the instance space. A decision tree consists of nodes that form a *Rooted Tree*, meaning it is a Directed Tree with a node called root that has no incoming edges. All other nodes have exactly one incoming edge. A node with outgoing edges is called internal node or test nodes. All other nodes are called leaves (also known as terminal nodes or decision nodes).

In a decision tree, each internal node splits the instance space into two or more subspaces according to a certain discrete function of the input attributes values. In the simplest and most frequent case each test considers a single attribute, such that the instance space is partitioned according to the attribute's value. In the case of numeric attributes the condition refers to a range.

Each leaf is assigned to one class representing the most appropriate target value. Usually the most appropriate target value is the class with the greatest representation, because selecting this value minimizes the zero-one loss. However if a different loss function is used then a different class may be selected in order to minimize the loss function. Alternatively the leaf may hold a probability vector indicating the probability of the target value having a certain value.

Instances are classified by navigating them from the root of the tree down to a leaf, according to the outcome of the tests along the path.

Figure 1.2 describes a decision tree to the classification problem illustrated in Table 1.3 (whether or not a potential customer will respond to a direct mailing). Internal nodes are represented as circles whereas leaves are denoted as triangles. The node "Last R" stands for the attribute "Last Reaction". Note that this decision tree incorporates both nominal and numeric attributes. Given this classifier, the analyst can predict the response of a potential customer (by sorting it down the tree), and understand the behavioral characteristics of the potential customers regarding direct mailing. Each node is labeled with the attribute it tests, and its branches are labeled with its corresponding values.

In case of numeric attributes, decision trees can be geometrically interpreted as a collection of hyperplanes, each orthogonal to one of the axes.

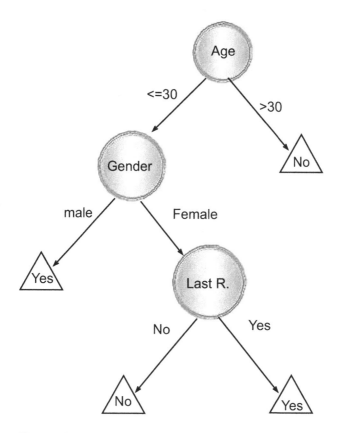

Fig. 1.2   Decision Tree Presenting Response to Direct Mailing.

Naturally, decision makers prefer a less complex decision tree, as it is considered more comprehensible. Furthermore, according to [Breiman *et al.* (1984)] the tree complexity has a crucial effect on its accuracy performance. Usually large trees are obtained by over fitting the data and hence exhibit poor generalization ability. Nevertheless a large decision tree can be accurate if it was induced without over fitting the data. The tree complexity is explicitly controlled by the stopping criteria used and the pruning method employed. Usually the tree complexity is measured by one of the following metrics: The total number of nodes, Total number of leaves, Tree

Depth and Number of attributes used.

Decision tree induction is closely related to rule induction. Each path from the root of a decision tree to one of its leaves can be transformed into a rule simply by conjoining the tests along the path to form the antecedent part, and taking the leaf's class prediction as the class value. For example, one of the paths in Figure 1.2 can be transformed into the rule: "If customer age $\leq$ 30, and the gender of the customer is "Male" — then the customer will respond to the mail". The resulting rule set can then be simplified to improve its comprehensibility to a human user, and possibly its accuracy [Quinlan (1987)]. A survey of methods for constructing decision trees can be found in the following chapter.

1.7   Bayesian Methods

1.7.1   *Overview*

Bayesian approaches employ probabilistic concept representations, and range from the Naïve Bayes [Domingos and Pazzani (1997)] to Bayesian networks. The basic assumption of Bayesian reasoning is that the relation between attributes can be represented as a probability distribution [Maimon and Last (2000)]. Moreover if the problem examined is supervised then the objective is to find the conditional distribution of the target attribute given the input attribute.

1.7.2   *Naïve Bayes*

1.7.2.1   *The Basic Naïve Bayes Classifier*

The most straightforward Bayesian learning method is the Naïve Bayesian classifier [Duda and Hart (1973)]. This method uses a set of discriminant functions for estimating the probability of a given instance to belong to a certain class. More specifically it uses Bayes rule to compute the probability of each possible value of the target attribute given the instance, assuming the input attributes are conditionally independent given the target attribute.

Due to the fact that this method is based on the simplistic, and rather unrealistic, assumption that the causes are conditionally independent given the effect, this method is well known as Naïve Bayes.

The predicted value of the target attribute is the one which maximizes the following calculated probability:

$$v_{MAP}(x_q) = \underset{c_j \in dom(y)}{\operatorname{argmax}} \hat{P}(y = c_j) \cdot \prod_{i=1}^{n} \hat{P}(a_i = x_{q,i} \mid y = c_j) \tag{1.2}$$

where $\hat{P}(y = c_j)$ denotes the estimation for the *a-priori* probability of the target attribute obtaining the value c_j. Similarly $\hat{P}(a_i = x_{q,i} \mid y = c_j)$ denotes the conditional probability of the input attribute a_i obtaining the value $x_{q,i}$ given that the target attribute obtains the value c_j. Note that the hat above the conditional probability distinguishes the probability estimation from the actual conditional probability.

A simple estimation for the above probabilities can be obtained using the corresponding frequencies in the training set, namely:

$$\hat{P}(y = c_j) = \frac{|\sigma_{y=c_j} S|}{|S|} \quad ; \quad \hat{P}(a_i = x_{q,i} \mid y = c_j) = \frac{|\sigma_{y=c_j \ AND \ a_i = x_{q,i}} S|}{|\sigma_{y=c_j} S|}$$

Using the Bayes rule, the above equations can be rewritten as:

$$v_{MAP}(x_q) = \underset{c_j \in dom(y)}{\operatorname{argmax}} \frac{\prod_{i=1}^{n} \hat{P}(y=c_j \mid a_i = x_{q,i})}{\hat{P}(y=c_j)^{n-1}} \tag{1.3}$$

Or alternatively, after using the log function as:

$$v_{MAP}(x_q) = \underset{c_j \in dom(y)}{\operatorname{argmax}} \log\left(\hat{P}(y = c_j)\right)$$
$$+ \sum_{i=1}^{n} \left(\log\left(\hat{P}(y = c_j \mid a_i = x_{q,i})\right) - \log\left(\hat{P}(y = c_j)\right)\right)$$

If the "naive" assumption is true, this classifier can easily be shown to be optimal (i.e. minimizing the generalization error), in the sense of minimizing the misclassification rate or zero-one loss (misclassification rate), by a direct application of Bayes' theorem. [Domingos and Pazzani (1997)] showed that the Naïve Bayes can be optimal under zero-one loss even when the independence assumption is violated by a wide margin. This implies that the Bayesian classifier has a much greater range of applicability than previously thought, for instance for learning conjunctions and disjunctions. Moreover, a variety of empirical research shows surprisingly that this method can perform quite well compared to other methods, even in domains where clear attribute dependencies exist.

The computational complexity of Naïve Bayes is considered very low compared to other methods like decision trees, since no explicit enumeration of possible interactions of various causes is required. More specifically since the Naïve Bayesian classifier combines simple functions of univariate densities, the complexity of this procedure is $O(nm)$.

Furthermore, Naïve Bayes classifiers are also very simple and easy to understand [Kononenko (1990)]. Other advantages of Naïve Bayes are the easy adaptation of the model to incremental learning environments and resistance to irrelevant attributes. The main disadvantage of Naïve Bayes is that it is limited to simplified models only, that in some cases are far from representing the complicated nature of the problem. To understand this weakness, consider a target attribute that cannot be explained by a single attribute, for instance, the Boolean exclusive or function (XOR).

The classification using the Naïve Bayesian classifier is based on all of the available attributes, unless a feature selection procedure is applied as a pre-processing step.

1.7.2.2   *Naïve Bayes for Numeric Attributes*

Originally Naïve Bayes assumes that all input attributes are nominal. If this is not the case then there are some options to bypass this problem:

(1) Pre-Processing: The numeric attributes should be discretized before using the Naïve Bayes. [Domingos and Pazzani (1997)] suggest discretizing each numeric attribute into ten equal-length intervals (or one per observed value, whichever was the least). Obviously there are many other more informed discretization methods that can be applied here and probably obtain better results.
(2) Revising the Naïve Bayes: [John and Langley (1995)] suggests using kernel estimation or single variable normal distribution as part of building the conditional probabilities.

1.7.2.3   *Correction to the Probability Estimation*

Using the probability estimation described above as-is will typically overestimate the probability. This can be problematic especially when a given class and attribute value never co-occur in the training set. This case leads to a zero probability that wipes out the information in all the other probabilities terms when they are multiplied according to the original Naïve Bayes equation.

There are two known corrections for the simple probability estimation which avoid this phenomenon. The following sections describe these corrections.

1.7.2.4 *Laplace Correction*

According to Laplace's law of succession [Niblett (1987)], the probability of the event $y = c_i$ where y is a random variable and c_i is a possible outcome of y which has been observed m_i times out of m observations is:

$$\frac{m_i + kp_a}{m + k}$$

where p_a is an *a-priori* probability estimation of the event and k is the equivalent sample size that determines the weight of the *a-priori* estimation relative to the observed data. According to [Mitchell (1997)] k is called "equivalent sample size" because it represents an augmentation of the m actual observations by additional k virtual samples distributed according to p_a. The above ratio can be rewritten as the weighted average of the *a-priori* probability and the posteriori probability (denoted as p_p):

$$\frac{m_i + k \cdot p_a}{m + k}$$
$$= \frac{m_i}{m} \cdot \frac{m}{m+k} + p_a \cdot \frac{k}{m+k}$$
$$= p_p \cdot \frac{m}{m+k} + p_a \cdot \frac{k}{m+k} =$$
$$= p_p \cdot w_1 + p_a \cdot w_2$$

In the case discussed here the following correction is used:

$$\hat{P}_{Laplace}(a_i = x_{q,i} \,|\, y = c_j) = \frac{\left|\sigma_{y=c_j \, AND \, a_i = x_{q,i}} S\right| + k \cdot p}{\left|\sigma_{y=c_j} S\right| + k} \qquad (1.4)$$

In order to use the above correction, the values of p and k should be selected. It is possible to use $p = 1/|dom(y)|$ and $k = |dom(y)|$. [Ali and Pazzani (1996)] suggest to use $k = 2$ and $p = 1/2$ in any case even if $|dom(y)| > 2$ in order to emphasize the fact that the estimated event is always compared to the opposite event. [Kohavi *et al.* (1997)] suggest to use $k = |dom(y)| / |S|$ and $p = 1/|dom(y)|$.

1.7.2.5 *No Match*

According to [Clark and Niblett (1989)] only zero probabilities are corrected and replaced by the following value: $p_a/|S|$. [Kohavi *et al.* (1997)] suggest to use $p_a = 0.5$. They also empirically compared the Laplace correction and the No-Match correction and indicate that there is no significant difference between them. However, both of them are significantly better than not performing any correction at all.

1.7.3 *Other Bayesian Methods*

A more complicated model can be represented by Bayesian belief networks [Pearl (1988)]. Usually each node in a Bayesian network represents a certain attribute. The immediate predecessors of a node represent the attributes on which the node depends. By knowing their values, it is possible to determine the conditional distribution of this node. Bayesian networks have the benefit of a clearer semantics than more ad hoc methods, and provide a natural platform for combining domain knowledge (in the initial network structure) and empirical learning (of the probabilities, and possibly of new structure). However, inference in Bayesian networks can have a high time complexity, and as tools for classification learning they are not yet as mature or well tested as other approaches. More generally, as [Buntine (1990)] notes, the Bayesian paradigm extends beyond any single representation, and forms a framework in which many learning tasks can be usefully studied.

1.8   Other Induction Methods

1.8.1 *Neural Networks*

Neural network methods are based on representing the concept as a network of nonlinear units [Anderson and Rosenfeld (2000)]. The most frequently used type of unit, incorporating a sigmoidal nonlinearity, can be seen as a generalization of a propositional rule, where numeric weights are assigned to antecedents, and the output is graded, rather than binary [Towell and Shavlik (1994)].

The multilayer feedforward neural network is the most widely studied neural network, because it is suitable for representing functional relationships between a set of input attributes and one or more target attributes. Multilayer feedforward neural network consists of interconnected units called neurons, which are organized in layers. Each neuron performs a simple task of information processing by converting received inputs into processed outputs. Figure 1.3 illustrates the most frequently used architecture of feedforward neural network. This network consists of neurons (nodes) organized in three layers: input layer, hidden layer, and output layer. The neurons in the input layer correspond to the input attributes and the neurons in the output layer correspond to the target attribute. Neurons in the hidden layer are connected to both input and output neurons and are key to inducing the classifier. Note that the signal flow is one directional from the input layer to the output layer and there are no feedback connections.

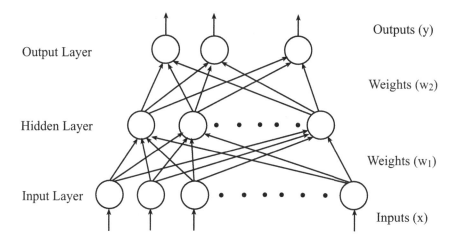

Fig. 1.3   Three-Layer Feedforward Neural Network.

Many search methods can be used to learn these networks, of which the most widely applied one is back propagation [Rumelhart *et al.* (1986)]. This method efficiently propagates values of the evaluation function backward from the output of the network, which then allows the network to be adapted so as to obtain a better evaluation score. Radial basis function (RBF) networks employ units with a Gaussian nonlinearity [Moody and Darken (1989)], and can be seen as a generalization of nearestneighbor methods with an exponential distance function [Poggio and Girosi (1990)]. Most ANNs are based on a unit called perceptron. A perceptron calculates a linear combination of its inputs, and outputs one of two values as a result. Figure 1.4 illustrates the perceptron. The activation function turns the weighted sum of inputs into a two-value output.

Using a single perceptron, it is possible to realize any decision function that can be represented as a hyper-plane in the input attribute space, so that any instance in one side of the plane is assigned to one class, and instances on the other side of the plane are assigned to the other class. The equation for this hyperplane is:

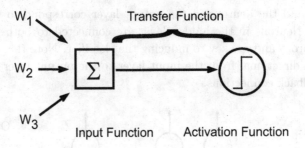

Fig. 1.4   The Perceptron.

$$\sum_{i=1}^{n} w_i \cdot x_i = 0$$

where each w_i is a real-valued weight, that determines the contribution of each input signal x_i to the perceptron output.

Neural networks are remarkable for their learning efficiency and tend to outperform other methods (like decision trees) when no highly relevant attributes exist, but many weakly relevant ones are present. Furthermore, ANN can easily be adjusted as new examples accumulate.

However according to [Lu *et al.* (1996)], the drawbacks of applying neural networks to data mining include: difficulty in interpreting the model, difficulty in incorporating prior knowledge about the application domain in a neural network, and, also, long learning time, both in terms of CPU time, and of manually finding parameter settings that will enable successful learning. The rule extraction algorithm, described in [Lu *et al.* (1996)], makes an effective use of the neural network structure, though the weights of the links between the nodes remain meaningless, and the rules are extracted in a deterministic (Boolean) form. The network is pruned by removing redundant links and units, but removal of entire attributes (Feature selection) is not considered.

1.8.2   *Genetic Algorithms*

Genetic algorithms are a search method that can be applied to learning many different representations, of which the most frequently used one is probably rule sets [Booker *et al.* (1989)]. Genetic algorithms maintain a population of classifiers during learning, as opposed to just one, and search for a better classifier by applying random mutations to them, and exchanging parts between pairs of classifiers that obtain high evaluation scores. This endows them with a potentially greater ability to avoid local minima than is possible with the simple greedy search employed in most learners, but can lead to high computational cost, and to higher risks of finding poor classifiers that appear good on the training data by chance.

1.8.3 *Instancebased Learning*

Instancebased learning algorithms [Aha *et al.* (1991)] are non-parametric general classification algorithms that simply search for similar instances in the labeled database in order to classify a new unlabeled instance. These techniques are able to induce complex frontiers from relatively few examples and are naturally suited to numeric domains, but can be very sensitive to irrelevant attributes and are unable to select different attributes in different regions of the instance space. Another disadvantage of instance-based methods is that it is relatively time consuming to classify a new instance.

The most basic and simplest Instance-based method is the nearest neighbor (NN) classifier, which was first examined by [Fix and Hodges (1957)]. It can be represented by the following rule: to classify an unknown pattern, choose the class of the nearest example in the training set as measured by a distance metric. A common extension is to choose the most common class in the *k nearest neighbors* (kNN).

Despite its simplicity, the nearest neighbor classifier has many advantages over other methods. For instance, it can generalize from a relatively small training set. Namely, compared to other methods, such as decision trees or neural network, nearest neighbor requires smaller training examples to provide effective classification. Moreover, it can incrementally add new information at runtime, thus the nearest neighbor can provide a performance that is competitive when compared to more modern methods such as decision trees or neural networks.

1.8.4 *Support Vector Machines*

Support Vector Machines [Vapnik (1995)] map the input space into a high-dimensional feature space through some non-linear mapping chosen *a-priori* and then construct an optimal separating hyperplan in the new feature space. The method searches for a hyperplan that is optimal according the VC-Dimension theory. Further details and pointers to the literature on these induction paradigms can be found in the above reference and in the following section.

1.9   Performance Evaluation

Evaluating the performance of an inducer is a fundamental aspect of machine learning. As stated above, an inducer receives a training set as input and constructs a classification model that can classify an unseen instance . Both the classifier and the inducer can be evaluated using an evaluation criteria. The evaluation is important for understanding the quality of the model (or inducer), for refining parameters in the KDD iterative process and for selecting the most acceptable model (or inducer) from a given set of models (or inducers).

There are several criteria for evaluating models and inducers. Naturally, classification models with high accuracy are considered better. However, there are other criteria that can be important as well, such as the computational complexity or the comprehensibility of the generated classifier.

1.9.1   *Generalization Error*

Let $I(S)$ represent a classifier generated by an inducer I on S. Recall that the generalization error of $I(S)$ is its probability to misclassify an instance selected according to the distribution D of the instance labeled space. The *Classification Accuracy* of a classifier is one minus the generalization error. The *Training Error* is defined as the percentage of examples in the training set correctly classified by the classifier, formally:

$$\hat{\varepsilon}(I(S), S) = \sum_{\langle x,y \rangle \in S} L\left(y, I(S)(x)\right) \tag{1.5}$$

where $L(y, I(S)(x))$ is the zero-one loss function defined in Equation 1.1.

In this book, classification accuracy is the primary evaluation criterion for experiments. A decomposition is considered beneficial if the accuracy of an inducer improves or remains the same.

Although generalization error is a natural criterion, its actual value is known only in rare cases (mainly synthetic cases). The reason for that is that the distribution D of the instance labeled space is not known.

One can take the training error as an estimation of the generalization error. However, using the training error as-is will typically provide an optimistically biased estimate, especially if the learning algorithm *over-fits* the training data. There are two main approaches for estimating the generalization error: Theoretical and Empirical. In the context of this book we utilize both approaches.

1.9.2 *Theoretical Estimation of Generalization Error*

A low training error does not guarantee low generalization error. There is often a trade-off between the training error and the confidence assigned to the training error as a predictor for the generalization error, measured by the difference between the generalization and training errors. The capacity of the inducer is a determining factor for this confidence in the training error. Indefinitely speaking, the capacity of an inducer indicates the variety of classifiers it can induce. The notion of VC-Dimension presented below can be used as a measure of the inducers capacity.

Inducers with a large capacity, e.g. a large number of free parameters, relative to the size of the training set are likely to obtain a low training error, but might just be memorizing or over-fitting the patterns and hence exhibit a poor generalization ability. In this regime, the low error is likely to be a poor predictor for the higher generalization error. In the opposite regime, when the capacity is too small for the given number of examples, inducers may under-fit the data, and exhibit both poor training and generalization error. For inducers with an insufficient number of free parameters, the training error may be poor, but it is a good predictor for the generalization error. In between these capacity extremes there is an optimal capacity for which the best generalization error is obtained, given the character and amount of the available training data.

In the book "Mathematics of Generalization", [Wolpert (1995)] discuss four theoretical frameworks for estimating the generalization error, namely: PAC, VC and Bayesian, and Statistical Physics. All these frameworks combine the training error (which can be easily calculated) with some penalty function expressing the capacity of the inducers. In this book we employ the VC framework, described in the next section.

1.9.2.1 *VC-Framework*

Of all the major theoretical approaches to learning from examples the Vapnik–Chervonenkis theory [Vapnik (1995)] is the most comprehensive, applicable to regression, as well as classification tasks. It provides general necessary and sufficient conditions for the consistency of the induction procedure in terms of bounds on certain measures. Here we refer to the classical notion of consistency in statistics: both the training error and the generalization error of the induced classifier must converge to the same minimal error value as the training set size tends to infinity. Vapnik's theory also defines a capacity measure of an inducer, the VC-dimension, which is widely used.

VC-theory describes a worst case scenario: the estimates of the difference between the training and generalization errors are bounds valid for any induction algorithm and probability distribution in the labeled space. The bounds are expressed in terms of the size of the training set and the VC-dimension of the inducer.

Theorem 1.1   *The bound on the generalization error of hypothesis space H with finite VC-Dimension d is given by:*

$$|\varepsilon(h, D) - \hat{\varepsilon}(h, S)| \leq \sqrt{\frac{d \cdot (\ln \frac{2m}{d} + 1) - \ln \frac{\delta}{4}}{m}} \quad \begin{array}{l} \forall h \in H \\ \forall \delta > 0 \end{array} \quad (1.6)$$

with probability of $1 - \delta$ where $\hat{\varepsilon}(h, S)$ represents the training error of classifier h measured on training set S of cardinality m and $\varepsilon(h, D)$ represents the generalization error of the classifier h over the distribution D.

The VC dimension is a property of a set of all classifiers, denoted by H, that have been examined by the inducer. For the sake of simplicity we consider classifiers that correspond to the two-class pattern recognition case. In this case, the VC dimension is defined as the maximum number of data points that can be shattered by the set of admissible classifiers. By definition, a set S of m points is shattered by H if and only if for every dichotomy of S there is some classifier in H that is consistent with this dichotomy. In other words, the set S is shattered by H if there are classifiers that split the points into two classes in all of the 2^m possible ways. Note that, if the VC dimension of H is d, then there exists at least one set of d points that can be shattered by H, but in general it will not be true that every set of d points can be shattered by H.

A sufficient condition for consistency of an induction procedure is that the VC-dimension of the inducer is finite. The VC-dimension of a linear classifier is simply the dimension n of the input space, or the number of free parameters of the classifier. The VC-dimension of a general classifier may however be quite different from the number of free parameters and in many cases it might be very difficult to compute it accurately. In this case it is useful to calculate a lower and upper bound for the VC-Dimension, for instance [Schmitt (2002)] have presented these VC bounds for neural networks.

1.9.2.2 *PAC-Framework*

The Probably Approximately Correct (PAC) learning model was introduced by [Valiant (1984)]. This framework can be used to characterize the concept class "that can be reliably learned from a reasonable number of randomly drawn training examples and a reasonable amount of computation" [Mitchell (1997)]. We use the following formal definition of PAC-learnable adapted from [Mitchell (1997)]:

Definition 1.1 Let C be a concept class defined over the input instance space X with n attributes. Let I be an inducer that considers hypothesis space H. C is said to be PAC-learnable by I using H if for all $c \in C$, distributions D over X, ε such that $0 < \varepsilon < 1/2$ and δ such that $0 < \delta < 1/2$, learner I with a probability of at least $(1 - \delta)$ will output a hypothesis $h \in H$ such that $\varepsilon(h, D) \leq \varepsilon$, in time that is polynomial in $1/\varepsilon$, $1/\delta$, n, and $size(c)$, where $size(c)$ represents the encoding length of c in C, assuming some representation for C.

The PAC learning model provides a general bound on the number of training examples sufficient for any consistent learner I examining a finite hypothesis space H with probability at least $(1 - \delta)$ to output a hypothesis $h \in H$ within error ε of the target concept $c \in C \subseteq H$. More specifically, the size of the training set should be: $m \geq \frac{1}{\varepsilon}(\ln(1/\delta) + \ln|H|)$

1.9.3 *Empirical Estimation of Generalization Error*

Another approach for estimating the generalization error is to split the available examples into two groups: training set and test set. First, the training set is used by the inducer to construct a suitable classifier and then we measure the misclassification rate of this classifier on the test set. This test set error usually provides a better estimation to the generalization error than the training error. The reason for that is the fact that the training error usually under-estimates the generalization error (due to the overfitting phenomena).

When data is limited, it is common practice to *resample* the data, that is, partition the data into training and test sets in different ways. An inducer is trained and tested for each partition and the accuracies averaged. By doing this, a more reliable estimate of the true generalization error of the inducer is provided.

Random subsampling and *n-fold cross-validation* are two common methods of resampling. In random subsampling, the data is randomly partitioned into disjoint training and test sets several times. Errors obtained from each partition are averaged. In n-fold cross-validation, the data is randomly split into n mutually exclusive subsets of approximately equal size. An inducer is trained and tested n times; each time it is tested on one of the k folds and trained using the remaining $n-1$ folds.

The cross-validation estimate of the generalization error is the overall number of misclassifications, divided by the number of examples in the data. The random subsampling method has the advantage that it can be repeated an indefinite number of times. However, it has the disadvantage that the test sets are not independently drawn with respect to the underlying distribution of examples. Because of this, using a t-test for paired differences with random subsampling can lead to increased chance of Type I error that is, identifying a significant difference when one does not actually exist. Using a t-test on the generalization error produced on each fold has a lower chance of Type I error but may not give a stable estimate of the generalization error. It is common practice to repeat n fold cross-validation n times in order to provide a stable estimate. However, this of course renders the test sets non-independent and increases the chance of Type I error. Unfortunately, there is no satisfactory solution to this problem. Alternative tests suggested by [Dietterich (1998)] have low chance of Type I error but high chance of Type II error — that is, failing to identify a significant difference when one does actually exist.

Stratification is a process often applied during random subsampling and n-fold crossvalidation. Stratification ensures that the class distribution from the whole dataset is preserved in the training and test sets. Stratification has been shown to help reduce the variance of the estimated error especially for datasets with many classes. Stratified random subsampling with a paired t-test is used herein to evaluate accuracy.

1.9.4 *Bias and Variance Decomposition*

It is well known that the error can be decomposed into three additive components [Kohavi and Wolpert (1996)]: the intrinsic error, the bias error and the variance error.

The intrinsic error represents the error generated due to noise. This quantity is the lower bound of any inducer, i.e. it is the expected error of the Bayes optimal classifier (also known as irreducible error). The bias error of an inducer is the persistent or systematic error that the inducer is expected to make. Variance is a concept closely related to bias. The variance captures random variation in the algorithm from one training set to another, namely it measures the sensitivity of the algorithm to the actual training set, or error due to the training set's finite size. The following equations are a possible mathematical definition for the various components in case of a zero-one loss.

$$t(I, S, c_j, x) = \begin{cases} 1 & \hat{P}_{I(S)}(y = c_j \,|x) > \hat{P}_{I(S)}(y = c^* \,|x) \,\forall c^* \in dom(y), \neq c_j \\ 0 & Otherwise \end{cases}$$

$$bias^2(P(y \,|x), \hat{P}_I(y \,|x)) =$$

$$\frac{1}{2} \sum_{c_j \in dom(y)} \left[P(y = c_j \,|x) - \sum_{\forall S, |S| = m} P(S \,|D) \cdot t(I, S, c_j, x) \right]^2$$

$$var(\hat{P}_I(y \,|x)) = \frac{1}{2} \left\{ 1 - \sum_{c_j \in dom(y)} \left[\sum_{\forall S, |S| = m} P(S \,|D) \cdot t(I, S, c_j, x) \right]^2 \right\}$$

$$var(P(y \,|x)) = \frac{1}{2} \left\{ 1 - \sum_{c_j \in dom(y)} [P(y = c_j \,|x)]^2 \right\}$$

Note that the probability to misclassify the instance x using inducer I and a training set of size m is:

$$\varepsilon(x) = bias^2(P(y \,|x), \hat{P}_I(y \,|x)) + var(\hat{P}_I(y \,|x)) + var(P(y \,|x))$$
$$= 1 - \sum_{c_j \in dom(y)} P(y = c_j \,|x) \cdot \sum_{\forall S, |S| = m} P(S \,|D) \cdot t(I, S, c_j, x)$$

It is important to note that in case of zero-one loss there are other definitions for the bias-variance components. These definitions are not necessarily consistent. In fact there is a considerable debate in the literature about what should be the most appropriate definition. For a complete list of these definitions please refer to [Hansen (2000)].

Nevertheless in context of regression a single definition of bias and variance has been adopted by the entire community. In this case it is useful to define the bias-variance components by referring to the quadratic loss, as follows:

$$E((f(x) - \hat{f}_R(x)^2) =$$
$$\text{var}(f(x)) + \text{var}(\hat{f}_R(x)) + bias^2(f(x), \hat{f}_R(x))$$

where $\hat{f}_R(x)$ represents the prediction of the regression model and $f(x)$ represents the actual value. The intrinsic variance and bias components are respectively defined as:

$$\text{var}(f(x)) = E((f(x) - E(f(x)))^2)$$
$$\text{var}(\hat{f}_R(x)) = E((\hat{f}_R(x) - E(\hat{f}_R(x)))^2)$$
$$bias^2(f(x), \hat{f}_R(x)) = E((E(\hat{f}_R(x)) - E(f(x)))^2$$

Simpler models tend to have a higher bias error and smaller variance error than complicated models. [Bauer and Kohavi (1999)] have provided an experimental result supporting the last argument for Naïve Bayes, while [Dietterich and Kong (1995)] have examined the bias-variance issue in decision trees. Figure 1.5 illustrates this argument. The figure shows that there is a trade-off between variance and bias. When the classifier is simple it has a large bias and small variance. As the classifier become more complicated, it has larger variance but smaller bias. The minimum generalization error is obtained somewhere in between, where both bias and variance are small.

1.9.5 *Computational Complexity*

Another useful criterion for comparing inducers and classifiers is their computational complexities. Strictly speaking computational complexity is the amount of CPU consumed by each inducer. It is convenient to differentiate between three metrics of computational complexity:

- Computational Complexity for generating a new classifier: This is the most important metric, especially when there is a need to scale the

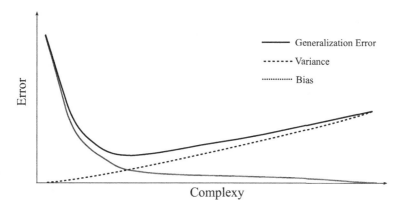

Fig. 1.5   Bias vs. Variance in the Deterministic Case: Hansen, 2000.

data mining algorithm to massive data sets. Because most of the algorithms have computational complexity, which is worse than linear in the numbers of tuples, mining massive data sets might be "prohibitively expensive".

- Computational Complexity for updating a classifier: Giving a new data — what is the computational complexity required for updating the current classifier such that the new classifier reflects the new data?
- Computational Complexity for classifying a new instance: Generally this type is neglected because it is relatively small. However, in certain methods (like k-Nearest Neighborhood) or in certain real time applications (like anti-missiles applications), this type can be critical.

1.9.6   *Comprehensibility*

Comprehensibility criterion (also known as Interpretability) refers to how well humans grasp the classifier induced. While the generalization error measures how the classifier fits the data, comprehensibility measures the "Mental fit" of that classifier.

Many techniques, like neural networks or SVM (Support Vector Machines), are designed solely to achieve accuracy. However, as their classifiers are represented using large assemblages of real valued parameters, they are also difficult to understand and are referred to as black-box models.

It is often important for the researcher to be able to inspect an induced classifier. For domains such as medical diagnosis, the users must understand how the system makes its decisions in order to be confident of the outcome.

Data mining can also play an important role in the process of scientific discovery. A system may discover salient features in the input data whose importance was not previously recognized. If the representations formed by the inducer are comprehensible, then these discoveries can be made accessible to human review [Hunter and Klein (1993)].

Comprehensibility can vary between different classifiers created by the same inducer. For instance, in the case of decision trees, the size (number of nodes) of the induced trees is also important. Smaller trees are preferred because they are easier to interpret. However, this is only a rule of thumb, in some pathologic cases a large and unbalanced tree can still be easily interpreted [Buja and Lee (2001)].

As the reader can see the accuracy and complexity factors can be quantitatively estimated, while the comprehensibility is more subjective.

Another distinction is that the complexity and comprehensibility depend mainly only on the induction method and much less on the specific domain considered. On the other hand, the dependence of error metric on specific domain can not be neglected.

1.10   "No Free Lunch" Theorem

Empirical comparison of the performance of different approaches and their variants in a wide range of application domains has shown that each performs best in some, but not all, domains. This has been termed the selective superiority problem [Brodley (1995)].

It is well known that no induction algorithm can be the best in all possible domains; each algorithm contains an explicit or implicit bias [Mitchell (1980)] that leads it to prefer certain generalizations over others, and it will be successful only insofar as this bias matches the characteristics of the application domain [Brazdil *et al.* (1994)]. Furthermore, other results have demonstrated the existence and correctness of the "conservation law" [Schaffer (1994)] or "no free lunch theorem" [Wolpert (1996)]: if one inducer is better than another in some domains, then there are necessarily other domains in which this relationship is reversed.

The "no free lunch theorem" implies that for a given problem a certain approach can yield more information from the same data than other approaches.

A distinction should be made between all the mathematically possible domains, which are simply a product of the representation languages used, and the domains that occur in the real world, and are therefore the ones of primary interest [Rao *et al.* (1995)]. Without doubt there are many domains in the former set that are not in the latter, and average accuracy in the realworld domains can be increased at the expense of accuracy in the domains that never occur in practice. Indeed, achieving this is the goal of inductive learning research. It is still true that some algorithms will match certain classes of naturallyoccurring domains better than other algorithms, and so achieve higher accuracy than these algorithms, and that this may be reversed in other realworld domains; but this does not preclude an improved algorithm from being as accurate as the best in each of the domain classes.

Indeed, in many application domains the generalization error of even the best methods is far above 0%, and the question of whether it can be improved, and if so how, is an open and important one. One part of answering this question is determining the minimum error achievable by any classifier in the application domain (known as the optimal Bayes error). If existing classifiers do not reach this level, new approaches are needed. Although this problem has received considerable attention (see for instance [Tumer and Ghosh (1996)]), no generally reliable method has so far been demonstrated.

The "no free lunch" concept presents a dilemma to the analyst approaching a new task: which inducer should be used?

If the analyst is looking for accuracy only, one solution is to try each one in turn, and by estimating the generalization error, to choose the one that appears to perform best [Schaffer (1994)]. Another approach, known as *multistrategy learning* [Michalski and Tecuci (1994)], attempts to combine two or more different paradigms in a single algorithm. Most research in this area has been concerned with combining empirical approaches with analytical methods (see for instance [Towell and Shavlik (1994)]. Ideally, a multistrategy learning algorithm would always perform as well as the best of its "parents" obviating the need to try each one and simplifying the knowledge acquisition task. Even more ambitiously, there is hope that this combination of paradigms might produce synergistic effects (for instance by allowing different types of frontiers between classes in different regions of the example space), leading to levels of accuracy that neither atomic approach by itself would be able to achieve.

Unfortunately, this approach has often been only moderately successful. Although it is true that in some industrial applications (like in the case of demand planning) this strategy proved to boost the error performance, in many other cases the resulting algorithms are prone to be cumbersome, and often achieve an error that lie between those of their parents, instead of matching the lowest.

The dilemma of what method to choose becomes even greater, if other factors such as comprehensibility are taken into consideration. For instance for a specific domain, neural network may outperform decision trees in accuracy. However, from the comprehensibility aspect, decision trees are considered better. In other words, in this case even if the researcher knows that neural network is more accurate, he still has a dilemma what method to use.

1.11   Scalability to Large Datasets

Obviously induction is one of the central problems in many disciplines like: machine learning, pattern recognition, and statistics.

However the feature that distinguishes data mining from traditional methods is its scalability to very large sets of varied types of input data. In this book the notion, "scalability" refers to datasets that fulfill at least one of the following properties: high number of records, high dimensionality, high number of classes or heterogeneousness.

"Classical" induction algorithms have been applied with practical success in many relatively simple and small-scale problems. However, trying to discover knowledge in real life and large databases, introduce time and memory problems.

As large databases have become the norm in many fields (including astronomy, molecular biology, finance, marketing, health care, and many others), the use of data mining to discover patterns in them has become a potentially very productive enterprise. Many companies are staking a large part of their future on these "data mining" applications, and looking to the research community for solutions to the fundamental problems they encounter.

While a very large amount of available data used to be a dream of any data analyst, nowadays the synonym for "very large" has become "terabyte", a hardly imaginable volume of information. Information-intensive organizations (like telecom companies and banks) are supposed to accumulate several terabytes of raw data every one to two years.

However, the availability of an electronic data repository (in its enhanced form known as a "data warehouse") has caused a number of previously unknown problems, which, if ignored, may turn the task of efficient data mining into mission impossible. Managing and analyzing huge data warehouses requires special and very expensive hardware and software, which often causes a company to exploit only a small part of the stored data.

According to [Fayyad *et al.* (1996)] the explicit challenges for the data mining research community is to develop methods that facilitate the use of data mining algorithms for real-world databases. One of the characteristics of a real world databases is high volume data.

Huge databases pose several challenges:

- Computing complexity: Since most induction algorithms have a computational complexity that is greater than linear in the number of attributes or tuples, the execution time needed to process such databases might become an important issue.
- Poor classification accuracy due to difficulties in finding the correct classifier. Large databases increase the size of the search space, and thus it increases the chance that the inducer will select an over fitted classifier that is not valid in general.
- Storage problems: In most machine learning algorithms, the entire training set should be read from the secondary storage (such as magnetic storage) into the computer's primary storage (main memory) before the induction process begins. This causes problems since the main memory's capability is much smaller than the capability of magnetic disks.

The difficulties in implementing classification algorithms as-is on high volume databases derives from the increase in the number of records/instances in the database and from the increase in the number of attributes/features in each instance (high dimensionality).

Approaches for dealing with a high number of records include:

- Sampling methods — statisticians are selecting records from a population by different sampling techniques.
- Aggregation — reduces the number of records either by treating a group of records as one, or by ignoring subsets of "unimportant" records.
- Massively parallel processing — exploiting parallel technology — to simultaneously solve various aspects of the problem.
- Efficient storage methods — enabling the algorithm to handle many records. For instance [Shafer *et al.* (1996)] presented the SPRINT which constructs an attribute list data structure.

- Reducing the algorithm's Search space — For instance the PUBLIC algorithm [Rastogi and Shim (2000)] integrates the growing and pruning of decision trees by using MDL cost in order to reduce the computational complexity.

1.12   The "Curse of Dimensionality"

High dimensionality of the input (that is, the number of attributes) increases the size of the search space in an exponential manner, and thus increases the chance that the inducer will find spurious classifiers that are not valid in general. It is well known that the required number of labeled samples for supervised classification increases as a function of dimensionality [Jimenez and Landgrebe (1998)]. [Fukunaga (1990)] showed that the required number of training samples is linearly related to the dimensionality for a linear classifier and to the square of the dimensionality for a quadratic classifier. In terms of nonparametric classifiers like decision trees, the situation is even more severe. It has been estimated that as the number of dimensions increases, the sample size needs to increase exponentially in order to have an effective estimate of multivariate densities ([Hwang et al. (1994)].

This phenomenon is usually called "curse of dimensionality". Bellman (1961) was the first to coin this term, while working on complicated signal processing. Techniques like decision trees inducers that are efficient in low dimensions fail to provide meaningful results when the number of dimensions increases beyond a "modest" size. Furthermore, smaller classifiers, involving fewer features (probably less than 10), are much more understandable by humans. Smaller classifiers are also more appropriate for user-driven data mining techniques such as visualization.

Most of the methods for dealing with high dimensionality focus on Feature Selection techniques, i.e. selecting a single subset of features upon which the inducer (induction algorithm) will run, while ignoring the rest. The selection of the subset can be done manually by using prior knowledge to identify irrelevant variables or by using proper algorithms.

In the last decade, Feature Selection has enjoyed increased interest by many researchers. Consequently many Feature Selection algorithms have been proposed, some of which have reported remarkable accuracy improvement. As it is too wide to survey here all methods, the reader is referred to the following sources: [Langley (1994)], [Liu and Motoda (1998)] for further reading.

Despite its popularity, the usage of feature selection methodologies for overcoming the obstacles of high dimensionality has several drawbacks:

- The assumption that a large set of input features can be reduced to a small subset of relevant features is not always true; in some cases the target feature is actually affected by most of the input features, and removing features will cause a significant loss of important information.
- The outcome (i.e. the subset) of many algorithms for Feature Selection (for example almost any of the algorithms that are based upon the wrapper methodology) is strongly dependent on the training set size. That is, if the training set is small, then the size of the reduced subset will be small also. Consequently, relevant features might be lost. Accordingly, the induced classifiers might achieve lower accuracy compared to classifiers that have access to all relevant features.
- In some cases, even after eliminating a set of irrelevant features, the researcher is left with relatively large numbers of relevant features.
- The backward elimination strategy, used by some methods, is extremely inefficient for working with large-scale databases, where the number of original features is more than 100.

A number of linear dimension reducers have been developed over the years. The linear methods of dimensionality reduction include projection pursuit [Friedman and Tukey (1973)], factor analysis [Kim and Mueller (1978)], and principal components analysis [Dunteman (1989)]. These methods are not aimed directly at eliminating irrelevant and redundant features, but are rather concerned with transforming the observed variables into a small number of "projections" or "dimensions". The underlying assumptions are that the variables are numeric and the dimensions can be expressed as linear combinations of the observed variables (and vice versa). Each discovered dimension is assumed to represent an unobserved factor and thus provide a new way of understanding the data (similar to the curve equation in the regression models).

The linear dimension reducers have been enhanced by constructive induction systems that use a set of existing features and a set of pre-defined constructive operators to derive new features [Pfahringer (1994); Ragavan and Rendell (1993)]. These methods are effective for high dimensionality applications only if the original domain size of the input feature can be in fact decreased dramatically.

One way to deal with the above mentioned disadvantages is to use a very large training set (which should increase in an exponential manner as the number of input features increases). However, the researcher rarely enjoys this privilege, and even if it does happen, the researcher will probably encounter the aforementioned difficulties derived from a high number of instances.

Practically most of the training sets are still considered "small" not due to their absolute size but rather due to the fact that they contain too few instances given the nature of the investigated problem, namely the instance space size, the space distribution and the intrinsic noise. Furthermore, even if a sufficient dataset is available, the researcher will probably encounter the aforementioned difficulties derived from high number of records.

Chapter 2

Decision Trees

2.1 Decision Trees

A Decision tree is a classifier expressed as a recursive partition of the instance space. The decision tree consists of nodes that form a Rooted Tree, meaning it is a Directed Tree with a node called root that has no incoming edges. All other nodes have exactly one incoming edge. A node with outgoing edges is called internal node or test nodes. All other nodes are called leaves (also known as terminal nodes or decision nodes). In the decision tree each internal node splits the instance space into two or more subspaces according to a certain discrete function of the input attributes values. In the simplest and most frequent case each test considers a single attribute, such that the instance space is partitioned according to the attribute's value. In the case of numeric attributes the condition refers to a range.

Each leaf is assigned to one class representing the most appropriate target value. Alternatively the leaf may hold a probability vector indicating the probability of the target attribute having a certain value. Instances are classified by navigating them from the root of the tree down to a leaf, according to the outcome of the tests along the path. Figure 2.1 describes a decision tree that reasons whether or not a potential customer will respond to a direct mailing. Internal nodes are represented as circles, whereas leaves are denoted as triangles. Note that this decision tree incorporates both nominal and numeric attributes. Given this classifier, the analyst can predict the response of a potential customer (by sorting it down the tree), and understand the behavioral characteristics of the entire potential customers population regarding direct mailing. Each node is labeled with the attribute it tests, and its branches are labeled with its corresponding values.

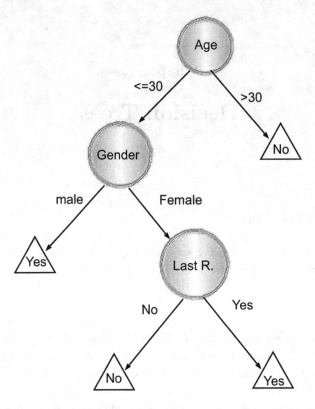

Fig. 2.1   Decision Tree Presenting Response to Direct Mailing.

In case of numeric attributes, decision trees can be geometrically interpreted as a collection of hyperplanes, each orthogonal to one of the axes. Naturally, decision makers prefer less complex decision tree, as it is considered more comprehensible. Furthermore, according to [Breiman *et al.* (1984)] the tree complexity has a crucial effect on its accuracy performance. The tree complexity is explicitly controlled by the stopping criteria used and the pruning method employed. Usually the tree complexity is measured by one of the following metrics: The Total Number of Nodes, Total Number of Leaves, Tree Depth and Number of Attributes Used. Decision tree induction is closely related to rule induction. Each path from the root of a decision tree to one of its leaves can be transformed into a rule simply by conjoining the tests along the path to form the antecedent part, and taking the leaf's class prediction as the class value. For example, one of the paths in Figure 2.1 can be transformed into the rule: "If customer age is is less than or equal to or equal to 30, and the gender of the customer is "Male" — then the customer will respond to the mail". The resulting rule set can then be simplified to improve its comprehensibility to a human user, and possibly its accuracy [Quinlan (1987)].

2.2 Algorithmic Framework for Decision Trees

Decision tree inducers are algorithms that automatically construct a decision tree from a given dataset. Typically the goal is to find the optimal decision tree by minimizing the generalization error. However, other target functions can be also defined, for instance: minimizing the number of nodes or minimizing the average depth.

Induction of an optimal decision tree from a given data is considered to be hard task. [Hancock *et al.* (1996)] have shown that finding a minimal decision tree consistent with the training set is NP-Hard. [Hyafil and Rivest (1976)] have shown that constructing a minimal binary tree with respect to the expected number of tests required for classifying an unseen instance is NP-complete. Even finding the minimal equivalent decision tree for a given decision tree [Zantema and Bodlaender (2000)] or building the optimal decision tree from decision tables is known to be NP-Hard [Naumov (1991)].

The above results indicate that using optimal decision tree algorithms is feasible only in small problems. Consequently, heuristics methods are required for solving the problem. Roughly speaking, these methods can be divided into two groups: Top-Down and Bottom-Up with clear preference in the literature to the first group.

There are various top-down decision trees inducers such as ID3 [Quinlan (1986)], C4.5 [Quinlan (1993)], CART [Breiman *et al.* (1984)]. Some of which consist of two conceptual phases: Growing and Pruning (C4.5 and CART). Other inducers perform only the growing phase.

Figure 2.2 presents a typical algorithmic framework for top-down inducing of a decision tree using growing and pruning. Note that these algorithms are greedy by nature and construct the decision tree in a top-down, recursive manner (also known as "divide and conquer"). In each iteration, the algorithm considers the partition of the training set using the outcome of a discrete function of the input attributes. The selection of the most appropriate function is made according to some splitting measures. After the selection of an appropriate split, each node further subdivides the training set into smaller subsets, until no split gains sufficient splitting measure or a stopping criteria is satisfied.

2.3   Univariate Splitting Criteria

2.3.1   *Overview*

In most of the cases the discrete splitting functions are univariate. Univariate means that an internal node is split according to the value of a single attribute. Consequently, the inducer searches for the best attribute upon which to split. There are various univariate criteria. These criteria can be characterized in different ways, such as:

- According to the origin of the measure: Information Theory, Dependence, and Distance.
- According to the measure structure: Impurity Based criteria, Normalized Impurity Based criteria and Binary criteria.

The following section describes the most common criteria in the literature.

2.3.2   *Impurity Based Criteria*

Given a random variable x with k discrete values, distributed according to $P = (p_1, p_2, \ldots, p_k)$, an impurity measure is a function $\phi{:}[0, 1]^k \rightarrow R$ that satisfies the following conditions:

- $\phi\,(\mathrm{P}){\geq}0$
- $\phi\,(\mathrm{P})$ is minimum if $\exists i$ such that component $p_i = 1$.
- $\phi\,(\mathrm{P})$ is maximum if $\forall i,\ 1 \leq i \leq k,\ p_i = 1/k$.
- $\phi\,(\mathrm{P})$ is symmetric with respect to components of P.
- $\phi\,(\mathrm{P})$ is smooth (differentiable everywhere) in its range.

Note: if the probability vector has a component of 1 (the variable x gets only one value), then the variable is defined as pure. On the other hand, if all components are equal the level of impurity reaches maximum.

Given a training set S the probability vector of the target attribute y is defined as:

$$P_y(S) = \left(\frac{|\sigma_{y=c_1}S|}{|S|}, \ldots, \frac{|\sigma_{y=c_{|dom(y)|}}S|}{|S|} \right)$$

TreeGrowing (S,A,y)

Where:

S - Training Set

A - Input Feature Set

y - Target Feature

Create a new tree T with a single root node.

IF One of 'the Stopping Criteria is fulfilled THEN

    Mark the root node in T as a leaf with the most

    common value of y in S as a label.

ELSE

    Find a discrete function $f(A)$ of the input

        attributes values such that splitting S

        according to $f(A)$'s outcomes $(v_1,\ldots,v_n)$ gains

        the best splitting metric.

    IF best splitting metric > threshold THEN

        Label t with $f(A)$

        FOR each outcome v_i of $f(A)$:

            Set $Subtree_i$= TreeGrowing $(\sigma_{f(A)=v_i}S, A, y)$.

            Connect the root node of t_T to $Subtree_i$ with

                an edge that is labelled as v_i

        END FOR

    ELSE

        Mark the root node in T as a leaf with the most

            common value of y in S as a label.

    END IF

END IF

RETURN T

TreePruning (S,T,y)

Where:

S - Training Set

y - Target Feature

T - The tree to be pruned

DO

    Select a node t in T such that pruning it

        maximally improve some evaluation criteria

    IF $t \neq \emptyset$ THEN $T = pruned(T,t)$

UNTIL $t = \emptyset$

RETURN T

Fig. 2.2   Top-Down Algorithmic Framework for Decision Trees Induction.

The goodness-of-split due to discrete attribute a_i is defined as reduction in impurity of the target attribute after partitioning S according to the values $v_{i,j} \in dom(a_i)$:

$$\Delta\Phi(a_i, S) = \phi(P_y(S)) - \sum_{j=1}^{|dom(a_i)|} \frac{|\sigma_{a_i=v_{i,j}} S|}{|S|} \cdot \phi(P_y(\sigma_{a_i=v_{i,j}} S))$$

2.3.3   Information Gain

Information Gain is an Impurity Based Criteria that uses the entropy measure (origin from information theory) as the impurity measure [Quinlan (1987)].

$$InformationGain(a_i, S) =$$
$$Entropy(y, S) - \sum_{v_{i,j} \in dom(a_i)} \frac{|\sigma_{a_i=v_{i,j}} S|}{|S|} \cdot Entropy(y, \sigma_{a_i=v_{i,j}} S)$$

where:

$$Entropy(y, S) = \sum_{c_j \in dom(y)} -\frac{|\sigma_{y=c_j} S|}{|S|} \cdot \log_2 \frac{|\sigma_{y=c_j} S|}{|S|}$$

2.3.4   Gini Index

Gini Index is an Impurity Based Criteria that measures the divergences between the probability distributions of the target attribute's values. The Gini index has been used in various works such as [Breiman *et al.* (1984)] and [Gelfand *et al.* (1991)] and it is defined as:

$$Gini(y, S) = 1 - \sum_{c_j \in dom(y)} \left(\frac{|\sigma_{y=c_j} S|}{|S|} \right)^2$$

Consequently the evaluation criterion for selecting the attribute a_i is defined as:

$$GiniGain(a_i, S) = Gini(y, S) - \sum_{v_{i,j} \in dom(a_i)} \frac{|\sigma_{a_i=v_{i,j}} S|}{|S|} \cdot Gini(y, \sigma_{a_i=v_{i,j}} S)$$

2.3.5   Likelihood Ratio Chi-Squared Statistics

The likelihood-ratio is defined as [Attneave (1959)]

$$G^2(a_i, S) = 2 \cdot \ln(2) \cdot |S| \cdot InformationGain(a_i, S)$$

This ratio is useful for measuring the statistical significance of the information gain criterion. The zero hypothesis (H_0) is that the input attribute and the target attribute are conditionally independent. If H_0 holds, the test statistic is distributed as χ^2 with degrees of freedom equal to: $(dom(a_i) - 1) \cdot (dom(y) - 1)$.

2.3.6 DKM Criterion

The DKM criterion is an impurity based splitting criteria designed for binary class attributes [Dietterich *et al.* (1996)] and [Kearns and Mansour (1999)]. The impurity based function is defined as:

$$DKM(y,S) = 2 \cdot \sqrt{\left(\frac{|\sigma_{y=c_1}S|}{|S|}\right) \cdot \left(\frac{|\sigma_{y=c_2}S|}{|S|}\right)}$$

[Kearns and Mansour (1999)] have theoretically proved that this criterion requires smaller trees for obtaining a certain error than other impurity based criteria (information gain and Gini index).

2.3.7 Normalized Impurity Based Criteria

The Impurity Based Criterion described above is biased towards attributes with larger domain values. Namely, it prefers input attributes with many values over attributes with less values [Quinlan (1986)]. For instance, an input attribute that represents the national security number will probably get the highest information gain. However, adding this attribute to a decision tree will result in a poor generalized accuracy. For that reason, it is useful to "normalize" the impurity based measures, as described in the following sections.

2.3.8 Gain Ratio

The Gain Ratio "normalizes" the information gain as following [Quinlan (1993)]:

$$GainRatio(a_i, S) = \frac{InformationGain(a_i, S)}{Entropy(a_i, S)}$$

Note that this ratio is not defined when the denominator is zero. Also the ratio may tend to favor attributes for which the denominator is very small. Consequently, it is suggested in two stages. First the information gain is calculated for all attributes. As a consequence taking into consideration only attributes that have performed at least as good as the average information gain, the attribute that has obtained the best ratio gain is selected. [Quinlan (1988)] has shown that the gain ratio tends to outperform simple information gain criteria, both from the accuracy aspect, as well as from classifier complexity aspects.

2.3.9 *Distance Measure*

The Distance Measure, like the Gain Ratio, normalizes the impurity measure. However, it suggests normalizing it in a different way [Lopez de Mantras (1991)]:

$$
\frac{\Delta\Phi(a_i, S)}{-\sum_{v_{i,j} \in dom(a_i)} \sum_{c_k \in dom(y)} \frac{|\sigma_{a_i=v_{i,j} \ AND \ y=c_k} S|}{|S|} \cdot \log_2 \frac{|\sigma_{a_i=v_{i,j} \ AND \ y=c_k} S|}{|S|}}
$$

2.3.10 *Binary criteria*

The binary criteria are used for creating binary decision trees. These measures are based on division of the input attribute domain into two subdomains.

Let $\beta(a_i, dom_1(a_i), dom_2(a_i), S)$ denote the binary criterion value for attribute a_i over sample S when $dom_1(a_i)$ and $dom_2(a_i)$ are its corresponding subdomains. The value obtained for the optimal division of the attribute domain into two mutually exclusive and exhaustive subdomains is used for comparing attributes, namely:

$$
\beta^*(a_i, S) = \max_{\substack{\forall dom_1(a_i); dom_2(a_i) \\ dom_1(a_i) \cup dom_2(a_i) = dom(a_i) \\ dom_1(a_i) \cap dom_2(a_i) = \emptyset}} \beta(a_i, dom_1(a_i), dom_2(a_i), S)
$$

2.3.11 *Twoing Criterion*

The Gini index may encounter problems when the domain of the target attribute is relatively wide [Breiman *et al.* (1984)]. In this case it is possible to employ binary criterion called Twoing Criterion. This criterion is defined as:

$$twoing(a_i, dom_1(a_i), dom_2(a_i), S) =$$
$$0.25 \cdot \frac{|\sigma_{a_i \in dom_1(a_i)} S|}{|S|} \cdot \frac{|\sigma_{a_i \in dom_2(a_i)} S|}{|S|} \cdot$$
$$\left(\sum_{c_i \in dom(y)} \left| \frac{|\sigma_{a_i \in dom_1(a_i) \ AND \ y=c_i} S|}{|\sigma_{a_i \in dom_1(a_i)} S|} - \frac{|\sigma_{a_i \in dom_2(a_i) \ AND \ y=c_i} S|}{|\sigma_{a_i \in dom_2(a_i)} S|} \right| \right)^2$$

When the target attribute is binary the Gini and twoing criteria are equivalent. For multi-class problems the twoing criteria prefers attributes with evenly divided splits.

2.3.12 Orthogonal Criterion

The ORT criterion was presented by [Fayyad and Irani (1992)]. This binary criterion is defined as:

$$ORT(a_i, dom_1(a_i), dom_2(a_i), S) = 1 - cos\theta(P_{y,1}, P_{y,2})$$

where $\theta(P_{y,1}, P_{y,2})$ is the angle between two vectors $P_{y,1}$ and $P_{y,2}$. These vectors represent the probability distribution of the target attribute in the partitions $\sigma_{a_i \in dom_1(a_i)} S$ and $\sigma_{a_i \in dom_2(a_i)} S$ respectively.

It has been shown that this criterion performs better than the information gain and the Gini index for specific problems constellation.

2.3.13 Kolmogorov–Smirnov Criterion

A binary criterion that uses Kolmogorov–Smirnov distance has been proposed by [Friedman (1977)] and [Rounds (1980)]. Assuming a binary target attribute, namely $dom(y) = \{c_1, c_2\}$, the criterion is defined as:

$$KS(a_i, dom_1(a_i), dom_2(a_i), S) =$$

$$\left| \frac{|\sigma_{a_i \in dom_1(a_i) \ AND \ y=c_1} S|}{|\sigma_{y=c_1} S|} - \frac{|\sigma_{a_i \in dom_1(a_i) \ AND \ y=c_2} S|}{|\sigma_{y=c_2} S|} \right|$$

This measure was extended by [Utgoff and Clouse (1996)] to handle target attribute with multiple classes and missing data values. Their results indicate that the suggested method outperforms the gain ratio criteria.

2.3.14   *AUC Splitting Criteria*

The idea of using the AUC metric as a splitting criterion was recently proposed by [Ferri *et al.* (2002)]. The attribute that obtains the maximal area under the convex hull of the ROC curve is selected. It has been shown that the AUC-based splitting criterion outperforms other splitting criteria both with respect to classification accuracy and area under the ROC curve. It is important to note that unlike impurity criteria, this criterion does not perform a comparison between the impurity of the parent node with the weighted impurity of the children after splitting.

2.3.15   *Other Univariate Splitting Criteria*

Additional univariate splitting criteria can be found in the literature, such as permutation statistic [Li and Dubes (1986)], mean posterior improvement [Taylor and Silverman (1993)] and hypergeometric distribution measure [(Martin (1997)].

2.3.16   *Comparison of Univariate Splitting Criteria*

Comparative studies of the splitting criteria described above, and others, have been conducted by several researchers during the last thirty years, such as [Breiman (1996)], [Baker and Jain (1976)], [BenBassat (1978)], [Mingers (1989)], [Fayyad and Irani (1992)], [Buntine and Niblett (1992)], [Loh and Shih (1997)], [Loh and Shih (1999)], [Lim *et al.* (2000)]. Most of these comparisons are based on empirical results, although there are some theoretical conclusions.

Most of the researchers point out that in most of the cases the choice of splitting criteria will not make much difference on the tree performance. Each criterion is superior in some cases and inferior in other, as the "No-Free Lunch" theorem suggests.

2.4   Multivariate Splitting Criteria

In Multivariate Splitting Criteria several attributes may participate in a single node split test. Obviously, finding the best multivariate criteria is more complicated than finding the best univariate split. Furthermore, although this type of criteria may dramatically improve the tree's performance, these criteria are much less popular than the univariate criteria.

Most of the Multivariate Splitting Criteria are based on the linear combination of the input attributes. Finding the best linear combination can be performed using greedy search ([Breiman *et al.* (1984)]; [Murthy (1998)]), linear programming ([Duda and Hart (1973)]; [Bennett and Mangasarian (1994)]), linear discriminant analysis ([Duda and Hart (1973)]; [Friedman (1977)]; [Sklansky and Wassel (1981)]; [Lin and Fu (1983)];[Loh and Vanichsetakul (1988)]; [John (1996)] and others ([Utgoff (1989a)]; [Lubinsky (1993)]; [Sethi and Yoo (1994)]).

2.5 Stopping Criteria

The growing phase continues until a stopping criterion is triggered. The following conditions are common stopping rules:

(1) All instances in the training set belong to a single value of y.
(2) The maximum tree depth has been reached.
(3) The number of cases in the terminal node is less than the minimum number of cases for parent nodes.
(4) If the node were split, the number of cases in one or more child nodes would be less than the minimum number of cases for child nodes.
(5) The best splitting criteria is not greater than a certain threshold.

2.6 Pruning Methods

2.6.1 *Overview*

Employing tightly stopping criteria tends to create small and under-fitted decision trees. On the other hand, using loosely stopping criteria tends to generate large decision trees that are over-fitted to the training set. Pruning methods originally suggested by [Breiman *et al.* (1984)] were developed for solving this dilemma. According to this methodology, a loosely stopping criterion is used, letting the decision tree to overfit the training set. Then the overfitted tree is cut back into a smaller tree by removing sub-branches that are not contributing to the generalization accuracy. It has been shown in various studies that employing pruning methods can improve the generalization performance of a decision tree, especially in noisy domains.

Another key motivation of pruning is "trading accuracy for simplicity" as presented by [Bratko and Bohanec (1994)]. When the goal is to produce a sufficiently accurate compact concept description, pruning is highly useful. Within this process the initial decision tree is seen as a completely accurate one, thus the accuracy of a pruned decision tree indicates how close it is to the initial tree.

There are various techniques for pruning decision trees. Most of them perform top down or bottom up traversal of the nodes. A node is pruned if this operation improves a certain criteria. The following subsections describe the most popular techniques.

2.6.2   Cost-Complexity Pruning

Cost complexity pruning (also known as weakest link pruning or error complexity pruning) proceeds in two stages [Breiman *et al.* (1984)]. In the first stage, a sequence of trees $T_0, T_1, \ldots, T_k$ are built on the training data where T_0 is the original tree before pruning and T_k is the root tree.

In the second stage, one of these trees is chosen as the pruned tree, based on its generalization error estimation.

The tree T_{i+1} is obtained by replacing one or more of the sub-trees in the predecessor tree T_i with suitable leaves. The sub-trees that are pruned are those that obtain the lowest increase in apparent error rate per pruned leaf:

$$\alpha = \frac{\varepsilon(pruned(T,t),S) - \varepsilon(T,S)}{|leaves(T)| - |leaves(pruned(T,t))|}$$

where $\varepsilon(T,S)$ indicates the error rate of the tree T over the sample S and $|leaves(T)|$ denotes the number of leaves in T. $pruned(T,t)$ denotes the tree obtained by replacing the node t in T with a suitable leaf.

In the second phase the generalization error of each pruned tree $T_0, T_1, \ldots, T_k$ is estimated. The best pruned tree is then selected. If the given dataset is large enough, the authors suggest breaking it into a training set and a pruning set. The trees are constructed using the training set and evaluated on the pruning set. On the other hand, if the given dataset is not large enough, they propose to use cross-validation methodology, despite the computational complexity implications.

2.6.3   Reduced Error Pruning

A simple procedure for pruning decision trees, known as Reduced Error Pruning, has been suggested by [Quinlan (1987)]. While traversing over the internal nodes from the bottom to the top, the procedure checks for each internal node, whether replacing it with the most frequent class does not reduce the tree's accuracy. In this case, the node is pruned. The procedure continues until any further pruning would decrease the accuracy.

In order to estimate the accuracy [Quinlan (1987)] proposes to use a pruning set. It can be shown that this procedure ends with the smallest accurate sub-tree with respect to a given pruning set.

2.6.4 *Minimum Error Pruning (MEP)*

The Minimum Error Pruning has been proposed by [Niblett and Bratko (1986)]. It performs bottom-up traversal of the internal nodes. In each node it compares the l-probability error rate estimation with and without pruning.

The l-probability error rate estimation is a correction to the simple probability estimation using frequencies. If S_t denotes the instances that have reached a leaf t, then the expected error rate in this leaf is:

$$\varepsilon'(t) = 1 - \max_{c_i \in dom(y)} \frac{|\sigma_{y=c_i} S_t| + l \cdot p_{apr}(y = c_i)}{|S_t| + l}$$

where $p_{apr}(y = c_i)$ is the *a-priori* probability of y getting the value c_i, and l denotes the weight given to the *a-priori* probability.

The error rate of an internal node is the weighted average of the error rate of its branches. The weight is determined according to the proportion of instances along each branch. The calculation is performed recursively up to the leaves.

If an internal node is pruned, then it becomes a leaf and its error rate is calculated directly using the last equation. Consequently, we can compare the error rate before and after pruning a certain internal node. If pruning this node does not increase the error rate, the pruning should be accepted.

2.6.5 *Pessimistic Pruning*

Pessimistic pruning avoids the need of pruning set or cross validation and uses the pessimistic statistical correlation test instead [Quinlan (1993)].

The basic idea is that the error ratio estimated using the training set is not reliable enough. Instead, a more realistic measure, known as the continuity correction for binomial distribution, should be used:

$$\varepsilon'(T, S) = \varepsilon(T, S) + \frac{|leaves(T)|}{2 \cdot |S|}$$

However, this correction still produces optimistic error rate. Consequently, [Quinlan (1993)] suggests pruning an internal node t if its error rate is within one standard error from a reference tree, namely:

$$\varepsilon'(pruned(T, t), S) \leq \varepsilon'(T, S) + \sqrt{\frac{\varepsilon'(T, S) \cdot (1 - \varepsilon'(T, S))}{|S|}}$$

The last condition is based on statistical confidence interval for proportions. Usually the last condition is used such that T refers to a sub-tree whose root is the internal node t and S denotes the portion of the training set that refers to the node t.

The pessimistic pruning procedure performs top-down traversing over the internal nodes. If an internal node is pruned, then all its descendants are removed from the pruning process, resulting in a relatively fast pruning.

2.6.6 *Error-Based Pruning (EBP)*

Error-Based Pruning is an evolution of the pessimistic pruning. It is implemented in the well-known C4.5 algorithm.

As in pessimistic pruning, the error rate is estimated using the upper bound of the statistical confidence interval for proportions.

$$\varepsilon_{UB}(T, S) = \varepsilon(T, S) + Z_\alpha \cdot \sqrt{\frac{\varepsilon(T, S) \cdot (1 - \varepsilon(T, S))}{|S|}}$$

where $\varepsilon(T, S)$ denotes the misclassification rate of the tree T on the training set S. Z is the inverse of the standard normal cumulative distribution and α is the desired significance level.

Let $subtree(T, t)$ denote the subtree rooted by the node t. Let $maxchild(T, t)$ denote the most frequent child node of t (namely most of the instances in S reach this particular child) and let S_t denote all instances in S that reach the node t.

The procedure performs bottom-up traversal over all nodes and compares the following values:

(1) $\varepsilon_{UB}(subtree(T, t), S_t)$
(2) $\varepsilon_{UB}(pruned(subtree(T, t), t), S_t)$

(3) $\varepsilon_{UB}(subtree(T, maxchild(T,t)), S_{maxchild(T,t)})$

According to the lowest value the procedure either leaves the tree as is, prune the node t, or replaces the node t with the subtree rooted by $maxchild(T,t)$.

2.6.7 Optimal Pruning

The issue of finding optimal pruning has been studied by [Bratko and Bohanec (1994)] and [Almuallim (1996)]. [Bratko and Bohanec (1994)] introduce an algorithm which guarantees optimality, knows as OPT. This algorithm finds the optimal pruning based on dynamic programming, with the complexity of $\Theta(|leaves(T)|^2)$, where T is the initial decision tree. [Almuallim (1996)] introduced an improvement of OPT called OPT-2, which also performs optimal pruning using dynamic programming. However, the time and space complexities of OPT-2 are both $\Theta(|leaves(T^*)| \cdot |internal(T)|)$, where T^* is the target (pruned) decision tree and T is the initial decision tree.

Since the pruned tree is habitually much smaller than the initial tree and the number of internal nodes is smaller than the number of leaves, OPT-2 is usually more efficient than OPT in terms of computational complexity.

2.6.8 Minimum Description Length Pruning

The Minimum Description Length can be used for evaluating the generalized accuracy of a node [Rissanen (1989)], [Quinlan and Rivest (1989)] and [Mehta et al. (1995)]. This method measures the size of a decision tree by means of the number of bits required to encode the tree. The MDL method prefers decision trees that can be encoded with fewer bits. [Mehta et al. (1995)] indicate that the cost of a split at a leaf t can be estimated as:

$$\text{Cost}(t) = \sum_{c_i \in dom(y)} |\sigma_{y=c_i} S_t| \cdot \ln \frac{|S_t|}{|\sigma_{y=c_i} S_t|} + \frac{|dom(y)|-1}{2} \ln \frac{|S_t|}{2} + \ln \frac{\pi^{\frac{|dom(y)|}{2}}}{\Gamma(\frac{|dom(y)|}{2})}$$

where S_t denotes the instances that have reached node t. The splitting cost of an internal node is calculated based on the cost aggregation of its children.

2.6.9   Other Pruning Methods

There are other pruning methods reported in the literature. [Wallace and Patrick (1993)] proposed a MML (Minimum Message Length) pruning method. [Kearns and Mansour (1998)] provide a theoretically-justified pruning algorithm. [Mingers (1989)] proposed the Critical Value Pruning (CVP). This method prunes an internal node if its splitting criterion is not greater than a certain threshold. By that it is similar to a stopping criterion. However, contrary to a stopping criterion, a node is not pruned if at least one of its children does not fulfill the pruning criterion.

2.6.10   Comparison of Pruning Methods

Several studies aim to compare the performance of different pruning techniques ([Quinlan (1987)], [Mingers (1989)] and [Esposito *et al.* (1997)]). The results indicate that some methods (such as Cost-Complexity Pruning, Reduced Error Pruning) tend to over-pruning, i.e. creating smaller but less accurate decision trees. Other methods (like Error Based Pruning, Pessimistic Error Pruning and Minimum Error Pruning) bias toward underpruning. Most of the comparisons concluded that the "No Free Lunch" theorem applies in this case also, namely there is no pruning method that in any case outperform other pruning methods.

2.7   Other Issues

2.7.1   Weighting Instances

Some decision trees inducers may give different treatments to different instances. This is performed by weighting the contribution of each instance in the analysis according to a provided weight (between 0 and 1).

2.7.2   Misclassification costs

Several decision trees inducers can be provided with numeric penalties for classifying an item into one class when it really belongs in another.

2.7.3   Handling Missing Values

Missing values are a common experience in real world data sets. This situation can complicate both induction (a training set where some of its values are missing) as well as classification a new instance that miss certain values).

This problem has been addressed by several researchers such as [Friedman (1977)], [Breiman *et al.* (1984)] and [Quinlan (1989)]. [Friedman (1977)] suggests handling missing values in the training set in the following way. Let $\sigma_{a_i=?}S$ indicate the subset of instances in S whose a_i values are missing. When calculating the splitting criteria using attribute a_i, simply ignore all instances that their values in attribute a_i are unknown, namely instead of using the splitting criteria $\Delta\Phi(a_i, S)$ it uses $\Delta\Phi(a_i, S - \sigma_{a_i=?}S)$.

On the other hand, [Quinlan (1989)] argues that in case of missing values the splitting criteria should be reduced proportionally as nothing has been learned from these instances. In other words, instead of using the splitting criteria $\Delta\Phi(a_i, S)$, it uses the following correction:

$$\frac{|S - \sigma_{a_i=?}S|}{|S|}\Delta\Phi(a_i, S - \sigma_{a_i=?}S).$$

In a case where the criterion value is normalized (like in the case of Gain Ratio), the denominator should be calculated as if the missing values represent an additional value in the attribute domain. For instance, the Gain Ratio with missing values should be calculated as follows:

$$GainRatio(a_i, S) =$$
$$\frac{\frac{|S - \sigma_{a_i=?}S|}{|S|}InformationGain(a_i, S - \sigma_{a_i=?}S)}{-\frac{|\sigma_{a_i=?}S|}{|S|}\log(\frac{|\sigma_{a_i=?}S|}{|S|}) - \sum_{v_{i,j} \in dom(a_i)}\frac{|\sigma_{a_i=v_{i,j}}S|}{|S|}\log(\frac{|\sigma_{a_i=v_{i,j}}S|}{|S|})}$$

Once a node is split, [Quinlan (1989)] suggests adding $\sigma_{a_i=?}S$ to each one of the outgoing edges with the following corresponding weight: $|\sigma_{a_i=v_{i,j}}S|/|S - \sigma_{a_i=?}S|$.

The same idea is used for classifying a new instance with missing attribute values. When an instance encounters a node where its splitting criteria can be evaluated due to a missing value, it is passed through to all outgoing edges. The predicted class will be the class with the highest probability in the weighted union of all the leaf nodes at which this instance ends up.

Another approach known as *surrogate splits* was presented by [Breiman *et al.* (1984)] and is implemented in the CART algorithm. The idea is to find for each split in the tree a surrogate split which uses a different input attribute and which most resembles the original split. If the value of the input attribute used in the original split is missing, then it is possible to use the surrogate split. The resemblance between two binary splits over sample S is formally defined as:

$$res(a_i, dom_1(a_i), dom_2(a_i), a_j, dom_1(a_j), dom_2(a_j), S) =$$

$$\frac{\left|\sigma_{a_i \in dom_1(a_i) \ AND \ a_j \in dom_1(a_j)} S\right|}{|S|} + \frac{\left|\sigma_{a_i \in dom_2(a_i) \ AND \ a_j \in dom_2(a_j)} S\right|}{|S|}$$

where the first split refers to attribute a_i and it splits $dom(a_i)$ into $dom_1(a_i)$ and $dom_2(a_i)$. The alternative split refers to attribute a_j and splits its domain to $dom_1(a_j)$ and $dom_2(a_j)$.

The missing value can be estimated based on other instances [Loh and Shih (1997)]. On the learning phase, if the value of a nominal attribute a_i in tuple q is missing, then it is estimated by it's mode over all instances having the same target attribute value. Formally,

$$estimate(a_i, y_q, S) = \underset{v_{i,j} \in dom(a_i)}{argmax} \left|\sigma_{a_i = v_{i,j} \ AND \ y = y_q} S\right|$$

where y_q denotes the value of the target attribute in the tuple q. If the missing attribute a_i is numeric then instead of using mode of a_i it is more appropriate to use its mean.

2.8   Decision Trees Inducers

2.8.1   *ID3*

The ID3 algorithm is considered as a very simple decision tree algorithm [Quinlan (1986)]. ID3 uses Information Gain as Splitting Criteria. The growing stops when all instances belong to a single value of target feature or when best information gain is not greater than zero. ID3 does not apply any pruning procedure. It does not handle numeric attributes neither missing values.

2.8.2   *C4.5*

C4.5 is an evolution of ID3, presented by the same author [Quinlan (1993)]. It uses Gain Ratio as splitting criteria. The splitting is ceased when the number of instances to be split is below a certain threshold. Error-Based Pruning is performed after the growing phase. C4.5 can handle numeric attributes. It can induce from a training set that incorporates missing values by using corrected Gain Ratio Criteria as presented above.

2.8.3 *CART*

CART stands for Classification and Regression Trees. It was developed by [Breiman *et al.* (1984)] and is characterized by the fact that it constructs binary trees, namely each internal node has exactly two outgoing edges. The splits are selected using the Twoing Criteria and the obtained tree is pruned by Cost-Complexity Pruning. When provided, CART can consider misclassification costs in the tree induction. It also enables users to provide prior probability distribution.

An important feature of CART is its ability to generate regression trees. Regression trees are trees where their leaf predicts a real number and not a class. In case of regression, CART looks for splits that minimize the prediction squared error (The Least-Squared Deviation). The prediction in each leaf is determined based on the weighted mean for node.

2.8.4 *CHAID*

Starting from early seventies, researchers in applied statistics have developed procedures for generating decision trees, such as: AID [Sonquist *et al.* (1971)], MAID [Gillo (1972)], THAID [Morgan and Messenger (1973)] and CHAID [Kass (1980)]. CHIAD (Chisquare-Automatic-Interaction-Detection) was originally designed to handle nominal attributes only. For each input attribute a_i, CHAID finds the pair of values in V_i that is least significantly different with respect to the target attribute. The significant difference is measured by the p value obtained from a statistical test. The statistical test used depends on the type of target attribute. If the target attribute is continuous, an F test is used, if it is nominal, then a Pearson chi-squared test is used, if it is ordinal, then a likelihood-ratio test is used.

For each selected pair CHAID checks if the p value obtained is greater than a certain merge threshold. If the answer is positive, it merges the values and searches for an additional potential pair to be merged. The process is repeated until no significant pairs are found.

The best input attribute to be used for splitting the current node is then selected, such that each child node is made of a group of homogeneous values of the selected attribute. Note that no split is performed if the adjusted p value of the best input attribute is not less than a certain split threshold. This procedure stops also when one of the following conditions is fulfilled:

(1) Maximum tree depth is reached.

(2) Minimum number of cases in node for being a parent is reached, so it can not be split any further.
(3) Minimum number of cases in node for being a child node is reached.

CHAID handles missing values by treating them all as a single valid category. CHAID does not perform pruning.

2.8.5 *QUEST*

The QUEST (Quick, Unbiased, Efficient, Statistical Tree) algorithm supports univariate and linear combination splits [Loh and Shih (1997)]. For each split, the association between each input attribute and the target attribute is computed using the ANOVA F-test or Levene's test (for ordinal and continuous attributes) or Pearson's chi-square (for nominal attributes). If the target attribute is multinomial, two-means clustering is used to create two super-classes. The attribute that obtains the highest association with the target attribute is selected for splitting. Quadratic Discriminant Analysis (QDA) is applied to find the optimal splitting point for the input attribute. QUEST has negligible bias and it yields a binary decision trees. Ten-fold cross-validation is used to prune the trees.

2.8.6 *Reference to Other Algorithms*

Table 2.1 describes other decision trees algorithms available in the literature. Obviously there are many other algorithms which are not included in this table. Nevertheless, most of these algorithms are a variation of the algorithmic framework presented above. A profound comparison of the above algorithms and many others has been conducted in [Lim *et al.* (2000)].

2.8.7 *Advantages and Disadvantages of Decision Trees*

Several advantages of the decision tree as a classification tool have been pointed out in the literature:

(1) Decision Trees are self-explanatory and when compacted they are also easy to follow, namely if the decision tree has a reasonable number of leaves it can be grasped by non-professional users. Furthermore decision trees can be converted to a set of rules. Thus, this representation is considered as comprehensible.
(2) Decision trees can handle both nominal and numeric input attributes.

Table 2.1   Additional Decision Tree Inducers.

Algorithm	Description	Reference
CAL5	Designed specifically for numerical-valued attributes	[Muller and Wysotzki (1994)]
FACT	An earlier version of QUEST. Uses statistical tests to select an attribute for splitting each node and then uses discriminant analysis to find the split point.	[Loh and Vanichsetakul (1988)]
LMDT	Constructs a decision tree based on multivariate tests are linear combinations of the attributes.	[Brodley and Utgoff (1995)]
T1	A one-level decision tree that classifies instances using only one attribute. Missing values are treated as a "special value". Support both continuous an nominal attributes.	[Holte (1993)]
PUBLIC	Integrates the growing and pruning by using MDL cost in order to reduce the computational complexity.	[Rastogi and Shim (2000)]
MARS	A multiple regression function is approximated using linear splines and their tensor products.	[Friedman (1991)]

(3) Decision tree representation is rich enough to represent any discrete-value classifier.

(4) Decision trees are capable to handle datasets that may have errors.

(5) Decision trees are capable to handle datasets that may have missing values.

(6) Decision trees are considered to be a nonparametric method; meaning decision trees have no assumptions on the space distribution and on the classifier structure.

On the other hand decision trees have disadvantages such as:

(1) Most of the algorithms (like ID3 and C4.5) require that the target attribute will have only discrete values.

(2) As decision trees use the "divide and conquer" method, they tend to perform well if a few highly relevant attributes exist, but less so if many complex interactions are present. One of the reasons for that is that

other classifiers can compactly describe a classifier that would be very challenging to represent using a decision tree. A simple illustration of this phenomenon is the replication problem of decision trees [Pagallo and Huassler (1990)]. Since most decision trees divide the instance space into mutually exclusive regions to represent a concept, in some cases the tree should contain several duplications of the same subtree in order to represent the classifier. For instance if the concept follows the following binary function: $y = (A_1 \cap A_2) \cup (A_3 \cap A_4)$ then the minimal univariate decision tree that represents this function is illustrated in Figure 2.3. Note that the tree contains two copies of the same subtree.

(3) The greedy characteristic of decision trees leads to another disadvantage that should be pointed out. This is its over-sensitivity to the training set, to irrelevant attributes and to noise [Quinlan (1993)].

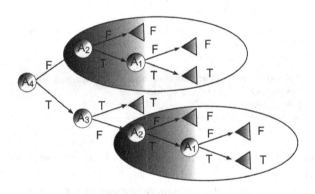

Fig. 2.3   Illustration of Decision Tree with Replication.

2.8.8   *Oblivious Decision Trees*

Oblivious Decision Trees are decision trees for which all nodes at the same level test the same feature. Despite its restriction, oblivious decision trees are found to be effective for feature selection. [Almuallim and Dietterich (1994)] as well as [Schlimmer (1993)] have proposed forward feature selection procedure by constructing oblivious decision trees, whereas [Langley and Sage (1994)] suggested backward selection using the same means. [Kohavi and Sommerfield (1998)] have shown that oblivious decision trees can be converted to a decision table. Recently [Maimon and Last (2000)] have suggested a new algorithm for constructing oblivious decision trees, called IFN (Information Fuzzy Network) that is based on information theory.

Figure 2.4 illustrates a typical oblivious decision tree with four input features: glucose level (G), age (A), Hypertension (H) and Pregnant (P) and the Boolean target feature representing whether that patient suffers from diabetes. Each layer is uniquely associated with an input feature by representing the interaction of that feature and the input features of the previous layers. The number that appears in the terminal nodes indicates the number of instances that fit this path. For example: regarding patients whose glucose level is less than 107 and their age is greater than 50, 10 of them are positively diagnosed with diabetes while 2 of them are not diagnosed with diabetes.

The principal difference between the oblivious decision tree and a regular decision tree structure is the constant ordering of input attributes at every terminal node of the oblivious decision tree, the property which is necessary for minimizing the overall subset of input attributes (resulting in dimensionality reduction). The arcs that connect the terminal nodes and the nodes of the target layer are labelled with the number of records that fit this path.

An oblivious decision tree is usually built by a greedy algorithm, which tries to maximize the mutual information measure in every layer. The recursive search for explaining attributes is terminated when there is no attribute that explains the target with statistical significance.

2.8.9 *Decision Trees Inducers for Large Datasets*

With the recent growth in the amount of data collected by information systems there is a need for decision trees that can handle large datasets. [Catlett (1991)] has examined two methods for efficiently growing decision trees from a large database by reducing the computation complexity required for induction. However, the Catlett method requires that all data will be loaded into the main memory before induction. Namely, the largest dataset that can be induced is bounded by the memory size. [Fifield (1992)] suggests parallel implementation of the ID3 Algorithm. However, like Catlett it assumes that all dataset can fit in the main memory. [Chan and Stolfo (1997)] suggest to partition the datasets into several disjointed datasets, such that each dataset is loaded separately into the memory and

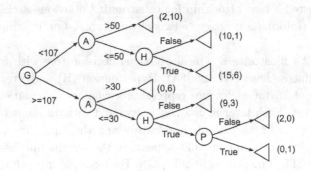

Fig. 2.4   Illustration of Oblivious Decision Tree.

used to induce a decision tree. The decision trees are then combined to create a single classifier. However, the experimental results indicate that partition may reduce the classification performance, meaning that the classification accuracy of the combined decision trees is not as good as the accuracy of a single decision tree induced from the entire dataset.

The SLIQ algorithm [Mehta *et al.* (1996)] does not require loading the entire dataset into the main memory, instead it uses a secondary memory (disk) namely a certain instance is not necessarily resident in the main memory all the time. SLIQ creates a single decision tree from the entire dataset. However, this method also has an upper limit for the largest dataset that can be processed, because it uses a data structure that scales with the dataset size and this data structure is required to be resident in main memory all the time. The SPRINT algorithm uses a similar approach [Shafer *et al.* (1996)]. This algorithm induces decision trees relatively quickly and removes all of the memory restrictions from decision tree induction. SPRINT scales any impurity based split criteria for large datasets. [Gehrke *et al.* (2000)] introduced RainForest; a unifying framework for decision tree classifiers that are capable to scale any specific algorithms from the literature (including C4.5, CART and CHAID). In addition to its generality, RainForest improves SPRINT on a factor of three. In contrast to SPRINT, however, RainForest requires a certain minimum amount of main memory, proportional to the set of distinct values in a column of the input relation. However, this requirement is considered modest and reasonable.

Other decision tree inducers for large datasets can be found in the works of [Alsabti *et al.* (1998)], [Freitas and Lavington (1998)] and [Gehrke *et al.* (1999)].

2.8.10 *Incremental Induction*

Most of the decision trees inducers require rebuilding the tree from scratch for reflecting new data that has become available. Several researchers have addressed the issue of updating decision trees incrementally. [Utgoff (1989b); Utgoff (1997)] presents several methods for updating decision trees incrementally. An extension to the CART algorithm that is capable to induce incrementally is described in [Crawford (1989)].

Chapter 3

Clustering Methods

3.1 Introduction

This chapter presents clustering methods. Clustering and classification are both fundamental tasks in data mining. In essence, the difference between clustering and classification lies in the custom in which knowledge is extracted from data: whereas classification is a supervised learning method, clustering is an unsupervised one. In other words, the goal of clustering is descriptive, whereas the goal of classification is predictive.

Another distinction between clustering and classification stems from their different goals. This difference, as indicated by [Veyssieres and Plant (1998)], involves the way that the groups resulting from each sort of analysis are assessed: Since the goal of clustering is to discover a new set of categories, the new groups are of interest in themselves and their assessment is intrinsic. In classification tasks, however, an important part of the assessment is extrinsic, since the groups must reflect some reference set of classes.

"Understanding our world requires conceptualizing the similarities and differences between the entities that compose it" [Tyron and Bailey (1970)].

Clustering does exactly so: it groups the data instances into subsets in such a manner that similar instances are grouped together, while different instances belong to different groups. The instances are thereby organized into an efficient representation that characterizes the population being sampled. Formally, the clustering structure is represented as a set of subsets $C = C_1, \ldots, C_k$ of S, such that: $S = \bigcup_{i=1}^{k} C_i$ and $C_i \cap C_j = \emptyset$ for $i \neq j$. Consequently, any instance in S belongs to exactly one and only one subset.

Clusters of objects is as ancient as the human need for describing the salient characteristics of men and objects and identifying them with a type. Therefore, it embraces various scientific disciplines: from mathematics and statistics to biology and genetics, each of which uses different terms to describe the topologies formed using this analysis. From biological "taxonomies", to medical "syndromes" and genetic "genotypes" — the problem is identical: forming categories of entities and assigning individuals to the proper groups within it.

3.2 Distance Measures

Since clustering is the grouping of similar instances/objects, some kind of measure that can determine whether two objects are similar or dissimilar is required. There are two main type of measures used to estimate this relation: Distance Measures and Similarity Measures.

Many clustering methods use distance measures to determine the similarity or dissimilarity between any pair of objects. It is useful to denote the distance between two instances x_i and x_j as: $\mathrm{d}(x_i, x_j)$. A valid distance measure should be symmetric and obtains its minimum value (usually zero) in case of identical vectors. The distance measure is called a metric distance measure if it also satisfies the following properties:

(1) Triangle inequality $\mathrm{d}(x_i, x_k) \leq \mathrm{d}(x_i, x_j) + \mathrm{d}(x_j, x_k) \quad \forall x_i, x_j, x_k \in S$.
(2) $\mathrm{d}(x_i, x_j) = 0 \Rightarrow x_i = x_j \quad \forall x_i, x_j \in S$.

3.2.1 *Minkowski: Distance Measures for Numeric Attributes*

Given two p-dimensional instances: $x_i = (x_{i1}, x_{i2}, \ldots, x_{ip})$ and $x_j = (x_{j1}, x_{j2}, \ldots, x_{jp})$, The distance between the two data instances can be calculated using the Minkowski metric [Han and Kamber (2001)]:

$$d(x_i, x_j) = (|x_{i1} - x_{j1}|^g + |x_{i2} - x_{j2}|^g + \ldots + |x_{ip} - x_{jp}|^g)^{1/g}$$

The commonly used Euclidean distance between two objects is achieved when $g = 2$. Given $g = 1$ the sum of absolute paraxial distances (Manhattan metric) is obtained, and with $g = \infty$ one gets the greatest of the paraxial distances (Chebychev metric).

The measurement unit used can affect the clustering analysis. To avoid the dependence on the choice of measurement units, the data should be standardized. Standardizing measurements attempts to give all variables an equal weight. However, if each variable is assigned with a weight according to its importance, then the weighted distance can be computed as:

$$d(x_i, x_j) = (w_1 |x_{i1} - x_{j1}|^g + w_2 |x_{i2} - x_{j2}|^g + \ldots + w_p |x_{ip} - x_{jp}|^g)^{1/g}$$

where $w_i \in [0, \infty)$

3.2.2 *Distance Measures for Binary Attributes*

The distance measure described in the last section may be easily computed for continuous-valued attributes. In the case of instances described by categorical, binary, ordinal or mixed type attributes, the distance measure should be revised.

In the case of binary attributes, the distance between objects may be calculated based on a contingency table, as shown in Table 3.1.

Table 3.1 Contingency Table for Binary Attributes.

		Instance j		
		1	0	sum
	1	q	r	q+r
Instance i	0	s	t	s+t
	Sum	q+s	r+t	p

where q is the number of variables that equal 1 for both objects, t is the number of variables that equal 0 for both objects, and s and r are the number of variables that are non equal for both objects. The total number of attributes is p.

A binary attribute is symmetric, if both of its states are equally valuable. In that case, using the simple matching coefficient can assess dissimilarity between two objects:

$$d(x_i, x_j) = \frac{r + s}{q + r + s + t}$$

A binary attribute is asymmetric, if its states are not equally important (usually the positive outcome considered more important). In this case the denominator ignores the unimportant negative matches (t). This is called the Jaccard coefficient:

$$d(x_i, x_j) = \frac{r + s}{q + r + s}$$

3.2.3 *Distance Measures for Nominal Attributes*

When the attributes are *nominal*, two main approaches may be used:

(1) Simple matching:

$$d(x_i, x_j) = \frac{p - m}{p}$$

   where p is the total number of attributes and m is the number of matches.
(2) Creating a binary attribute for each state of each nominal attribute, and computing their dissimilarity as described above.

3.2.4 *Distance Metrics for Ordinal Attributes*

When the attributes are *ordinal* the sequence of the values is meaningful. In such cases, the attributes can be treated as numeric ones after mapping their range onto [0,1]. Such mapping may be carried out as follows:

$$z_{i,n} = \frac{r_{i,n} - 1}{M_n - 1}$$

where $z_{i,n}$ is the standardized value of attribute a_n of object i. $r_{i,n}$ is that value before standardization, and M_n is the upper limit of the domain of attribute a_n (assuming the lower limit is 1).

3.2.5 *Distance Metrics for Mixed-Type Attributes*

In the case that the instances are characterized by attributes of *mixed-type*, one may calculate the distance by combining the methods mentioned above. For instance, when calculating the distance between instances i and j using a metric such as the Euclidean distance, one may calculate the difference between nominal and binary attributes as 0 or 1 ("match" or "mismatch", respectively), and the difference between numeric attributes as the difference between their normalized values. The square of each such difference will be added to the total distance. Such calculation is employed in many clustering algorithms presented below.

The dissimilarity $d(x_i, x_j)$ between two instances, containing p attributes of mixed types, is defined as:

$$d(x_i, x_j) = \frac{\sum\limits_{n=1}^{p} \delta_{ij}^{(n)} d_{ij}^{(n)}}{\sum\limits_{n=1}^{p} \delta_{ij}^{(n)}}$$

where the indicator $\delta_{ij}^{(n)}$ =0 if one of the values is missing. The contribution of attribute n to the distance between the two objects $d^{(n)}(x_i, x_j)$ is computed according to its type:

- If the attribute is binary or categorical, $d^{(n)}(x_i, x_j) = 0$ if $x_{in} = x_{jn}$, otherwise $d^{(n)}(x_i, x_j)$=1.
- If the attribute is continuous-valued, $d_{ij}^{(n)} = \frac{|x_{in} - x_{jn}|}{\max_h x_{hn} - \min_h x_{hn}}$, where h runs over all non-missing objects for attribute n.
- If the attribute is ordinal, the standardized values of the attribute are computed first and then, $z_{i,n}$ is treated as continues-valued.

3.3 Similarity Functions

An alternative concept to that of the distance is the similarity function $s(x_i, x_j)$ that compares the two vectors x_i and x_j [Duda *et al.* (2001)]. This function should be symmetrical (namely $s(x_i, x_j) = s(x_j, x_i)$) and have a large value when x_i and x_j are somehow "similar" and the largest value for identical vectors.

A similarity function where the target range is [0,1] is called a dichotomous similarity function. In fact, the methods described in the previous sections for calculating the "distances" in the case of binary and nominal attributes may be considered as similarity functions, rather than distances.

3.3.1 *Cosine Measure*

When the angle between the two vectors is a meaningful measure of their similarity, the normalized inner product may be an appropriate similarity measure:

$$s(x_i, x_j) = \frac{x_i^T \cdot x_j}{\|x_i\| \cdot \|x_j\|}$$

3.3.2   Pearson Correlation Measure

The normalized Pearson correlation is defined as:

$$s(x_i, x_j) = \frac{(x_i - \bar{x}_i)^T \cdot (x_j - \bar{x}_j)}{\|x_i - \bar{x}_i\| \cdot \|x_j - \bar{x}_j\|}$$

where $\bar{x}_i$ denotes the average feature value of x over all dimensions.

3.3.3   Extended Jaccard Measure

The extended Jaccard measure was presented by [Strehl and Ghosh (2000)] and it is defined as:

$$s(x_i, x_j) = \frac{x_i^T \cdot x_j}{\|x_i\|^2 + \|x_j\|^2 - x_i^T \cdot x_j}$$

3.3.4   Dice Coefficient Measure

The dice coefficient measure is similar to the extended Jaccard measure and it is defined as:

$$s(x_i, x_j) = \frac{2x_i^T \cdot x_j}{\|x_i\|^2 + \|x_j\|^2}$$

3.4   Evaluation Criteria Measures

Evaluating if a certain clustering is good or not is a problematic and controversial issue. In fact [Bonner (1964)] was the first to argue that there is no universal definition for what is a good clustering. The evaluation remains mostly in the eye of the beholder. Nevertheless, several evaluation criteria have been developed in the literature. These criteria are usually divided into two categories: Internal and External.

3.4.1   Internal Quality Criteria

Internal quality metrics usually measure the compactness of the clusters using some similarity measure. It usually measures the intra-cluster homogeneity, the inter-cluster separability or a combination of these two. It does not use any external information beside the data itself.

3.4.1.1 *Sum of Squared Error (SSE)*

SSE is the simplest and most widely used criterion measure for clustering. It is calculated as:

$$SSE = \sum_{k=1}^{K} \sum_{i=1}^{N_k} \|x_i - \mu_k\|^2$$

where N_k is the number of instances belonging to cluster k. Note that:

$$\sum_{k=1}^{K} N_k = m$$

where m is the total number of data instances. μ_k is the mean of cluster no. k, calculated as:

$$\mu_{k,i} = \frac{1}{N_k} \sum_{q=1}^{N_k} x_{q,i} \quad \forall i$$

Clustering methods that minimize the SSE criterion are often called minimum variance partitions, since by simple algebraic manipulation the SSE criterion may be written as:

$$SSE = \frac{1}{2} \sum_{k=1}^{K} N_k \bar{S}_k$$

where:

$$\bar{S}_k = \frac{1}{N_k^2} \sum_{x_i, x_j \in C_k} \|x_i - x_j\|^2$$

(C_k=cluster k)

The SSE criterion function is suitable for cases in which the clusters form compact clouds that are well separated from one another [Duda *et al.* (2001)].

3.4.1.2 *Other Minimum Variance Criteria*

Additional minimum criteria to SSE may be produced by replacing the value of S_k with expressions such as:

$$\bar{S}_k = \frac{1}{N_k^2} \sum_{x_i, x_j \in C_k} s(x_i, x_j)$$

or:

$$\bar{S}_k = \min_{x_i, x_j \in C_k} s(x_i, x_j)$$

3.4.1.3 Scatter Criteria

The scalar scatter criteria are derived from the scatter matrices, reflecting the within-cluster scatter, the between-cluster scatter and their summation — the total scatter matrix. For the kth cluster, the scatter matrix may be calculated as:

$$S_k = \sum_{x \in C_k} (x - \mu_k)(x - \mu_k)^T$$

The within-cluster scatter matrix is calculated as the summation of the last definition over all clusters:

$$S_W = \sum_{k=1}^{K} S_k$$

The between-cluster scatter matrix may be calculated as:

$$S_B = \sum_{k=1}^{K} N_k (\mu_k - \mu)(\mu_k - \mu)^T$$

where μ is the total mean vector and is defined as:

$$\mu = \frac{1}{m} \sum_{k=1}^{K} N_k \mu_k$$

The total scatter matrix should be calculated as:

$$S_T = \sum_{x \in C_1, C_2, \dots, C_K} (x - \mu)(x - \mu)^T$$

Three scalar criteria may be derived from S_W, S_B and S_T:

- **The trace criterion** — the sum of the diagonal elements of a matrix. Minimizing the trace of S_W is similar to minimizing SSE and is therefore acceptable. This criterion, representing the within-cluster scatter, is calculated as:

$$J_e = tr[S_W] = \sum_{k=1}^{K} \sum_{x \in C_k} \|x - \mu_k\|^2$$

Another criterion, which may be maximized, is the between cluster criterion:

$$tr[S_B] = \sum_{k=1}^{K} N_k \|\mu_k - \mu\|^2$$

- **The determinant criterion** — the determinant of a scatter matrix roughly measures the square of the scattering volume. Since *SB* will be singular if the number of clusters is less than or equal to the dimensionality, or if $m - c$ is less than the dimensionality, its determinant is not an appropriate criterion. If we assume that SW is nonsingular, the determinant criterion function using this matrix may be employed:

$$J_d = |S_W| = \left| \sum_{k=1}^{K} S_k \right|$$

- **The invariant criterion** — the eigenvalues $\lambda_1, \lambda_2, \ldots, \lambda_d$ of

$$S_W^{-1} S_B$$

are the basic linear invariants of the scatter matrices. Good partitions are ones for which the nonzero eigenvalues are large. As a result, several criteria may be derived including the eigenvalues. Three such criteria are:

(1) $tr[S_W^{-1} S_B] = \sum_{i=1}^{d} \lambda_i$

(2) $J_f = tr[S_T^{-1} S_W] = \sum_{i=1}^{d} \frac{1}{1+\lambda_i}$

(3) $\frac{|S_W|}{|S_T|} = \prod_{i=1}^{d} \frac{1}{1+\lambda_i}$

3.4.1.4 *Condorcet's Criterion*

Another appropriate approach is to use the Condorcet's solution (1785) to the ranking problem [Marcotorchino and Michaud (1979)]. In this case the criterion is calculated as following:

$$\sum_{\substack{C_i \in C}} \sum_{\substack{x_j, x_k \in C_i \\ x_j \neq x_k}} s(x_j, x_k) + \sum_{\substack{C_i \in C}} \sum_{\substack{x_j \in C_i; x_k \notin C_i}} d(x_j, x_k)$$

where $s(x_j, x_k)$ and $d(x_j, x_k)$ measures the similarity and distance of the vectors x_j and x_k.

3.4.1.5   *The C-Criterion*

The C-criterion [Fortier and Solomon (1996)] is an extension of the Condorcet's criterion and is defined as:

$$\sum_{\substack{C_i \in C}} \sum_{\substack{x_j, x_k \in C_i \\ x_j \neq x_k}} (s(x_j, x_k) - \gamma) + \sum_{\substack{C_i \in C}} \sum_{\substack{x_j \in C_i; x_k \notin C_i}} (\gamma - s(x_j, x_k))$$

where γ is a threshold value.

3.4.1.6   *Category Utility Metric*

The category utility [Gluck and Corter (1985)] is defined as the increase of the expected number of feature values that can be correctly predicted given a certain clustering. This metric is useful for problems that contain a relatively small number of nominal features each having small cardinality.

3.4.1.7   *Edge Cut Metrics*

In some cases it can be useful to represent the clustering problem as an edge cut minimization problem. In this case the quality is measured as the ratio of the remaining edge weights to the total precut edge weights. If there is no restriction on the size of the clusters, finding the optimal value is easy. As a result of this the min-cut measure is revised to penalize imbalanced structures.

3.4.2   *External Quality Criteria*

External measures can be useful to examine whether the structure of the clusters match to some predefined classification of the instances.

3.4.2.1 *Mutual Information Based Measure*

The mutual information criterion can be used as an external measure for clustering [Strehl *et al.* (2000)]. The measure for m instances clustered using $C = \{C_1, \ldots, C_g\}$ and referring to the target attribute y whose domain is $dom(y) = \{c_1, \ldots, c_k\}$ is defined as follows:

$$C = \frac{2}{m} \sum_{l=1}^{g} \sum_{h=1}^{k} m_{l,h} \log_{g \cdot k} \left(\frac{m_{l,h} \cdot m}{m_{.,l} \cdot m_{l,.}} \right)$$

where $m_{l,h}$ indicate the number of instances that are in cluster C_l and also in class c_h. $m_{.,h}$ denotes the total number of instances in the class c_h. Similarly $m_{l,.}$ indicates the number of instances in cluster C_l.

3.4.2.2 *Precision-Recall Measure*

The precision-recall measure from information retrieval can be used as an external measure for evaluating clusters. The Cluster is viewed as the results of a query for a specific class. Precision is the fraction of correctly retrieved instances, while recall is the fraction of correctly retrieved instances out of all matching instances. A combined F-measure can be useful for evaluating a clustering structure [Larsen and Aone (1999)].

3.4.2.3 *Rand Index*

The Rand index [Rand (1971)] is a simple criterion used to compare an induced clustering structure (C_1) to a given clustering structure (C_2). Let a be the number of pairs of instances that are assigned to the same cluster in C_1 and in the same cluster in C_2, b be the number of pairs of instances that are in the same cluster in C_1, but not in the same cluster in C_2, c be the number of pairs of instances that are in the same cluster in C_2, but not in the same cluster in C_1, and d be the number of pairs of instances that are assigned to different clusters in C_1 and C_2. The quantities a and d can be interpreted as agreements, and b and c as disagreements. The Rand index is defined as:

$$RAND = \frac{a + d}{a + b + c + d}$$

The Rand index lies between 0 and 1. When the two partitions agree perfectly, the Rand index is 1.

A problem with the Rand index is that its expected value of two random clustering does not take a constant value (such as zero). [Hubert and Arabie (1985)] suggest an adjusted Rand index that overcomes this disadvantage.

3.5   Clustering Methods

In this section we describe the most well-known clustering algorithms. According to [Estivill-Castro (2000)] the main reason for having many clustering methods is the fact that the notion of "cluster" is not precisely defined. Consequently many clustering methods have been developed, each of which uses a different induction principle. [Farley and Raftery (1998)] suggest to divide the clustering methods into two main groups: Hierarchical and Partitioning methods. [Han and Kamber (2001)] suggest categorizing the methods into additional three main categories: *Density based methods*, *Model based clustering* and *Grid-based methods*. An alternative categorization based on the induction principle of the various clustering methods is presented in [Estivill-Castro (2000)].

3.5.1   *Hierarchical Methods*

These methods construct the clusters by recursively partitioning the instances in either a top-down or bottom-up fashion. These methods can be sub-divided as following:

- Agglomerative hierarchical clustering — each object initially represents a cluster of its own. Then clusters are successively merged until the desired cluster structure is obtained.
- Divisive hierarchical clustering — All objects initially belong to one cluster. Then the cluster is divided into sub clusters, which are successively divided into sub clusters of their own. This process continues until the desired clusters structure is obtained.

The result of the hierarchical methods is a dendrogram, representing the nested grouping of objects and similarity levels at which groupings change. A clustering of the data objects is obtained by cutting the dendrogram at the desired similarity level. Figure 3.1 illustrates the differences between these two approaches.

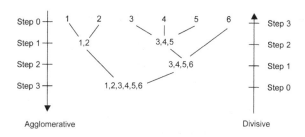

Fig. 3.1   Agglomerative and Divisive Hierarchical Clustering.

The merging or division of clusters is performed according to some similarity measure, chosen so as to optimize some criterion (such as a sum of squares). The hierarchical clustering methods could be further divided according to the manner that the similarity measure is calculated [Jain *et al.* (1999)]:

- **Single-link clustering** (also called the connectedness, the minimum method or the nearest neighbor method) — methods that consider the distance between two clusters to be equal to the shortest distance from any member of one cluster to any member of the other cluster. If the data consist of similarities, the similarity between a pair of clusters is considered to be equal to the greatest similarity from any member of one cluster to any member of the other cluster. This idea has been used in [Kaufmann and Rousseeuw (1990)] and in [Sneath and Sokal (1973)].
- **Complete-link clustering** (also called the diameter, the maximum method or the furthest neighbor method) — methods that consider the distance between two clusters to be equal to the longest distance from any member of one cluster to any member of the other cluster. An example for complete link clustering may be found in [King (1967)].
- **Average-link clustering** (also called minimum variance method) — methods that consider the distance between two clusters to be equal to the average distance from any member of one cluster to any member of the other cluster. Such clustering algorithms may be found in [Ward (1963)] and [Murtagh (1984)].

The disadvantages of the single-link clustering and the average-link clustering can be summarized as follows [Guha *et al.* (1998)]:

- Single-link clustering has a drawback known as the "chaining effect": A few points that form a bridge between two clusters cause the single-link clustering to unify these two clusters into one.

- Average-link clustering may cause elongated clusters to split and portions of neighboring elongated clusters to merge.

The complete-link clustering methods produce more compact clusters than the single-link clustering methods and produce more useful hierarchies in many applications, yet the single-link methods are more versatile.

Generally, hierarchical methods are characterized with the following strengths:

- Versatility — the single-link methods, for example, maintain good performance on data sets containing non-isotropic clusters, including well-separated, chain-like and concentric clusters (see Figure 3.2).
- Multiple partitions — hierarchical methods produce not one partition, but multiple nested partitions, which allows different users to choose different partitions, according to the desired similarity level. The hierarchical partition is presented using the dendrogram.

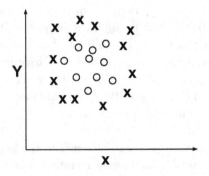

Fig. 3.2   Two Concentric Clusters.

The main disadvantages of Hierarchical methods include:

- Inability to scale well — the time complexity of hierarchical algorithms is at least $O(m^2)$ (where m is the total number of instances), which is non-linear with the number of objects. Clustering a large number of objects using a hierarchical algorithm is also characterized by huge I/O costs.
- Hierarchical methods can never undo what was done previously. Namely there is no back-tracking capability.

3.5.2 *Partitioning Methods*

Partitioning methods relocate instances, by moving them from one cluster to another, starting from an initial partitioning. Such methods typically require that the number of clusters will be pre-set by the user. To achieve global optimality in partitioned-based clustering, an exhaustive enumeration process of all possible partitions is required. Because this is not feasible, certain greedy heuristics are used in the form of iterative optimization. Namely, a relocation method iteratively relocates points between the k clusters. The following subsections present various type of partitioning methods.

3.5.2.1 *Error Minimization Algorithms*

These algorithms, which tend to work well with isolated and compact clusters, are the most intuitive and frequently used methods. The basic idea is to find a clustering structure that minimizes a certain error criterion which measures the "distance" of each instance to its representative value. The most well known criterion is the Sum of Squared Error (SSE), which measures the total squared Euclidian distance of instances to their representative values. SSE may be globally optimized by exhaustively enumerating all partitions, which is highly time-consuming, or rather be given an approximate solution (not necessarily leading to a global minimum) using heuristics, being the common course of action.

The simplest and most commonly used algorithm, employing a squared error criterion is the K-means algorithm. This algorithm partitions the data into K clusters $(C_1, C_2, \ldots, C_K)$, represented by their centers or means. The center of each cluster is calculated as the mean of all the instances belonging to that cluster.

Figure 3.3 presents the pseudo-code of the K-means algorithm. The algorithm starts with an initial set of cluster centers, chosen at random or according to some heuristic procedure. In each iteration, each instance is assigned to its nearest cluster center according to the Euclidean distance between the two. Then the cluster centers are re-calculated.

The center of each cluster is calculated as the mean of all the instances belonging to that cluster:

$$\mu_k = \frac{1}{N_k} \sum_{q=1}^{N_k} x_q$$

where N_k is the number of instances belonging to cluster k and μ_k is the mean of the cluster k.

A number of convergence conditions are possible. For example, the search may stop when the partitioning error is not reduced by the relocation of the centers. This indicates that the present partition is locally optimal. Other stopping criteria can be used also such as exceeding a pre-defined number of iterations.

```
K-Mean Clustering (S,K)
Where:
S - Instances Set
K - Number of Clusters
Initialize K cluster centers.
WHILE termination condition is not satisfied {
    Assign instances to the closest cluster center.
    Update cluster centers using the instances assignment
}
```

Fig. 3.3 K-means Algorithm.

The K-means algorithm may be viewed as a gradient-decent procedure, which begins with an initial set of K cluster-centers and iteratively updates it so as to decrease the error function.

A rigorous proof of the finite convergence of the K-means type algorithms is given in [Selim and Ismail (1984)]. The complexity of T iterations of the K-means algorithm performed on a sample size of m instances, each characterized by N attributes is: $O(T \cdot K \cdot m \cdot N)$.

This linear complexity is one of the reasons for the popularity of the K-means algorithms: Even if the number of instances is substantially large (which often is the case nowadays) — this algorithm is computationally attractive. Thus, the K-means algorithm has an advantage in comparison to other clustering methods (e.g. hierarchical clustering methods), which have non-linear complexity.

Other reasons for the algorithm's popularity are its ease of interpretation, simplicity of implementation, speed of convergence and adaptability to sparse data [Dhillon and Modha (2001)].

The Achilles heel of the K-means algorithm involves the selection of the initial partition. The algorithm is very sensitive to this selection, which may make the difference between global and local minimum.

Being a typical partitioning algorithm, the K-means algorithm works well only on data sets having isotropic clusters, and is not as versatile as single link algorithms, for instance.

In addition, this algorithm is sensitive to noisy data and outliers (a single outlier can increase the squared error dramatically), applicable only when mean is defined (namely, for numeric attributes) and requires the number of clusters in advance, which is not trivial when no prior knowledge is available.

The use of the K-means algorithm is often limited to numeric attributes. [Haung (1998)] presented the K-prototypes algorithm, which is based on the K-means algorithm but removes numeric data limitations whilst preserving its efficiency. The algorithm clusters objects with numeric and categorical attributes in a way similar to the K-means algorithm. The similarity measure on numeric attributes is the square Euclidean distance, whereas the similarity measure on the categorical attributes is the number of mismatches between objects and the cluster prototypes.

Another partitioning algorithm, which attempts to minimize the SSE is the K-medoids or PAM (partition around medoids — [Kaufmann and Rousseeuw (1987)]). This algorithm is very similar to the K-means algorithm. It defers from the latter mainly in its representation of the different clusters. Each cluster is represented by the most centric object in the cluster, rather than by the implicit mean that may not belong to the cluster.

The K-medoids method is more robust than the K-means algorithm in the presence of noise and outliers because a medoid is less influenced by outliers or other extreme values than a mean. However, its processing is more costly than the K-means method. Both methods require the user to specify K, the number of clusters.

Other error criteria can be used instead of the SSE. [Estivill-Castro (2000)] has analyzed the total absolute error criterion. Namely instead of summing up the squared error, he suggests to sum up the absolute error. While this criterion is superior on notion of robustness, it requires more computational effort.

3.5.2.2 *Graph-Theoretic Clustering*

Graph theoretic methods are methods that produce clusters via graphs. The edges of the graph connect the instances represented as nodes. A well-known graph-theoretic algorithm is based on the Minimal Spanning Tree — MST [Zahn (1971)]. Inconsistent edges are edges whose weight (in the case of clustering-length) is significantly larger than the average of nearby edge lengths. Another graph-theoretic approach constructs graphs based on limited neighborhood sets [Urquhart (1982)].

There is also a relation between hierarchical methods and graph theoretic clustering:

- Single-link clusters are subgraphs of the MST of the data instances. Each subgraph is a *connected component*, namely a set of instances in which each instance is connected to at least one other member of the set, so that the set is maximal with respect to this property. These subgraphs are formed according to some similarity threshold.
- Complete-link clusters are *maximal complete subgraphs*, formed using a similarity threshold. A maximal complete subgraph is a subgraph such that each node is connected to every other node in the subgraph and the set is maximal with respect to this property.

3.5.3   *Density Based Methods*

Density based methods assume that the points that belong to each cluster are drawn from a specific probability distribution [Banfield and Raftery (1993)]. The overall distribution of the data is assumed to be a mixture of several distributions.

Therefore, the aim of these methods is to identify the clusters and their distribution parameters. These methods are designed for discovering clusters of arbitrary shape which are not necessarily convex, namely:

$$x_i, x_j \in C_k$$

Does not necessarily imply that:

$$\alpha \cdot x_i + (1 - \alpha) \cdot x_j \in C_k$$

The idea is to continue growing the given cluster as long as the density (number of objects or data points) in the neighborhood exceeds some threshold. Namely, the neighborhood of a given radius has to contain at least a minimum number of objects. When each cluster is characterized by local mode or maxima of the density function, these methods are called mode-seeking

Much work in this field has been based on the underlying assumption that the component densities are multivariate Gaussian (in case of numeric data) or multinominal (in case of nominal data).

An acceptable solution in this case will be using the maximum likelihood principle. According to this principle one should choose the clustering structure and parameters such that the probability of the data being generated by such clustering structure and parameters is maximized. The expectation maximization algorithm — EM — [Dempster *et al.* (1977)], which is a general-purpose maximum likelihood algorithm for missing-data problems, has been applied to the problem of parameter estimation. This algorithm begins with an initial estimate of the parameter vector and then alternates between two steps [Farley and Raftery (1998)]: an "E-step", in which the conditional expectation of the complete data likelihood given the observed data and the current parameter estimates is computed, and an "M-step", in which parameters that maximize the expected likelihood from the E-step are determined. This algorithm was shown to converge to a local maximum of the observed data likelihood.

The K-means algorithm may be viewed as degenerate EM algorithm, in which:

$$p(k/x) = \begin{cases} 1 & k = \underset{k}{\mathrm{argmax}}\{\hat{p}(k/x)\} \\ 0 & \text{otherwise} \end{cases}$$

Assigning instances to clusters in the K-means may be considered as the E-step, whereas computing new cluster centers may be regarded to be the M-step.

DBSCAN algorithm (density-based spatial clustering of applications with noise) discovers clusters of arbitrary shapes and is efficient for large spatial databases. The algorithm searches for clusters by searching the neighborhood of each object in the database and checks if it contains more than the minimum number of objects [Ester *et al.* (1996)].

AUTOCLASS is a widely used algorithm that covers a broad variety of distributions, including Gaussian, Bernoulli, Poisson, and log-normal distributions [Cheeseman and Stutz (1996)]. Other well known density based methods include: SNOB [Wallace and Dowe (1994)] and MCLUST [Farley and Raftery (1998)].

Density-based clustering may also employ nonparametric methods, such as searching for bins with large counts in a multidimensional histogram of the input instance space [Jain *et al.* (1999)].

3.5.4   *Model Based Clustering*

These methods attempt to optimize the fit between the given data and some mathematical models. Unlike conventional clustering, which identifies groups of objects, those methods also find characteristic descriptions for each group, where each group represents a concept or class. The most frequently used induction methods are decision trees and neural networks.

3.5.4.1   *Decision Trees*

In decision trees the data is represented by a hierarchical tree, in which each node refers to a concept and contains a probabilistic description of that concept. Several algorithms produce classification trees for representing the unlabelled data. The most well-known algorithms are:

COBWEB — this algorithm assumes that all attributes are independent (an often too naive assumption). Its aim is to achieve high predictability of nominal variable values, given a cluster. This algorithm is not suitable for clustering large database data [Fisher (1987)]. CLASSIT — an extension of COBWEB for continuous—valued data, which unfortunately has similar problems as COBWEB algorithm.

3.5.4.2   *Neural Networks*

This type of algorithm represents each cluster by a neuron or "prototype". The input data is also represented by neurons, which are connected to the prototype neurons. Each such connection has a weight, which is learned adaptively during learning.

A very popular neural algorithm for clustering is the self-organizing map (SOM). This algorithm constructs a single-layered network. The learning process takes place in a "winner-takes-all" fashion:

- The prototype neurons compete for the current instance. The winner is the neuron whose weight vector is closest to the instance currently presented.
- The winner and its neighbors learn by having their weights adjusted.

The SOM algorithm is successfully used for vector quantization and speech recognition. It is useful for visualizing high-dimensional data in 2D or 3D space. However, it is sensitive to the initial selection of weight vector, as well as to its different parameters, such as the learning rate and neighborhood radius.

3.5.5   Grid-Based Methods

These methods quantisize the space into a finite number of cells that form a grid structure on which all of the operations for clustering are performed. The main advantage of the approach is its fast processing time [Han and Kamber (2001)].

3.5.6   Fuzzy Clustering

Traditional clustering approaches generate partitions; in a partition, each instance belongs to one and only one cluster. Hence, the clusters in a hard clustering are disjoint. Fuzzy clustering (see for instance [Hoppner *et al.* (1999)]) extends this notion and suggests a *soft clustering* schema. In this case each pattern is associated with every cluster using some sort of membership function, namely each cluster is a fuzzy set of all the patterns. Larger membership values indicate higher confidence in the assignment of the pattern to the cluster. A hard clustering can be obtained from a fuzzy partition by using a threshold of the membership value.

The most popular fuzzy clustering algorithm is the fuzzy c-means (FCM) algorithm. Even though it is better than the hard K-means algorithm at avoiding local minima, FCM can still converge to local minima of the squared error criterion. The design of membership functions is the most important problem in fuzzy clustering; different choices include those based on similarity decomposition and centroids of clusters. A generalization of the FCM algorithm was proposed through a family of objective functions. A fuzzy c-shell algorithm and an adaptive variant for detecting circular and elliptical boundaries was presented.

3.5.7   Evolutionary Approaches for Clustering

Evolutionary techniques are stochastic general purpose methods for solving optimization problems. As clustering problem can be defined as an optimization problem, evolutionary approaches may be appropriate here. The idea is to use evolutionary operators and a population of clustering structures to converge into a globally optimal clustering. Candidate clustering are encoded as chromosomes. The most commonly used evolutionary operators are: selection, recombination, and mutation. A fitness function evaluated on a chromosome determines a chromosome's likelihood of surviving into the next generation. The most frequently used evolutionary technique in clustering problems is genetic algorithms (GAs). Figure 3.4

presents a high-level pseudo-code of a typical GA for clustering. A fitness value is associated with each clusters structure. A higher fitness value indicates a better clusters structure. A suitable fitness function is the inverse of the squared error value. Clusters structure with a small squared error will have a larger fitness value.

GA-Clustering (S,K,n)

Where:

S - Instances Set

K - Number of Clusters

n - Population size

Randomly create a *population* of n structures, each corresponds to a valid K-clusters of the data.

DO {

    Associate a fitness value $\forall structure \in population$.

    Regenerate a new generation of structures.

} UNTIL some termination condition is satisfied

RETURN the best structure

Fig. 3.4   GA for Clustering.

The most obvious way to represent structures is to use strings of length m (where m is the number of instances in the given set). The i-th entry of the string denotes the cluster to which the i-th instance belongs. Consequently, each entry can have values from 1 to K. An improved representation scheme is proposed where an additional separator symbol is used along with the pattern labels to represent a partition. Using this representation permits them to map the clustering problem into a permutation problem such as the travelling salesman problem, which can be solved by using the permutation crossover operators. This solution also suffers from permutation redundancy.

In GAs, a selection operator propagates solutions from the current generation to the next generation based on their fitness. Selection employs a probabilistic scheme so that solutions with higher fitness have a higher probability of getting reproduced.

There are a variety of recombination operators in use; *crossover* is the most popular. Crossover takes as input a pair of chromosomes (called parents) and outputs a new pair of chromosomes (called children or offspring). In this way the GS explores the search space. Mutation is used to make sure that the algorithm is not trapped in local optimum.

More recently investigated is the use of edge-based crossover to solve the clustering problem. Here, all patterns in a cluster are assumed to form a complete graph by connecting them with edges. Offspring are generated from the parents so that they inherit the edges from their parents. In a hybrid approach proposed, the GAs is used only to find good initial cluster centers and the K-means algorithm is applied to find the final partition. This hybrid approach performed better than the GAs.

A major problem with GAs is their sensitivity to the selection of various parameters such as population size, crossover and mutation probabilities, etc. Several researchers have studied this problem and suggested guidelines for selecting these control parameters. However, these guidelines may not yield good results on specific problems like pattern clustering. It was reported that hybrid genetic algorithms incorporating problem-specific heuristics are good for clustering. A similar claim is made about the applicability of GAs to other practical problems. Another issue with GAs is the selection of an appropriate representation which is low in order and short in defining length.

There are other evolutionary techniques such as evolution strategies (ESs), and evolutionary programming (EP). These techniques differ from the GAs in solution representation and the type of mutation operator used; EP does not use a recombination operator, but only selection and mutation. Each of these three approaches have been used to solve the clustering problem by viewing it as a minimization of the squared error criterion. Some of the theoretical issues such as the convergence of these approaches were studied. GAs perform a globalized search for solutions whereas most other clustering procedures perform a localized search. In a localized search, the solution obtained at the 'next iteration' of the procedure is in the vicinity of the current solution. In this sense, the K-means algorithm and fuzzy clustering algorithms are all localized search techniques. In the case of GAs, the crossover and mutation operators can produce new solutions that are completely different from the current ones.

It is possible to search for the optimal location of the centroids rather than finding the optimal partition. This idea permits the use of ESs and EP, because centroids can be coded easily in both these approaches, as they support the direct representation of a solution as a real-valued vector.

ESs were used on both hard and fuzzy clustering problems and EP has been used to evolve fuzzy min-max clusters. It has been observed that they perform better than their classical counterparts, the K-means algorithm and the fuzzy c-means algorithm. However, all of these approaches are over sensitive to their parameters setting. Consequently, for each specific problem, the user is required to tune the parameter values to suit the application.

3.5.8   *Simulated Annealing for Clustering*

Another general-purpose stochastic search technique that can be used for clustering is simulated annealing (SA). The simulated annealing approach (SA) is a sequential stochastic search technique, which is designed to avoid local optima. This is accomplished by accepting with some probability a new solution for the next iteration of lower quality (as measured by the criterion function). The probability of acceptance is governed by a critical parameter called the temperature (by analogy with annealing in metals), which is typically specified in terms of a starting (first iteration) and final temperature value. [Selim and Al-Sultan (1991)] studied the effects of control parameters on the performance of the algorithm. SA is statistically guaranteed to find the global optimal solution. Figure 3.5 presents a high-level pseudo-code of the SA algorithm for clustering.

The SA algorithm can be slow in reaching the optimal solution, because optimal results require the temperature to be decreased very slowly from iteration to iteration. Tabu search, like SA, is a method designed to cross boundaries of feasibility or local optimality and to systematically impose and release constraints to permit exploration of otherwise forbidden regions. [Al-Sultan (1995)] suggests to use Tabu search as an alternative to SA.

3.5.9   *Which Technique to Use?*

An empirical study of K-means, SA, TS, and GA was presented by [Al-Sultan and Khan (1996)]. TS, GA and SA were judged comparable in terms of solution quality, and all were better than K-means. However, the K-means method is the most efficient in terms of execution time; other schemes took more time (by a factor of 500 to 2500) to partition a data set of size 60 into 5 clusters. Furthermore, GA has obtained the best solution faster than TS and SA; SA took more time than TS to reach the best clustering. However, GA took the maximum time for convergence, that is, to

```
SA Clustering  (S,K,T₀,Tƒ,c)
```

Where:

S - Instances Set

K - Number of Clusters

T_0 - Initial Temperature

T_f - Final Temperature

c - Temperature Reducing constant

Randomly select an initial valid K-partition of S (p_0), and compute its squared error value $E(p_0)$.

While $(T_0 > T_f$) {

    Select a neighbor p_1 of the last partition p_0.

    If $E(p_1) > E(p_0)$ then

        $p_0 \leftarrow p_1$ with a probability that depends on T_0

    Else

        $p_0 \leftarrow p_1$

    $T_0 \leftarrow c \cdot T_0$

}

Fig. 3.5   Clustering Based on Simulated Annealing.

obtain a population of only the best solutions, followed by TS and SA.

An additional empirical study has compared the performance of the following clustering algorithms: SA, GA, TS, randomized branch-and-bound (RBA), and hybrid search (HS) [Mishra and Raghavan (1994)]. The conclusion was that GA performs well in the case of one-dimensional data, while its performance on high dimensional data sets is not impressive. The convergence pace of SA is too slow, RBA and TS performed best and HS is good for high dimensional data. However, none of the methods was found to be superior to others by a significant margin.

It is important to note that both [Mishra and Raghavan (1994)] and [Al-Sultan and Khan (1996)] have used relatively small data sets in their experimental studies.

In summary, only the K-means algorithm and its ANN equivalent, the Kohonen net, have been applied on large data sets; other approaches have been tested, typically, on small data sets. This is because obtaining suitable learning/control parameters for ANNs, GAs, TS, and SA is difficult and their execution times are very high for large data sets. However, it has been shown that the K-means method converges to a locally optimal solution. This behavior is linked with the initial seed election in the K-means algorithm. Therefore, if a good initial partition can be obtained quickly using any of the other techniques, then K-means would work well even on problems with large data sets. Even though various methods discussed in this section are comparatively weak, it was revealed through experimental studies that combining domain knowledge would improve their performance. For example, ANNs work better in classifying images represented using extracted features rather than with raw images, and hybrid classifiers work better than ANNs. Similarly, using domain knowledge to hybridize a GA improves its performance. Therefore it may be useful in general to use domain knowledge along with approaches like GA, SA, ANN, and TS. However, these approaches (specifically, the criteria functions used in them) have a tendency to generate a partition of hyperspherical clusters, and this could be a limitation. For example, in cluster-based document retrieval, it was observed that the hierarchical algorithms performed better than the partitioning algorithms.

3.6   Clustering Large Data Sets

There are several applications where it is necessary to cluster a large collection of patterns. The definition of 'large' is vague. In document retrieval, millions of instances with a dimensionality of more than 100 have to be clustered to achieve data abstraction. A majority of the approaches and algorithms proposed in the literature cannot handle such large data sets. Approaches based on genetic algorithms, tabu search and simulated annealing are optimization techniques and are restricted to reasonably small data sets. Implementations of conceptual clustering optimize some criterion functions and are typically computationally expensive.

The convergent K-means algorithm and its ANN equivalent, the Kohonen net, have been used to cluster large data sets. The reasons behind the popularity of the K-means algorithm are:

(1) Its time complexity is $O(mkl)$, where m is the number of instances, k is the number of clusters, and l is the number of iterations taken by the algorithm to converge. Typically, k and l are fixed in advance and so the algorithm has linear time complexity in the size of the data set.

(2) Its space complexity is $O(k + m)$. It requires additional space to store the data matrix. It is possible to store the data matrix in a secondary memory and access each pattern based on need. However, this scheme requires a huge access time because of the iterative nature of the algorithm, and as a consequence, processing time increases enormously.

(3) It is order-independent; for a given initial seed set of cluster centers, it generates the same partition of the data irrespective of the order in which the patterns are presented to the algorithm.

However, the K-means algorithm is sensitive to initial seed selection and even in the best case, it can produce only hyperspherical clusters. Hierarchical algorithms are more versatile. But they have the following disadvantages:

(1) The time complexity of hierarchical agglomerative algorithms is $O(m^2 \cdot \log m)$.

(2) The space complexity of agglomerative algorithms is $O(m^2)$. This is because a similarity matrix of size m^2 has to be stored. It is possible to compute the entries of this matrix based on need instead of storing them.

A possible solution to the problem of clustering large data sets while only marginally sacrificing the versatility of clusters is to implement more efficient variants of clustering algorithms. A hybrid approach was used, where a set of reference points is chosen as in the K-means algorithm, and each of the remaining data points is assigned to one or more reference points or clusters. Minimal spanning trees (MST) are obtained for each group of points separately. These MSTs are merged to form an approximate global MST. This approach computes similarities between only a fraction of all possible pairs of points. It was shown that the number of similarities computed for 10,000 instances using this approach is the same as the total number of pairs of points in a collection of 2,000 points. [Bentley and Friedman (1978)] presents an algorithm that can compute an approximate MST in $O(m \log m)$ time. A scheme to generate an approximate dendrogram incrementally in $O(n \log n)$ time was presented.

CLARANS (Clustering Large Applications based on RANdom Search) have been developed by [Ng and Han (1994)]. This method identifies candidate cluster centroids by using repeated random samples of the original data. Because of the use of random sampling, the time complexity is $O(n)$ for a pattern set of n elements.

The BIRCH algorithm (Balanced Iterative Reducing and Clustering) stores summary information about candidate clusters in a dynamic tree data structure. This tree hierarchically organizes the clusters represented at the leaf nodes. The tree can be rebuilt when a threshold specifying cluster size is updated manually, or when memory constraints force a change in this threshold. This algorithm has a time complexity linear in the number of instances.

All algorithms presented till this point assume that the entire dataset can be accommodated in the main memory. However, there are cases in which this assumption is not true. There are currently three possible approaches to solve this problem, as described in the following subsections.

3.6.1 *Decomposition Approach*

The dataset can be stored in a secondary memory (i.e. hard disk) and subsets of this data clustered independently, followed by a merging step to yield a clustering of the entire dataset.

In initial step the data is decomposed into number of subsets. Each subset is sent to the main memory in turn and it is clustered into k clusters using a standard algorithm.

In order to join the various clustering structures obtained from each subset, a representative sample from each cluster of each structure is stored in the main memory. Then these representative instances are further clustered into k clusters and the cluster labels of these representative instances are used to re-label the original dataset. It is possible to extend this algorithm to any number of iterations; more levels are required if the data set is very large and the main memory size is very small.

3.6.2 *Incremental Clustering*

Incremental clustering is based on the assumption that it is possible to consider instances one at a time and assign them to existing clusters. Here, a new instance is assigned to a cluster without affecting the existing clusters significantly. Only the cluster representations are stored in the main memory to alleviate the space limitations.

Figure 3.6 presents a high level pseudo-code of a typical incremental clustering algorithm.

The major advantage with the incremental clustering algorithms is that it is not necessary to store the entire dataset in the memory. Therefore, the

---

SA Clustering $(S, K, Threshold)$

Where:

S - Instances Set

K - Number of Clusters

$Threshold$ - For assigning an instance to an existing cluster

$Clusters \leftarrow \emptyset$

$\forall x_i \in S \, \{$

    $As\_F = false$

    $\forall Cluster \in Clusters \, \{$

        IF $\|x_i - centroid(Cluster)\| < threshold$ THEN $\{$

            $update \, centroid(Cluster)$

            $ins\_counter(Cluster) + +$

            $As\_F = true$

            EXIT LOOP

        $\}$

    $\}$

    IF NOT(As_F) THEN $\{$

        $centroid(newCluster) = x_i$

        $ins\_counter(newCluster) = 1$

        $Clusters \leftarrow Clusters \cup newCluster$

    $\}$

$\}$

Fig. 3.6   An Incremental Clustering Algorithm.

space requirements of incremental algorithms are very small and also their time requirements are also small. There are several incremental clustering algorithms:

(1) The leader clustering algorithm is the simplest in terms of time complexity which is O(mk). It has gained popularity because of its neural network implementation, the ART network and is very easy to implement as it requires only $O(k)$ space.

(2) The shortest spanning path (SSP) algorithm, as originally proposed for data reorganization, was successfully used in automatic auditing of records. Here, the SSP algorithm was used to cluster 2000 patterns

using 18 features. These clusters are used to estimate missing feature values in data items and to identify erroneous feature values.

(3) The *COBWEB* system is an incremental conceptual clustering algorithm. It has been successfully used in engineering applications.

(4) An incremental clustering algorithm for dynamic information processing was presented by [Can (1993)]. The motivation behind this work is that in dynamic databases items might get added and deleted over time. These changes should be reflected in the partition generated without significantly affecting the current clusters. This algorithm was used to cluster incrementally an INSPEC database of 12,684 documents corresponding to computer science and electrical engineering.

Order-independence is an important property of clustering algorithms. An algorithm is *order-independent* if it generates the same partition for any order in which the data is presented, otherwise, it is *order-dependent*. Most of the incremental algorithms presented above are order-dependent. For instance the SSP algorithm and cobweb are order-dependent.

3.6.3 *Parallel Implementation*

Recent work demonstrates that a combination of algorithmic enhancements to a clustering algorithm and distribution of the computations over a network of workstations can allow a large dataset to be clustered in a few minutes. Depending on the clustering algorithm in use, parallelization of the code and replication of data for efficiency may yield large benefits. However, a global shared data structure, namely the cluster membership table, remains and must be managed centrally or replicated and synchronized periodically. The presence or absence of robust, efficient parallel clustering techniques will determine the success or failure of cluster analysis in large-scale data mining applications in the future.

3.7 Determining the Number of Clusters

As mentioned above, many clustering algorithms require that the number of clusters will be pre-set by the user. It is well known that this parameter affects the performance of the algorithm significantly. This poses a serious question as to which K should be chosen when prior knowledge regarding the cluster quantity is unavailable.

Note that most of the criteria that have been used to lead the construction of the clusters (such as SSE) are monotonically decreasing in K. Therefore using these criteria for determining the number of clusters result with a trivial clustering in which each instance is a cluster by itself. Consequently, different criteria are needed to be applied here. Many methods were offered to determine which K is preferable. These methods are usually heuristics, involving the calculation of clustering criteria measures for different values of K, thus enabling the evaluation of which K was preferable.

3.7.1 *Methods Based on Intra Cluster Scatter*

Many of the methods for determining K are based on the intra-cluster (within-cluster) scatter. This category includes the within cluster depression decay ([Tibshirani *et al.* (2000)]; [Wang and Yu (2001)]), which computes an error measure W_K, for each K chosen, as follows:

$$W_K = \sum_{k=1}^{K} \frac{1}{2N_k} D_k$$

where D_k is the sum of pairwise distances for all instances in cluster k:

$$D_k = \sum_{x_i, x_j \in Ck} \|x_i - x_j\|$$

In general, as the number of clusters increases, the within cluster decay first declines rapidly. From a certain K the curve flattens. That elbow is considered to be the appropriate K according to this method.

Other heuristics relate to the intra-cluster distance as the sum of squared Euclidean distances between the data instances and their cluster centers (the sum of squares error the algorithm attempts to minimize). They range from simple methods, such as the PRE method, to more sophisticated, statistics-based methods.

An example of a simple method which works well in most databases is, as mentioned above, the proportional reduction in error (PRE) method. PRE is the ratio of reduction in the sum of squares to the previous sum of squares when comparing the results of using $K + 1$ clusters to the results of using K clusters. Increasing the number of clusters by 1 is justified for PRE rates of about 0.4 or larger.

It is also possible to examine the SSE decay, which behaves similarly to the within cluster depression described above. The manner of determining K according to both measures is also similar.

An approximate F statistic can be used to test the significance of the reduction in the sum of squares as we increase the number of clusters [Hartigan (1975)]. The method obtains this F statistic as follows:

Suppose that $P(m, k)$ is the partition of m instances into k clusters, and $P(m, k+1)$ is obtained from $P(m, k)$ by splitting one of the clusters. Also assume that the clusters are selected without regard to $x_{qi} \sim N(\mu_i, \sigma^2)$ independently over all q and i. Then the overall mean square ratio is calculated and distributed as follows:

$$R = \left(\frac{e(P(m, k)}{e(P(m, k+1)} - 1 \right) (m - k - 1) \approx F_{N, N(m-k-1)}$$

where $e(P(m, k))$ is the sum of squared Euclidean distances between the data instances and their cluster centers.

In fact this F distribution is not accurate since it is based on inaccurate assumptions:

- K-means is not a hierarchical clustering algorithm, but a relocation method. Therefore, the partition $P(m, k+1)$ is not necessarily obtained by splitting one of the clusters in $P(m, k)$.
- Each x_{qi} influences the partition.
- The assumptions as to the normal distribution and independence of x_{qi} are not valid in all databases.

As the F statistic, as described above, is imprecise, Hartigan offers a crude rule of thumb: only large values of the ratio (say, larger than 10) justify increasing the number of partitions from K to $K + 1$.

3.7.2   Methods Based on Both the Inter and Intra Cluster Scatter

All the methods described so far for estimating the number of clusters are quite reasonable. However, they all suffer the same deficiency: None of these methods examines the inter cluster distances. Thus, if the K-means algorithm partitions an existing distinct cluster in the data into sub-clusters (which is undesired), it is possible that none of the above methods would indicate this situation.

In light of this observation, it may be preferable to minimize the intra-cluster scatter and at the same time maximize the inter-cluster scatter. [Ray and Turi (1999)], for example, strive for this goal by setting a measure that equals the ratio of intra-cluster scatter and inter-cluster scatter. Minimizing this measure is equivalent to both minimizing the intra-cluster scatter and maximizing the inter-cluster scatter.

Another method for evaluating the "optimal" K using both inter and intra cluster scatter is the validity index method, proposed by [Kim *et al.* (2001)]. These researchers examine 2 measures:

- MICD — mean intra-cluster distance; defined for the kth cluster as:

$$MD_k = \sum_{x_i \in C_k} \frac{\|x_i - \mu_k\|}{N_k}$$

- ICMD — inter-cluster minimum distance; defined as:

$$d_{\min} = \min_{i \neq j} \|\mu_i - \mu_j\|$$

in order to create cluster validity index, the behavior of these two measures around the real number of clusters (K^*) should be used.

When the data are under-partitioned ($K < K^*$), at least one cluster maintains large MICD. As the partition state moves towards over-partitioned ($K > K^*$), the large MICD abruptly decreases.

The ICMD is large when the data are under-partitioned or optimally partitioned. It becomes very small when the data enters the over-partitioned state, since at least one of the compact clusters is subdivided.

Two additional measure functions may be defined in order to find the under-partitioned and over-partitioned states. These functions depend, among other variables, on the vector of the clusters centers $\mu = [\mu_1, \mu_2, \ldots \mu_K]^T$:

(1) Under-partition measure function:

$$v_u(K, \mu; X) = \frac{\sum_{k=1}^{K} MD_k}{K} \quad 2 \leq K \leq K_{\max}$$

This function has very small values for $K \geq K^*$ and relatively large values for $K < K^*$. Thus, it helps determine whether the data is under-partitioned.

(2) Over-partition measure function:

$$v_o(K, \mu) = \frac{K}{d_{\min}} \quad 2 \leq K \leq K_{\max}$$

This function has very large values for $K \geq K^*$, and relatively small values for $K < K^*$. Thus, it helps determine whether the data is over-partitioned.

The validity index uses the fact that both functions have small values only at $K = K^*$. The vectors of both partition functions are defined as following:

$$V_u = [v_u(2, \mu; X), \ldots, v_u(K_{\max}, \mu; X)]$$

$$V_o = [v_o(2, \mu), \ldots, v_o(K_{\max}, \mu)]$$

Before finding the validity index, each element in each vector is normalized to the range [0,1], according to its minimum and maximum values. For instance, for the V_u vector:

$$v_u^*(K, \mu; X) = \frac{v_u(K, \mu; X)}{\max\limits_{K=2,\ldots,K_{\max}} \{v_u(K, \mu; X)\} - \min\limits_{K=2,\ldots,K_{\max}} \{v_u(K, \mu; X)\}}$$

The process of normalization is done the same way for the V_o vector. The validity index vector is calculated as the sum of the two normalized vectors:

$$v_{sv}(K, \mu; X) = v_u^*(K, \mu; X) + v_o^*(K, \mu)$$

Since both partition measure functions have small values only at $K = K^*$, the smallest value of v_{sv} is chosen as the optimal number of clusters.

3.7.3   *Criteria Based on Probabilistic*

When clustering is performed using a density based method, the determination of the most suitable number of clusters K becomes a more tractable task as clear probabilistic foundation can be used. The question is whether adding new parameters results in a better way of fitting the data by the model. In Bayesian theory the likelihood of a model is also affected by the number of parameters which are proportional to K. Suitable criteria that can used here include BIC (Bayesian Information Criterion), MML (Minimum Message Length) and MDL (Minimum Description Length).

Chapter 4

Ensemble Methods

4.1 Multiple Classifiers

The idea of building a classifier by integrating multiple classifiers has been under investigation for a long time. In fact [Selfridge (1958)] was the first to examine this idea. Later on [Kanal (1974)] explained why the multiple classifiers idea is appealing:

> It is now recognized that the key to pattern recognition problems does not lie wholly in learning machines, statistical approaches spatial, filtering, ..., or in any other particular solution which has been vigorously advocated by one or another group during the last one and a half decades, as the solution to the pattern recognition problem. No single model exists for all pattern recognition problems and no single technique is applicable to all problems. Rather what we have is a bag of tools and a bag of problems.

Moreover [Minsky (1991)] expressed his thoughts as to why this issue is important:

> In the 1960s and 1970s, students frequently asked, "Which kind of representation is best," and I usually replied that we'd need more research before answering that. But now I would give a different reply: To solve really hard problems, we'll have to use several different representations. ... It is time to stop arguing over which type of patternclassification technique is best. ... Instead we should work at a higher level of organization and discover how to build anagerial systems to exploit the different virtues and evade the different limitations of each of these ways of comparing things.

The Multiple Classifier approach can be divided into two sub-types: Ensemble Methodology and Decomposition Methodology. In both cases the final classifier is a composite of multiple classifiers combined in some fashion. However, [Sharkey (1996)] distinguishes between these methodologies in the following way: The main idea of ensemble methodology is to combine a set of classifiers, each of which solves the same original task. The purpose of ensemble methodology is to obtain a more accurate and reliable performance than using a single classifier. In a typical ensemble setting, each classifier is trained on data taken or re-sampled from a common data set as in the case of bagging). On the other hand, the purpose of decomposition methodology is to break down a complex problem into several manageable problems, such that each inducer aims to solve a different task. Therefore, in ensemble methodology, any classifier can provide a sufficient solution to the original task. On the other hand, in decomposition methodology a combination of all classifiers is mandatory for obtaining a reliable solution, namely individual classifiers cannot provide a solution to the original task. Moreover, it is possible to construct an ensemble such that each classifier is built using the decomposition methodology [Sharkey (1996)]. [Tumer and Ghosh (2000)] indicate that in case of ensemble methodology, the individual classifier performance "will be (relatively) comparable in any region of the problem space". Nevertheless, there are many researchers that disagree with this ensemble-decomposition distinction and refer to both as ensemble methods [Avnimelech and Intrator (1999)].

4.2   Ensemble Methodology

The main idea of ensemble methodology is to combine a set of classifiers, each of which solves the same original task (see for instance [Ali and Pazzani (1996)]), in order to obtain a better composite global classifier, with more accurate and reliable estimates or decisions than using a single classifier.

In the past few years, vast of experimental studies conducted by the machine learning community show that combining the outputs of multiple classifiers reduce the generalization error (see for instance [Domingos (1996)], [Quinlan (1996)], [Bauer and Kohavi (1999)] and [Opitz and Maclin (1999)]). Ensemble methods are very effective, mainly due to the phenomenon that various types of classifiers have different "inductive biases" ([Geman *et al.* (1995)]; [Mitchell (1997)]). Indeed, ensemble methods can effectively make use of such diversity to reduce the variance-error ([Tumer and Ghosh (1999)], [Ali and Pazzani (1996)]) without increasing the bias-error. In certain situations, an ensemble can also reduce bias-error, as shown by the theory of large margin classifiers ([Bartlett and Shawe-Taylor (1998)]).

Given the potential usefulness of ensemble methods, it is not surprising that a vast number of methods is now available to researchers and practitioners. This chapter aims to organize all significant methods developed in this field into a coherent and unified catalog. There are several factors that differentiate between the various ensembles methods. The main factors are:

(1) Inter-Classifiers relationship: How does each classifier affect another classifier? The ensemble methods can be divided into two main types: sequential and concurrent.

(2) Combining method — This strategy involves combining the classifiers generated by an induction algorithm. The simplest combiner determines the output solely from the outputs of the individual inducers. [Ali and Pazzani (1996)] have compared several combination methods: uniform voting, Bayesian combination, distribution summation and likelihood combination. Moreover, theoretical analysis has been developed for estimating the classification improvement (see, for instance, [Tumer and Ghosh (1999)]). Along with simple combiners, there are other more sophisticated methods, such as stacking [Wolpert (1992)] and arbitration [Chan and Stolfo (1995)].

(3) Diversity generator — In order to make the ensemble efficient, there should be some sort of diversity between the classifiers. Diversity may be obtained through different presentations of the input data, as in bagging, variations in learner design, or by adding a penalty to the outputs to encourage diversity.

(4) Ensemble size — The number of classifiers in the ensemble.

The following sections discuss and describe each one of these factors.

4.3 Sequential Methodology

In sequential approaches for learning ensembles, there is an interaction between the learning runs. Thus it is possible to take advantage of knowledge generated in previous iterations to guide the learning in the next iterations. [Provost and Kolluri (1997)] distinguish between two main approaches for sequential learning, as described in the following sections.

4.3.1 *Model Guided Instance Selection*

In this sequential approach the classifiers that were constructed in previous iterations are used for manipulation of the training set for the following iteration (see Figure 4.1). One can embed this process within the basic learning algorithm. These methods, which are also known as constructive or conservative methods, usually ignore all data instances on which their initial classifier is correct and learn from misclassified instances only.

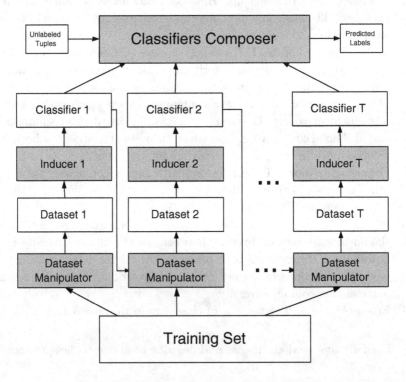

Fig. 4.1   Model Guided Instance Selection Diagram.

There are several methods which embed the sample selection at each run of the learning algorithm, as described in the following sections.

4.3.1.1 *Uncertainty Sampling*

This method is useful in scenarios where unlabeled data is plentiful and the labeling process is expensive. [Lewis and Gale (1994)] define uncertainty sampling as an iterative process of manual labeling of examples, classifier fitting from those examples, and use of the classifier to select new examples whose class membership is unclear. A teacher or an expert is asked to label unlabeled instances whose class membership is uncertain. The pseudo-code is described in Figure 4.2.

Uncertainty Sampling (I,b,U,E)

Where:

I is a method for building the classifier.

b is the selected bulk size.

U is a set on unlabled instances.

E is an Expert capable to label instances.

$X_{new} \leftarrow Random\ set\ of\ size\ b\ selected\ from\ U$

$Y_{new} \leftarrow E(X_{new})$

$S \leftarrow (X_{new}, Y_{new})$

$C \leftarrow I(S)\ U \leftarrow U - X_{new}$

WHILE E is willing to label instances DO:

$\quad X_{new} \leftarrow$ Select a subset of U of size b such that

$\quad\quad\quad\quad\quad$ C is least certain of its classification.

$\quad Y_{new} \leftarrow E(X_{new})$

$\quad S \leftarrow S \cup (X_{new}, Y_{new})$

$\quad C \leftarrow I(S)$

$\quad U \leftarrow U - X_{new}$

END WHILE

RETURN C

Fig. 4.2 Pseudo-Code for Uncertainty Sampling.

It has been shown that using uncertainty sampling method in text categorization tasks can reduce by a factor of up to 500 the amount of data that had to be labeled to obtain a given accuracy level [Lewis and Gale (1994)].

Simple uncertainty sampling requires the construction of many classifiers. The necessity of a cheap classifier now results. The cheap classifier selects instances "in the loop" and then uses those instances for training another, more expensive inducer. Therefore [Lewis and Catlett (1994)] introduced the *Heterogeneous Uncertainty Sampling* method which achieves a given error rate by using a cheaper kind of classifier (both to build and run) and by that reducing computational cost and run time.

Unfortunately, an uncertainty sampling tends to create a training set that contains a disproportionately large number of instances from rare classes. In order to balance this effect, [Lewis and Catlett (1994)] developed a modified version of C4.5 decision tree, which accepts a parameter called loss ratio (LR). The parameter specifies the relative cost of two types of errors: false positives (where negative instance is classified positive) and false negatives (where positive instance is classified negative). Choosing a loss ratio greater than 1 indicates that false positives errors are more costly than the false negative. Therefore, setting the LR above 1 will counterbalance the over representation of positive instances. Choosing the exact value of LR requires sensitivity analysis of the effect of the specific value on the accuracy of the classifier produced.

The original C4.5 determines the class value at the leaves by checking whether the split decreases the error rate, the final class value is determined by majority vote. In modified C4.5 the leaf's class is determined by comparison with a probability threshold of $LR/(LR+1)$ (or its reciprocal as appropriate). [Lewis and Catlett (1994)] showed that their method led to significant higher accuracy than in the case of using random samples ten times larger.

4.3.1.2 *Boosting*

Boosting (also know as arcing — Adaptive Resampling and Combining) is a general method for improving the performance of any learning algorithm. The method works by repeatedly running a weak learner (such as classification rules or decision trees), on various distributed training data. The classifiers produced by the weak learners are then combined into a single composite strong classifier in order to achieve a higher accuracy than the weak learner's classifiers would had.

Schapire introduced the first boosting algorithm in 1990. In 1995 Freund and Schapire introduced the AdaBoost algorithm. The main idea of the algorithm is to assign a weight in each example in the training set. At the beginning, all weights are equal, but in every round, the weights of all misclassified instances are increased where the weights of correctly classified instances are decreased. As a consequence, the weak learner is forced to focus on the difficult instances of the training set. This procedure provides a series of classifiers that complement one another.

The pseudo-code of the AdaBoost algorithm is described in Figure 4.3. The algorithm assumes that the training set consists of m instances, labeled as -1 or +1. The classification of a new instance is made by voting on all classifiers $\{C_t\}$, each having a weight of α_t. Mathematically it can be written as:

$$H(x) = sign(\sum_{t=1}^{T} \alpha_t \cdot C_t(x))$$

The basic AdaBoost algorithm, described in Figure 4.3, deals with binary classification. [Freund and Schapire (1996)] described two versions of the AdaBoost algorithm (AdaBoost.M1, AdaBoost.M2), which are equivalent for binary classification and differ in their handling of multiclass classification problems. Figure 4.4 describes the pseudo-code of AdaBoost.M1. The classification of a new instance is performed according to the following equation:

$$H(x) = \operatorname*{argmax}_{y \in dom(y)} (\sum_{t:C_t(x)=y} \log \frac{1}{\beta_t})$$

All bosting algorithms presented here assume that the provided weak inducers can cope with weighted instances. If it is not the case, an unweighted dataset is generated from the weighted data by a resampling technique. Namely, instances are chosen with probability according to their weights (until the dataset becomes as large as the original training set).

Boosting seems to improve performances for two main reasons:

(1) It generates a final classifier whose error on the training set is small by combining many hypotheses whose error may be large.
(2) It produces a combined classifier whose variance is significantly lower than those produced by the weak learner.

On the other hand, boosting sometimes leads to deterioration in generalization performance. According to [Quinlan (1996)] the main reason for boosting's failure is overfitting. The objective of boosting is to construct a composite classifier that performs well on the data, but a large number

---

Boosting (I,T,S)

Where:

I is a weak inducer.

T is the number of iterations.

S is the a training set; $S = \{(x_1, y_1), \ldots, (x_m, y_m)\}; y_i \in \{-1, +1\}$

$t \leftarrow 1$

$D_1(i) \leftarrow 1/m; i = 1, \ldots, m$

DO

    Build Classifier C_t using I and distribution D_t

    $\varepsilon_t \leftarrow \displaystyle\sum_{i:C_t(x_i) \neq y_i} D_t(i)$

    IF $\varepsilon_t > 0.5$ THEN

        $T \leftarrow t - 1$

        EXIT Loop.

    END IF

    $\alpha_t \leftarrow \frac{1}{2} \ln(\frac{1-\varepsilon_t}{\varepsilon_t})$

    $D_{t+1}(i) = D_t(i) \cdot e^{-\alpha_t y_t C_t(x_i)}$

    Normalize D_{t+1} to be a proper distribution.

    $t++$

UNTIL $t > T$

RETURN $C_t, \alpha_t; t = 1, \ldots, T$

Fig. 4.3   The AdaBoost Algorithm.

of iterations may create a very complex composite classifier: it can generate a classifier that is significantly less accurate than a single classifier. A possible way to avoid overfitting is by keeping the number of iterations as small as possible.

Another important drawback of boosting is that it is difficult to understand. The resulted ensemble is considered to be less comprehensible since the user is required to capture several classifiers instead of a single classifier. Despite the above drawbacks, [Breiman (1996)] refers to the boosting idea as the most significant development in classifier design in the 90's.

AdaBoost.M1 (I,T,S)

Where:

I is a weak inducer.

T is the number of iterations.

S is the a training set;

$S = \{(x_1, y_1), \ldots, (x_m, y_m)\}; y_i \in \{c_1, c_2, \ldots, c_{|dom(y)|}\}$

$t \leftarrow 1$

$D_1(i) \leftarrow 1/m; i = 1, \ldots, m$

DO

    Build Classifier C_t using I and distribution D_t

    $\varepsilon_t \leftarrow \sum\limits_{i:C_t(x_i) \neq y_i} D_t(i)$

    IF $\varepsilon_t > 0.5$ THEN

        $T \leftarrow t - 1$

        EXIT Loop.

    END IF

    $\beta_t \leftarrow \frac{\varepsilon_t}{1 - \varepsilon_t}$

    $D_{t+1}(i) = D_t(i) \cdot \begin{cases} \beta_t & C_t(x_i) = y_i \\ 1 & Otherwise \end{cases}$

    Normalize D_{t+1} to be a proper distribution.

    $t++$

UNTIL $t > T$

RETURN $C_t, \beta_t; t = 1, \ldots, T$

Fig. 4.4   The AdaBoost.M.1 Algorithm.

4.3.1.3 *Windowing*

Windowing is a general method aiming to improve the efficiency of inducers by reducing the complexity of the problem. It has been initially proposed as a supplement to the ID3 decision tree in order to address complex classification tasks that could have exceeded the memory capacity of computers. Windowing is performed by using a sub-sampling procedure. The method could be summarized as follows: a random subset of the training instances is selected (a window), the subset is used for training a classifier, which is tested on the remaining training data. If the accuracy of the induced classifier is not sufficient, the misclassified test instances are removed from the test set and are added to the training set of the next iteration. [Quinlan (1993)] mentions two different ways of forming a window: in the first, the current window is extended up to some specified limit. In the second, several "key" instances in the current window are identified and the rest are replaced, thus the size of the window stays constant. The process continues until the sufficient accuracy is obtained, and the classifier constructed at the last iteration is chosen as the final classifier. Figure 4.5 presents the pseudo—code of the windowing procedure.

Windowing (I,S,r,t)

Where:

I is an inducer.

S is the a training set;
$S = \{(x_1, y_1), \ldots, (x_m, y_m)\}; y_i \in \{c_1, c_2, \ldots, c_{|dom(y)|}\}$

r is the inital window size.

t is the maximum allowed windows size increase for sequential iterations.

Window $\leftarrow$ Select randomly r instances from S.

Test $\leftarrow$ S-Window

DO

    $C \leftarrow I(Window)$

    $Inc \leftarrow 0$

    $\forall (x_i, y_i) \in Test$

        IF $C(x_i) \neq y_i$ THEN

            $Test \leftarrow Test - (x_i, y_i)$

            $Window = Window \cup (x_i, y_i)$

            $Inc + +$

        END IF

        IF $Inc = t$ THEN EXIT Loop

    END FOR

UNTIL $Inc = 0$

RETURN C

Fig. 4.5   The Windowing Procedure.

The windowing method has been examined also for separate-and-conquer rule induction algorithms [Furnkranz (1997)]. This research has shown that for this type of algorithm, significant improvement in efficiency is possible in noise free domains. Contrary to the basic windowing algorithm, this one removes all instances that have been classified by consistent rules from this window, in addition to adding all instances that have been misclassified. Removal of instances from the window keeps its size small and thus decreases induction time.

In conclusion, both windowing and uncertainty sampling build a sequence of classifiers only for obtaining an ultimate sample. The difference between them lies in the fact that in windowing the instances are labeled in advance, while in uncertainty, this is not so. Therefore, new training instances are chosen differently. Boosting also builds a sequence of classifiers, but combines them in order to gain knowledge from them all. Windowing and uncertainty sampling do not combine the classifiers, but use the best classifier.

4.3.2 *Incremental Batch Learning*

In this method the classifier produced in one iteration is given as "prior knowledge" to the learning algorithm in the following iteration (along with the subsample of that iteration). The learning algorithm uses the current subsample to evaluate the former classifier, and uses the former one for building the next classifier. The classifier constructed at the last iteration is chosen as the final classifier.

4.4 Concurrent Methodology

Figure 4.6 illustrates the concurrent ensemble method. In this the original dataset is partitioned into a subset from which multiple classifiers are induced concurrently. The subsets created from the training data may be disjoint (mutually exclusive) or overlapping. A combining procedure is then applied in order to produce a single classification for a given instance. Since the method for combining the results of induced classifiers is usually independent of the induction algorithms, it can be used with different inducers at each subset. These concurrent methods aim at improving the predictive power of classifiers, or decrease the total execution time. The following sections describe several algorithms that implement this methodology.

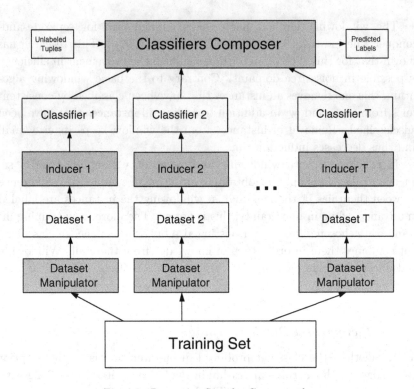

Fig. 4.6   Processing Samples Concurrently.

4.4.0.1 *Bagging*

The most well-known method that process samples concurrently is Bagging (bootstrap aggregating). The method aims to improve the accuracy by creating an improved composite classifier,I^*, by amalgamating the various outputs of learned classifiers into a single prediction.

Figure 4.7 presents the pseudo-code of the bagging algorithm [Breiman (1996)]. Each classifier is trained on a sample of instances taken with replacement from the training set. Usually each sample size is equal to the size of the original training set.

Note that since sampling with replacement is used, some of the original instances of S may appear more than once in S_t and some may not be included at all. So the training sets S_t are different from each other, but are certainly not independent. To classify a new instance, each classifier returns the class prediction for the unknown instance. The composite bagged classifier,I^*, returns the class that has been predicted most often

---

Bagging (I,T,S)

Where:

I is an inducer.

T is the number of iterations.

S is the original training set.

N the subsample size.

$t \leftarrow 1$

DO

    $S_t \quad \leftarrow$ Sample N instances from S with replacment.

    Build Classifier C_t using I on S_t

    $t++$

UNTIL $t > T$

RETURN $C_t; t = 1, \ldots, T$

Fig. 4.7   The Bagging Algorithm.

(voting method). The result is that bagging produces a combined model that often performs better than the single model built from the original single data. [Breiman (1996)] notes that this is true especially for unstable inducers because bagging can eliminate their instability. In this context, an inducer is considered unstable if perturbing the learning set can cause significant changes in the classifier constructed. However, the Bagging method is rather hard to analyze and it is not easy to understand by intuition as to what are the factors and reasons for the improved decisions.

Bagging, like boosting, is a technique for improving the accuracy of a classifier by producing different classifiers and combining multiple models. They both use a kind of voting for classification in order to combine the outputs of the different classifiers of the same type. In boosting unlike bagging, each classifier is influenced by the performance of those built before, so the new classifier tries to pay more attention to errors that were made in the previous ones and to their performances. In bagging, each instance is chosen with equal probability, while in boosting, instances are chosen with probability proportional to their weight. Furthermore, according to [Quinlan (1996)], as mentioned above, bagging requires that the learning system should not be stable, where boosting does not preclude the use of instable learning systems, provided that their error rate can be kept below 0.5.

4.4.0.2   *Cross-validated Committees*

This procedure creates k classifiers by partitioning the training set into k-equal sized sets and in turn, training on all but the i-th set. This method was first used by [Gams (1989)] that employed 10 folds partitioning. [Parmanto *et al.* (1996)] have also used this idea for creating ensemble of neural networks. [Domingos (1996)] has used cross-validated committees to speed up his own rule induction algorithm RISE, whose complexity is $O(n^2)$, making it unsuitable for processing large databases. In this case, partitioning is applied by predetermining a maximum number of examples to which the algorithm can be applied at once. The full training set is randomly divided into approximately equal sized partitions. RISE is then run on each partition separately, each set of rules grown from the examples in partition p is tested on the examples in partition p+1, in order to reduce overfitting and improve accuracy.

4.5   Combining Classifiers

The way of combining the classifiers may be divided to two main groups: simple multiple classifiers combinations and meta-combiners. The simple combining methods are best suited for problems where the individual classifiers perform the same task and have comparable success. However, such combiners are more vulnerable to outliers and to unevenly performing classifiers. On the other hand, the meta-combiners are theoretically more powerful but are susceptible to all the problems associated with the added learning (such as over-fitting, long training time).

4.5.1   *Simple Combining Methods*

Following, we describe several simple combining methods. The reader may refer to the following sources for more details: [Ali and Pazzani (1996)] and [Tresp and Taniguchi (1995)].

4.5.1.1   *Uniform Voting*

In this combining schema each classifier has the same weight. A classification of an unlabeled instance is performed according to the class that obtains the highest number of votes. Mathematically it can be written as:

$$Class(x) = \underset{c_i \in dom(y)}{\operatorname{argmax}} \sum_{k:c_i = \underset{c_j \in dom(y)}{\operatorname{argmax}} \hat{P}_{M_k}(y=c_j|x)} 1$$

where M_k denotes classifier k and $\hat{P}_{M_k}(y = c|x)$ is the probability of y obtaining the value c given an instance x.

4.5.1.2 *Distribution Summation*

This combining method was presented by [Clark and Boswell (1991)]. The idea is to sum up the conditional probability vector obtained from each classifier. The selected class is chosen according to the highest value in the total vector. Mathematically it can be written as:

$$Class(x) = \underset{c_i \in dom(y)}{\operatorname{argmax}} \sum_k \hat{P}_{M_k}(y = c_i|x)$$

4.5.1.3 *Bayesian Combination*

This combining method was investigated by [Buntine (1990)]. The idea is that the weight associated with each classifier is the posterior probability of the classifier given the training set.

$$Class(x) = \underset{c_i \in dom(y)}{\operatorname{argmax}} \sum_k P(M_k|S) \cdot \hat{P}_{M_k}(y = c_i|x)$$

where $P(M_k|S)$ denotes the probability that the classifier M_k is correct giving the training set S. The estimation of $P(M_k|S)$ depends on the classifier's representation. [Buntine (1990)] demonstrates how to estimate this value for decision trees.

4.5.1.4 *Dempster–Shafer*

The idea of using the Dempster–Shafer theory of evidence [Buchanan and Shortliffe (1984)] for combining models has been suggested by [Shilen (1990); Shilen (1992)]. This method uses the notion of Basic Probability Assignment defined for a certain class c_i given the instance x:

$$bpa(c_i, x) = 1 - \prod_k \left(1 - \hat{P}_{M_k}(y = c_i|x)\right)$$

Consequently, the selected class is the one that maximizes the value of the belief function:

$$Bel(c_i, x) = \frac{1}{A} \cdot \frac{bpa(c_i, x)}{1 - bpa(c_i, x)}$$

where A is a normalization factor defined as:

$$A = \sum_{\forall c_i \in dom(y)} \frac{bpa(c_i, x)}{1 - bpa(c_i, x)} + 1$$

4.5.1.5 *Naïve Bayes*

Using Bayes rule one can extend the Naïve Bayes idea for combination various classifiers:

$$class(x) = \underset{\substack{c_j \in dom(y) \\ \hat{P}(y = c_j) > 0}}{\operatorname{argmax}} \hat{P}(y = c_j) \cdot \prod_{k=1} \frac{\hat{P}_{M_k}(y = c_j \mid x)}{\hat{P}(y = c_j)}$$

4.5.1.6 *Entropy Weighting*

The idea in this combining method is to give each classifier a weight that is inversely proportional to the entropy of its classification vector.

$$Class(x) = \underset{c_i \in dom(y)}{\operatorname{argmax}} \sum_{\substack{k:c_i = \operatorname*{argmax}_{c_j \in dom(y)} \hat{P}_{M_k}(y = c_j \mid x)}} Ent(M_k, x)$$

where:

$$Ent(M_k, x) = - \sum_{c_j \in dom(y)} \hat{P}_{M_k}(y = c_j \mid x) \log \left(\hat{P}_{M_k}(y = c_j \mid x) \right)$$

4.5.1.7 *Density Based Weighting*

If the various classifiers were trained using datasets obtained from different regions of the instance space, it might be useful to weight the classifiers according to the probability of sampling x by classifier M_k, namely:

$$Class(x) = \underset{c_i \in dom(y)}{\operatorname{argmax}} \sum_{\substack{k:c_i = \operatorname*{argmax}_{c_j \in dom(y)} \hat{P}_{M_k}(y = c_j \mid x)}} \hat{P}_{M_k}(x)$$

The estimation of $\hat{P}_{M_k}(x)$ depend on the classifier representation and can not always be estimated.

4.5.1.8 *DEA Weighting Method*

Recently [Sohn and Choi (2001)] have suggested to use the DEA (Data Envelop Analysis) methodology ([Charnes *et al.* (1978)]) in order to assign weight to different classifiers. They argue that the weights should not be specified based on a single performance measure, but on several performance measures. Because there is a trade-off among the various performance measures, the DEA is employed in order to figure out the set of efficient classifiers. In addition, DEA provides inefficient classifiers with the benchmarking point.

4.5.1.9 *Logarithmic Opinion Pool*

According to the logarithmic opinion pool [Hansen (2000)] the selection of the preferred class is performed according to:

$$Class(x) = \underset{c_j \in dom(y)}{\operatorname{argmax}} \; e^{\sum_k \alpha_k \cdot \log\left(\hat{P}_{M_k}(y=c_j|x)\right)}$$

where α_k denotes the weight of the k-th classifier, such that:

$$\alpha_k \geq 0; \sum \alpha_k = 1$$

4.5.1.10 *Order Statistics*

Order statistics can be used to combine classifiers [Tumer and Ghosh (2000)]. These combiners have the simplicity of a simple weighted combining method with the generality of meta combining methods (see the following section). The robustness of this method is helpful when there are significant variations among classifiers in some part of the instance space.

4.5.2 *Meta Combining Methods*

Meta learning means learning from the classifiers produced by the inducers and from the classifications of these classifiers on training data. The following sections describe the most well known meta-combining methods.

4.5.2.1 *Stacking*

Stacking is a technique whose purpose is to achieve the highest generalization accuracy. By using a meta-learner, this method tries to induce which classifiers are reliable and which are not. Stacking is usually employed to combine models built by different inducers. The idea is to create a meta-dataset containing a tuple for each tuple in the original dataset. However, instead of using the original input attributes, it uses the predicted classification of the classifiers as the input attributes. The target attribute remains as in the original training set. Table 4.1 illustrates the meta-dataset used by the stacking procedure.

Table 4.1   Creating the Stacking Training Set.

C_1	C_2	...	C_k	y
$C_1(x_1)$	$C_2(x_1)$	...	$C_k(x_1)$	y_1
$C_1(x_2)$	$C_2(x_2)$	...	$C_k(x_2)$	y_2
$\vdots$	$\vdots$		$\vdots$	$\vdots$
$C_1(x_m)$	$C_2(x_m)$	...	$C_k(x_m)$	Y_m

Test instance is first classified by each of the base classifiers. These classifications are fed into a meta-level training set from which a meta-classifier is produced. This classifier combines the different predictions into a final one. It is recommended that the original dataset will be partitioned into two subsets. The first subset is reserved to form the meta-dataset and the second subset is used to build the base-level classifiers. Consequently the meta-classifier predications reflect the true performance of base-level's learning algorithms. Stacking performances could be improved by using output probabilities for every class label from the base-level classifiers, in that case the number of input attributes in the meta-dataset is multiplied by the number of classes.

4.5.2.2   *Arbiter Trees*

This approach, which was first introduced by [Chan and Stolfo (1993)], builds an arbiter tree in a bottom-up fashion. Initially the training set is randomly partitioned into k disjoint subsets. The arbiter is induced from a pair of classifiers and recursively a new arbiter is induced from the output of two arbiters. Consequently for k classifiers, there are $\log_2(k)$ levels in the generated arbiter tree.

The creation of The arbiter is performed as follows. For each pair of classifiers, the union of their training dataset is classified by the two classifiers. A selection rule compares the classifications of the two classifiers and selects instances from the union set to form the training set for the arbiter. The arbiter is induced from this set with the same learning algorithm used in the base level. The purpose of the arbiter is to provide an alternate classification when the base classifiers present diverse classifications. This arbiter, together with an arbitration rule, decides on a final classification outcome, based upon the base predictions. Figure 4.8 shows how the final classification is selected based on the classification of two base classifiers and a single arbiter:

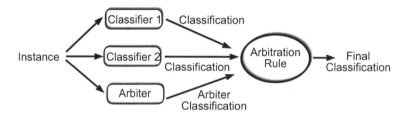

Fig. 4.8   A Prediction from Two Base Classifiers and a Single Arbiter.

The process of forming the union of data subsets, classifying it using a pair of arbiter trees, comparing the classifications, forming a training set, training the arbiter and picking one of the predictions, is recursively performed until the root arbiter is formed. Figure 4.9 illustrate an arbiter tree created for $k = 4$. $T_1 - T_4$ are the initial four training datasets from which four classifiers $C_1 - C_4$ are generated concurrently. T_{12} and T_{34} are the training sets generated by the rule selection from which arbiters are produced. A_{12} and A_{34} are the two arbiters. Similarly, T_{14} and A_{14} (root arbiter) are generated and the arbiter tree is completed.

Several schemes of arbiter trees were examined and differentiated from each other by the selection rule used. Here are three versions of rule selection:

- Only instances with classifications that disagree are chosen (group 1).
- Like group 1 defined above, plus instances that their classifications agree but are incorrect (group 2).
- Like groups 1 and 2 defined above, plus instances that have the same correct classifications (group 3).

Two versions of arbitration rules have been implemented; each one corresponds to the selection rule used for generating the training data at that level:

- For selection rule 1 and 2, a final classification is made by a majority

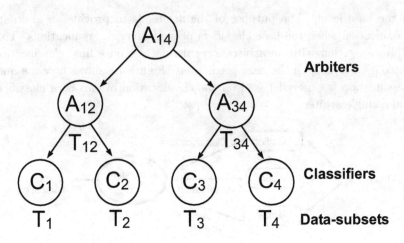

Fig. 4.9   Sample Arbiter Tree.

vote of the classifications of the two lower levels and the arbiter's own classification, with preference given to the latter.

- For selection rule 3, if the classifications of the two lower levels are not equal, the classification made by the sub arbiter based on the first group is chosen. In case this is not true and the classification of the sub-arbiter constructed on the third group equals those of the lower levels — then this is the chosen classification. In any other case, the classification of the sub arbiter constructed on the second group is chosen. [Chan and Stolfo (1993)] achieved the same accuracy level as in the single mode applied to the entire dataset but with less time and memory requirements. It has been shown that this meta-learning strategy required only around 30% of the memory used by the single model case at any processing sight. The last fact, combined with the independent nature of the various learning processes, make this method robust and effective for massive amounts of data. Nevertheless, the accuracy level depends on several factors such as: the distribution of the data among the subsets and the pairing scheme of learned classifiers and arbiters in each level. The decision in any of these issues may influence performance, but the optimal decisions are not necessarily known in advance, nor initially set by the algorithm.

4.5.2.3   Combiner Trees

The way combiner trees are generated is very similar to arbiter trees. A combiner tree is trained bottom-up, however a combiner, instead of an arbiter, is placed in each non-leaf node of a combiner tree [Chan and Stolfo (1997)]. In the combiner strategy, the classifications of the learned base classifiers form the basis of the meta-learner's training set. A composition rule determines the content of training examples from which a combiner (meta classifier) will be generated. In classifying an instance, the base classifiers first generate their classifications and based on the composition rule, a new instance is generated. The aim of this strategy is to combine the classifications from the base classifiers by learning the relationship between these classifications and the correct classification. Figure 4.10 illustrates the result obtained from two base classifiers and a single combiner.

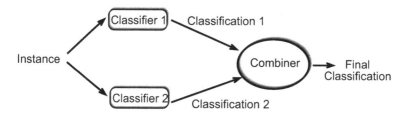

Fig. 4.10   A Prediction from Two Base Classifiers and a Single Combiner.

Two schemes of composition rule were proposed. The first one is the stacking schema. The second is like stacking with the addition of the instance input attributes. [Chan and Stolfo (1995)] showed that the stacking schema per se does not perform as well as the second schema. Although there is information loss due to data partitioning, combiner trees can sustain the accuracy level achieved by a single classifier. In a few cases the single classifier's accuracy was consistently exceeded.

4.5.2.4   Grading

This technique which was introduced by [Seewald and Furnkranz (2001)], uses "graded" classifications as meta-level classes. The term graded is used in the sense of classifications that have been marked as correct or incorrect. The method transforms the classification made by the k different classifiers into k training sets by using the instances k times and attaching them to a new binary class in each occurrence. This class indicates whether the k-th classifier yielded a correct or incorrect classification, compared to the real class of the instance.

For each base classifier, one meta-classifier is learned whose task is to classify when the base classifier will misclassify. At classification time, each base classifier classifies the unlabeled instance. The final classification is derived from the classifications of those base classifiers that are classified to be correct by the meta-classification schemes. In case several base classifiers with different classification results are classified to be correct, voting, or a combination considering the confidence estimates of the base classifiers, is performed. Grading may be considered as a generalization of cross validation selection [Schaffer (1993)], which divides the training data into k subsets, builds $k-1$ classifiers by dropping one subset at a time and then using it to find a misclassification rate. Finally, the procedure simply chooses the classifier corresponding to the subset with the smallest misclassification. Grading tries to make this decision separately for each and every instance by using only those classifiers that are predicted to classify that instance correctly. The main difference between grading and combiners (or stacking) are that the former does not change the instance attributes by replacing them with class predictions or class probabilities (or adding them to it), instead it modifies the class values. Furthermore, in grading several sets of meta-data are created, one for each base classifier, from those sets several meta-level classifiers are learned.

The main difference between grading and arbiters is that arbiters use information about the disagreements of classifiers for selecting a training set, while grading uses disagreement with the target function to produce a new training set.

4.6   Ensemble Size

4.6.1   *Selecting the Ensemble Size*

An important aspect of ensemble methods is to define how many component classifiers should be used. This number is usually defined based on the following issues:

- Desired accuracy — [Hansen (1990)] argue that ensemble containing ten classifiers is sufficient for reducing the error rate. [Opitz and Maclin (1999)], on the other hand, have empirically showed that in case of AdaBoost using decision trees, error reduction is observed in even relatively large ensembles containing 25 classifiers. In the disjoint partitioning approaches there may be a tradeoff between the number of subsets and the final accuracy. The size of each subset cannot be too small because sufficient data must be available for each learning process to produce an effective classifier. [Chan and Stolfo (1993)] varied the number of subsets in the arbiter trees from 2 to 64 and examined the effect of the predetermined number of subsets on the accuracy level.

- User preferences — Increasing the number of classifiers usually increase computational complexity and decrease the comprehensibility. For that reason, users may set their preferences by predefining the ensemble size limit.

- Number of processors available — In concurrent approaches, the number of processors available for parallel learning could be put as an upper bound on the number of classifiers that are treated in paralleled process.

4.6.2 *Pruning Ensembles*

Like in decision trees induction, it is sometime useful to let the ensemble grow freely and then prune the ensemble in order to get more effective and more compact ensembles. [Margineantu and Dietterich (1997)] examined the idea of pruning the ensemble obtained by AdaBoost. They found out that pruned ensembles may obtain similar accuracy performance as the original ensemble.

The efficiency of pruning methods when meta combining methods are used have been examined by [Prodromidis *et al.* (1999)]. In this case the pruning methods can be divided into two groups: pre-training pruning methods and post-training pruning methods. Pre-training pruning is performed before combining the classifiers. Classifiers that seem to be attractive are included in the meta-classifier. On the other hand, post-training pruning methods, remove classifiers based on their effect on the meta-classifier. [Prodromidis *et al.* (1999)] examined three methods for pre-training pruning (based on an individual classification performance on a separate validation set, diversity metrics, the ability of classifiers to classify correctly specific classes) and two methods for post-training pruning (based on decision tree pruning and correlation of the base classifier to the unpruned meta-classifier). As in the case of [Margineantu and Dietterich (1997)] it has been shown that by using pruning, one can obtain similar or better accuracy performance, while compacting the ensemble.

The GASEN algorithm was developed for selecting the most appropriate classifiers in a given ensemble [Zhou *et al.* (2002)]. In the initialization phase, GASEN assigns a random weight to each of the classifiers. Consequently, it uses genetic algorithm to evolve those weights so that they can characterize to some extent the fitness of the classifiers in joining the ensemble. Finally, it removes from the ensemble the classifiers whose weight is less than a predefined threshold value. Recently [Zhou and Tang (2003)] have suggested a revised version of the GASEN algorithm called GASEN-b. In this algorithm, instead of assigning a weight to each classifier, a bit is assigned to each classifier indicating whether it will be used in the final ensemble. They show that the obtained ensemble is not only smaller in size, but in some cases has better generalization performance.

4.7   Ensemble Diversity

In an ensemble, the combination of the output of several classifiers is only useful if they disagree on some inputs [Tumer and Ghosh (1996)]. According to [Hu (2001)] diversified classifiers lead to uncorrelated errors, which in turn improve classification accuracy.

4.7.1   *Manipulating the Inducer*

A simple method for gaining diversity is to manipulate the inducer used for creating the classifiers. [Ali and Pazzani (1996)] propose to change the rule learning HYDRA algorithm in the following way: Instead of selecting the best literal in each stage (using for instance information gain measure), the literal is selected randomly such that its probability to be selected is proportional to its measure value. [Dietterich (2000a)] has implemented a similar idea for C4.5 decision tree. Instead of selecting the best attribute in each stage, it selects randomly (with equal probability) an attribute from the set of the best 20 attributes. The simplest way to manipulate the back-propagation inducer is to assign different initial weights to the network ([Kolen and Pollack (1991)]). [Neal (1993)] used MCMC (Markov Chain Monte Carlo) methods for introducing randomness in the induction process.

4.7.2 Manipulating the Training Set

Most of ensemble methods construct the set of classifiers by manipulating the training instances. [Dietterich (2000b)] distinguishes between three main methods to manipulate the dataset.

4.7.2.1 Manipulating the Tuples

In this method each classifier is trained on a different subset of the original dataset. This method is useful for inducers whose variance-error factor is relatively large (such as decision trees and neural networks), namely small changes in the training set may cause a major change in the obtained classifier. This category contains procedures such as bagging, boosting and cross-validated committees.

The distribution of tuples among the different subsets could be random as in the bagging algorithm or in the arbiter trees. Other methods distribute the tuples based on the class distribution such that the class distribution in each subset is approximately the same as that in the entire dataset. Proportional distribution was used in combiner trees ([Chan and Stolfo (1993)]). It has been shown that proportional distribution can achieve higher accuracy than random distribution.

4.7.2.2 Manipulating the Input Feature Set

Another less common strategy for manipulating the training set is to manipulate the input attribute set. The idea is to simply give each classifier a different projection of the training set. In the literature there are several works that fit this idea. [Bay (1999)] presented an algorithm called MFS which combines multiple Nearest Neighbor classifiers, each using only a subset of random features. Experiments show MFS can improve the standard Nearest Neighbor classifiers. [Kusiak (2000)] proposed a different method for manipulating the input attributes in which features are grouped according to the type that is handled by a particular feature extraction algorithm, for instance, nominal value features, numeric value features and text value features. A similar approach was used by [Gama (2000)] for developing the Linear-Bayes classifier. The basic idea consists of aggregating the features into two subsets: the first subset containing only the nominal features and the second subset only the continuous features. [Hu (2001)] presented an approach for constructing ensemble of classifiers using rough set theory. His declared goal was to construct an ensemble such that different classifiers use different attributes as much as possible. The method searched for a set of reducts, which included all the indispensable attributes. A reduct represents the minimal set of attributes which has the same classification power as the entire attribute set.

The features set can be decomposed according to the target class [Tumer and Ghosh (1996)]. For each class the features with low correlation to that class have been removed. This method has been applied on a feature set of 25 sonar signals where the target was to identify the meaning of the sound (whale, cracking ice, etc.). [Cherkauer (1996)] used similar idea for radar volcanoes recognition. In this case the original feature set of 119 had been manually decomposed into 8 subsets. Features that are based on different image processing operations were grouped together. Then for each subset, four neural networks with different sizes were built. Combining the classifications of these networks has reached the performance of human expert. [Chen *et al.* (1997)] have proposed a new combining framework for feature set decomposition and demonstrate its applicability in text-independent speaker identification.

A quite different approach was proposed by [Liao and Moody (2000)]. According to this approach all input features are grouped by using a hier-archical clustering algorithm based on pairwise mutual information, such that statistically similar features are assigned to the same group. Then, several feature subsets are constructed by selecting one feature from each group. Subsequently for each subset a neural network is constructed, all of which are then combined.

Feature selection can be used for creating the various subsets [Zenobi and Cunningham (2001)]. The feature selection is performed using a hill-climbing strategy based on the classifier error rate and diversity. The suggested procedure ensures that each classifier obtains metrics that comply with a certain pre-defined threshold.

A feature set manipulation has been proposed by [Blum and Mitchell (1998)] for classifying Web pages. They suggested a paradigm, termed Co-Training, for learning with labeled and unlabeled data. This paradigm is useful when there is a large sample of data, of which only a small part is labeled. In many applications unlabeled examples are significantly easier to collect than labeled ones [Blum and Mitchell (1998); Duda and Hart (1973)]. This is especially true when the labeling process is time-consuming or expensive such as in medical applications. According to the Co-Training paradigm, the input space is divided into two different views (i.e. two independent and redundant sets of features). For each view

Blum and Mitchell built a different classifier to classify unlabeled data. The newly labeled data of each classifier is then used to retrain the other classifier. [Blum and Mitchell (1998)] have shown both empirically and theoretically that unlabeled data can be used to augment labeled data.

4.7.2.3 *Manipulating the Target Attribute*

The idea to decompose a K class classification problem into K two class classification problems has been proposed by [Anand *et al.* (1995)]. Each problem considers the discrimination of one class to the other classes. [Lu and Ito (1999)] extends Anand's method and proposes a new method for manipulating the data based on the class relations among training data. They have examined this idea using neural networks.

Another method for manipulating the target attribute is Error-correcting output coding (ECOC). This method decomposes a multi-class problems into multiple, two-class problems [Dietterich and Bakiri (1995)]. A classifier is built for each possible binary partition of the classes. Experiments show that ECOC improves the accuracy of neural networks and decision trees on several multi-class problems from the UCI repository.

4.7.3 *Measuring the Diversity*

Usually for regression problems *variance* is used to measure diversity [Krogh and Vedelsby (1995)]. In this case it can be easily shown that the ensemble error can be reduced by increasing ensemble diversity while maintaining the average error of a single model.

In classification problems, a more complicated measure is required to evaluate the diversity. [Kuncheva and Whitaker (2003)] compared several measures of diversity and concluded that most of them are correlated. Furthermore, it is usually assumed that increasing diversity may decrease ensemble error ([Zenobi and Cunningham (2001)]).

Chapter 5

Elementary Decomposition Framework

5.1 Decomposition Framework

One of the explicit challenges in data mining is to develop methods that will be feasible for complicated real-world problems. In many disciplines, when a problem becomes more complex, there is a general tendency to try to break it down into smaller, distinct, but connected pieces. The concept of breaking down a system into smaller pieces is generally referred to as *decomposition*. The purpose of decomposition methodology is to break down a complex problem into several smaller, less complex and more manageable sub-problems that are solvable by using existing tools, then joining them together to solve the initial problem. Decomposition methodology can be considered as an effective strategy for changing the representation of a classification problem. Indeed, [Kusiak (2000)] considers decomposition as the "most useful form of transformation of data sets".

The decomposition approach is frequently used in statistics, operations research and engineering. For instance, decomposition of time series is considered to be a practical way to improve forecasting. The usual decomposition into trend, cycle, seasonal and irregular components was motivated mainly by business analysts, who wanted to get a clearer picture of the state of the economy [Fisher (1995)]. Although the operations research community has extensively studied decomposition methods to improve computational efficiency and robustness, identification of the partitioned problem model has largely remained an ad hoc task [He *et al.* (2000)].

In engineering design, problem decomposition has received considerable attention as a means of reducing multidisciplinary design cycle time and of streamlining the design process by adequate arrangement of the tasks [Kusiak *et al.* (1991)]. Decomposition methods are also used in decision-making theory; a typical example is the AHP method [Saaty (1993)]. In artificial intelligence, according to [Michie (1995)], finding a good decomposition is a major tactic, both for ensuring the transparent end-product and for avoiding a combinatorial explosion.

Research has shown that no single learning approach is clearly superior for all cases. In fact, the task of discovering regularities can be made easier and less time consuming by decomposition of the task. However, as [Buntine (1996)] notes, decomposition methodology has not attracted as much attention in the KDD and machine learning community.

Although decomposition is a promising technique and presents an obviously natural direction to follow, there are hardly any works in the data mining literature that consider the subject directly. Instead, there are abundant practical attempts to apply decomposition methodology to specific, real life applications (like in the case of [Buntine (1996)]). There are also plentiful discussions on closely related problems, largely in the context of distributed and parallel learning [Zaki and Ho (2000)] or ensembles classifiers (see Chapter 4). Nevertheless, there are a few important works that consider decomposition methodology directly. [Kusiak (2000)] presents various decomposition methods, however he does not discuss how these decomposition structures should be obtained. [Bhargava (1999)] suggests decomposing the exploratory data analysis process into 3 parts: *model search*, *pattern search*, and *attribute search*. However,in this case the notion of "decomposition" refers to the entire KDD process,while this book focuses on decomposition of the model search.

In the neural network community several researchers have examined the decomposition methodology [Hansen (2000)]. [Nowlan and Hinton (1991)] have examined the *"mixture-of-experts"* (ME) method that decomposes the input space, such that each expert examines a different part of the space. However, the subspaces have soft "boundaries", namely subspaces are allowed to overlap. Figure 5.1 illustrates an n-expert structure. Each expert outputs the conditional probability of the target attribute given the input instance. A gating network is responsible for combining the various experts by assigning a weight to each network. These weights are not constant but are functions of the input instance x.

An extension to the basic mixture of experts, known as hierarchical mixtures of experts (HME), has been proposed by [Jordan and Jacobs (1994)]. This extension decomposes the space into subspaces, and then recursively decomposes each subspace to subspaces.

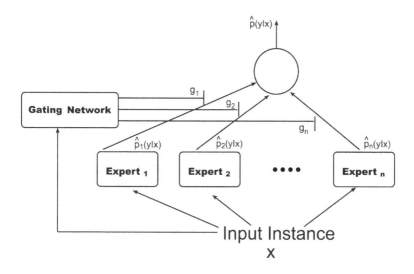

Fig. 5.1   Illustration of n-Expert Structure.

Variation of the basic mixtures of experts methods have been developed to accommodate specific domain problems. [Hampshire and Waibel (1992)] and [Peng *et al.* (1995)] have used a specialized modular network called the Meta-p_i network to solve the vowel-speaker problem. [Weigend *et al.* (1995)] proposed nonlinear gated experts for time-series. [Ohno-Machado and Musen (1997)] have used revised modular network for predicting the survival of AIDS patients. [Rahman and Fairhurst (1997)] have proposed a new approach for combining multiple experts for improving handwritten numerals recognition.

However, none of these works presents a complete framework that considers the coexistence of different decomposition methods, namely: When should we prefer a specific method and whether it is possible to solve a given problem using a hybridization of several decomposition methods.

5.2   Decomposition Advantages

5.2.1   *Increasing Classification Performance (Classification Accuracy)*

Decomposition methods can improve the predictive accuracy of regular methods. In fact [Sharkey (1999)] argues that improving performance is the main motivation for decomposition. Although this might look surprising at first, it can be explained by the bias-variance tradeoff. Since decomposition methodology constructs several simpler sub-models instead a single complicated model, we might gain better performance by choosing the appropriate sub-models' complexities (i.e. finding the best bias-variance tradeoff). Figure 5.2 illustrates this idea. As it can be seen in the figure, a single decision tree that attempts to model the entire instance space usually has high variance and small bias. On the other hand, Naïve Bayes can be seen as a composite of single-attribute decision trees (each one of these trees contains only one unique input attribute). The bias of the Naïve Bayes is large (as it can not represent a complicated classifier) but on the other hand, its variance is small. Decomposition can potentially obtain a set of decision trees, such that each one of the trees is more complicated than a single-attribute tree (thus it can represent a more complicated classifier and it has lower bias than the Naïve Bayes) but not complicated enough to have high variance.

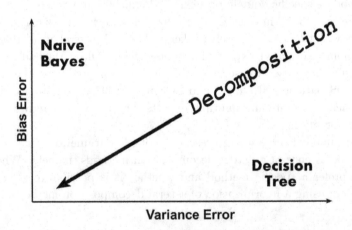

Fig. 5.2   Bias-Variance Tradeoff.

There are other justifications for the performance improvement of decomposition methods, such as the ability to exploit the specialized capabilities of each component, and consequently achieve results which would not be possible in a single model. [Baxt (1990)] has presented an excellent example of the contributions that decomposition methodology may provide. In this research the main goal was to identify a certain clinical diagnosis. Decomposing the problem and building two neural networks significantly increased the correct classification rate.

5.2.2 *Scalability to Large Databases*

One of the explicit challenges for the KDD research community is to develop methods that facilitate the use of data mining algorithms for real-world databases. In the information age, data is automatically collected and therefore the database available for mining can be quite large, as a result of an increase in the number of records in the database and the number of fields/attributes in each record (high dimensionality).

As stated in the first chapter, approaches for dealing with huge databases include: sampling methods; massively parallel processing, efficient storage methods and dimension reduction. This book suggests an alternative way to deal with the aforementioned problems by reducing the volume of data to be processed at a time. Decomposition methods break the original problem into several subproblems, each one with relatively small dimensionality. In this way, decomposition reduces training time and makes it possible to apply standard machine learning algorithms to large databases [Sharkey (1999)].

5.2.3 *Increasing Comprehensibility*

Decomposition methods suggest a conceptual simplification of the original complex problem. Instead of getting a single and complicated model, decomposition methods create several sub-models, which are more comprehensible. This motivation has often been noted in the literature [Pratt *et al.* (1991); Hrycej (1992); Sharkey (1999)]. Smaller models are also more appropriate for user-driven data mining that is based on *Visualization Techniques*. Furthermore, if the decomposition structure is induced by automatic means, it can provide new insight about the explored domain.

5.2.4 *Modularity*

Modularity eases the maintenance of the classification model. Since new data is being collected all the time, it is essential to execute a rebuild process to the entire model once in a while. However, if the model is built from several sub-models, and the new data collected effect only part of the sub-models, a more simple re-building process may be sufficient. This justification has often been noted [Kusiak (2000)].

5.2.5 *Suitability for Parallel Computation*

If there are no dependencies between the various sub-components, then parallel techniques can be applied. By using parallel computation the time needed to solve a mining problem can be shortened.

5.2.6 *Flexibility in Techniques Selection*

Decomposition methodology suggests the ability to use different inducers for individual subproblems or even to use the same inducer but with a different setup. For instance, it is possible to use neural networks having different topologies (different number of hidden nodes). The researcher can exploit this freedom of choice to boost classifier performance.

The first three advantages are of particular importance in commercial and industrial data mining. However, as it will be demonstrated later, not all decomposition methods display the same advantages.

5.3 The Elementary Decomposition Methodology

We believe that finding an optimal or quasi-optimal decomposition for a certain supervised learning problem might be hard or impossible. For that reason our approach is to use elementary decomposition steps. The basic idea is to develop a meta-algorithm that recursively decomposes a classification problem using elementary decomposition methods. We use the term "elementary decomposition" to describe a type of simple decomposition that can be used to build up a more complicated decomposition. Given a certain problem, we first select the most appropriate elementary decomposition to that problem, then a suitable decomposer decomposes the problem, and finally a similar procedure is performed on each sub-problem. This approach agrees with the "no free lunch theorem" described in the first chapter, namely if one decomposition is better than another in some domains, then there are necessarily other domains in which this relationship is reversed.

For implementing this decomposition methodology, one might consider the following issues:

- What type of elementary decomposition methods exist for classification inducers?
- Which elementary decomposition type performs best for which problem? What factors should one take into account when choosing the appropriate decomposition type?
- Given an elementary type, how should we infer the best decomposition structure automatically?
- How should the subproblems be recomposed to represent the original concept learning?
- How can we utilize prior knowledge for improving decomposing methodology?

We start by answering the first question. Figure 5.3 illustrates a novel approach for arranging the different elementary types of decomposition in supervised learning [Maimon and Rokach (2002)]. A simple illustration of each type can be found in the following section.

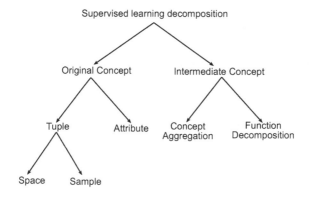

Fig. 5.3   Elementary Decomposition Methods in Classification.

In *Intermediate Concept* decomposition, instead of inducing a single complicated classifier, several subproblems with different and more simple concepts are defined. The intermediate concepts can be based on an aggregation of the original concept's values (*Concept Aggregation*) or not (*Function Decomposition*).

Classical concept aggregation replaces the original target attribute with a function, such that the domain of the new target attribute is smaller than the original one.

$$f(y) : dom(y) \mapsto dom(y*) \; |dom(y*)| < |dom(y)|$$

Nevertheless the condition that $|dom(y*)| < |dom(y)|$ is not mandatory. Furthermore, in some cases it might be convenient to use the input attributes for performing the transformation:

$$f(x,y) : X \times dom(y) \mapsto dom(y*) \; |dom(y*)| < |dom(y)|$$

Concept aggregation has been used to classify free text documents into predefined topics [Buntine (1996)]. This paper suggests breaking the topics up into groups (co-topics). Instead of predicting the document's topic directly, the document is first classified into one of the co-topics. Another model is then used to predict the actual topic in that co-topic.

A general concept aggregation algorithm called *Error-Correcting Output Coding* (ECOC) which decomposes multi-class problems into multiple, two-class problems has been suggested by [Dietterich and Bakiri (1995)]. A classifier is built for each possible binary partition of the classes. Experiments show that ECOC improves the accuracy of neural networks and decision trees on several multi-class problems from the UCI repository.

The idea to decompose a K class classification problems into K two class classification problems has been proposed by [Anand *et al.* (1995)]. Each problem considers the discrimination of one class to the other classes. [Lu and Ito (1999)] extends Anand's method and proposes a new method for manipulating the data based on the class relations among training data. By using this method, they divide a K class classification problem into a series of $K(K-1)/2$ two-class problems where each problem considers the discrimination of one class to each one of the other classes. They have examined this idea using neural networks.

Function decomposition was originally developed in the fifties and sixties for designing switching circuits. [Samuel (1967)] proposed a function decomposition method based on a signature table system as an evaluation mechanism for his checkers playing programs. This approach was later improved by [Biermann *et al.* (1982)]. Recently the machine learning community has adopted this approach. [Michie (1995)] used a manual decomposition of the problem and an expert-assisted selection of examples to construct rules for the concepts in the hierarchy. In comparison with standard decision tree induction techniques, structured induction exhibits about the same degree of classification accuracy with the increased transparency and lower complexity of the developed models. [Zupan *et al.* (1998)] presented a general-purpose function decomposition approach for machine learning. According to this approach, attributes are transformed into new concepts in an iterative manner and create a hierarchy of concepts. Recently [Long (2003)] has suggested using a different function decomposition known as Bi-Decomposition and shows it applicability in data mining.

Original Concept decomposition means dividing the original problem into several sub-problems by partitioning the training set into smaller training sets. A classifier is trained on each sub-sample seeking to solve the original problem. Note that this resembles ensemble methodology but with the following distinction: each inducer uses only a portion of the original training set and ignores the rest. After a classifier is constructed for each portion separately, the models are combined in some fashion, either at learning or classification time.

There are two obvious ways to break up the original dataset: tuple oriented or attribute oriented. It is worth to mention that some researchers prefer the terms "Horizontal Decomposition" and "Vertical Decomposition" for describing "Space Decomposition" and "Attribute Decomposition" respectively [Ronco *et al.* (1996)]. Tuple decomposition by itself can be divided into two different types: sample and space. In sample decomposition (also known as partitioning), the goal is to partition the training set into several sample sets, such that each sub-learning task considers the entire space.

In space decomposition, on the other hand, the original instance space is divided into several sub-spaces. Each sub-space is considered independently and the total model is a (possibly soft) union of such simpler models.

Space decomposition also includes the divideandconquer approaches such as mixturesofexperts, local linear regression, CART/MARS, adaptive subspace models, etc., [Johansen and Foss (1992); Jordan and Jacobs (1994); Ramamurti and Ghosh (1999); Holmstrom *et al.* (1997)].

5.3.1 *Illustrative Example of Elementary Decomposition*

5.3.1.1 *Overview*

This section illustrates the elementary decomposition methods presented in the last section. Consider the training set in Table 5.1 containing data about twenty health insurance policyholder. Each policyholder is characterized by four attributes: Asset Ownership (Whether the person holds a house, tenement or none). The last attribute describes whether that person was willing to purchase a complementary insurance and what type of complementary insurance he was willing to buy (Silver or Gold).

Table 5.1   Training Set for Illustrative Examples.

Asset Ownership	Education (years)	Car Engine Volume (cc)	Employment Status	Target
Tenement	15	1200	Employee	Silver
House	12	2200	Self	Gold
None	11	0	None	Silver
Tenement	13	1100	Employee	None
Tenement	19	1800	Employee	Silver
House	12	3000	Self	Gold
None	12	2500	Self	Gold
Tenement	12	1600	Employee	Silver
House	12	1500	None	Gold
None	14	1800	Employee	Silver
Tenement	15	2000	Self	Gold
Tenement	12	1100	Employee	None
None	12	0	None	Silver
Tenement	15	1600	Self	Gold
House	16	1200	Employee	Silver
None	17	1800	None	None
Tenement	9	1200	Employee	None
Tenement	12	1000	None	Silver
House	12	1300	Self	Gold
None	12	0	Employee	Silver
Tenement	8	1800	Employee	Silver
Tenement	10	1000	None	Silver
House	12	2000	Employee	None

5.3.1.2   *Feature Set Decomposition*

The feature set is decomposed into mutually exclusive or partially overlapping subsets. For each subset, a different classifier is trained. Using the C4.5 algorithm, the two decision trees presented in Figure 5.4 and Figure 5.5 were generated to describe the target attribute. The first decision tree uses the attributes Asset Ownership and Volume, while the second uses the attributes Employment Status and Education. Note that each classifier was induced by using a different projection of the original dataset presented in Table 5.1.

```
if Asset Ownership == House
    then -> Gold
if Asset Ownership == Tenement
    and Volume > 1000
    and Volume <=1300
    then -> None
if Asset Ownership == None
    then -> Silver
if Asset Ownership == Tenement
    and (Volume<=1000 or Volume>1300)
    then -> Silver
```

Fig. 5.4   Decision Tree for Attributes Asset Ownership and Volume.

```
if Employment Status == Employee and Education > 12
    then -> Silver
if Employment Status == Employee and Education <= 12
    then -> none
if Employment Status == Self
    then -> Gold
if Employment Status == None
    then -> Silver
```

Fig. 5.5   Decision Tree for Attributes Employment Status and Education.

5.3.1.3   *Sample Decomposition*

The tuples from Table 5.1 are decomposed into two equal-size groups. Figure 5.6 shows the decision tree extracted from the first half of the tuples in Table 5.1. While Figure 5.7 presents the decision tree generated from the second half.

5.3.1.4   *Space Decomposition*

In this decomposition mode, the entire input space is decomposed into several subspaces. The tuples in Table 5.1 are separated into two subsets based on the value of the Education attribute. The first group relates to

```
if Employment Status==Employee
    and Asset Ownership== House
    then->None
if Employment Status==Employee
    and Asset Ownership == None
    then -> Silver
if Employment Status==Employee
    and Asset Ownership ==Tenement
    and Volume =< 1300
    then -> None
if Employment Status==Employee
    and Asset Ownership ==Tenement
    and Volume > 1300
    then -> Silver
if Employment Status == None
    then -> Silver
if Employment Status == Self
    then -> Gold
```

Fig. 5.6   Decision Tree for the First Half Tuples.

subspace where Education is less than 15 and the second group relate to the remaining tuples. The decision trees extracted for each of the subspaces are shown in Figure 5.8 and Figure 5.9.

5.3.1.5   *Concept Aggregation*

In concept aggregation the domain values of the target attribute is decomposed into several sub-domains. A model is trained for classifying tuples to one of the sub-domains. Then for each sub-domain, a more specific classifier is trained in order to classify the tuple to the target class. For instance, in the training set presented in Table 5.1, target attribute domain {None, Gold, Silver} can be decomposed into two sub-domains: No = {None} and Yes={Gold, Silver}.

Figure 5.10 shows a classification model to the sub-domains. Figure 5.11 classifies a tuple that was already classified to the "Yes" group into more specific values, i.e. Silver or Gold.

```
if Employment Status == Self
    then -> Gold
if Volume <= 1100 and Employment Status == Employee
    then -> None
if Volume > 1100 and Employment Status == Employee
    then -> Silver
if Employment Status == None
    then -> Silver
```

Fig. 5.7   Decision Tree for the Second Half Tuples.

```
if Employment Status == Self
    then -> Gold
if Education <= 17 and Employment Status == Employee
    then -> None
if Education > 17 and Employment Status == Employee
    then -> Silver
if Employment Status == None
    then -> Silver
```

Fig. 5.8   Decision Tree for Subspace Education >= 15.

```
if Volume > 1000
    then -> Gold
if Volume <= 1000
    then -> Silver
```

Fig. 5.9   Decision Tree for Subspace Education < 15.

5.3.1.6   *Function Decomposition*

In function decomposition, the idea is to look for intermediate concepts. In this example, an intermediate concept named "wealth" is defined (see Figure 5.12). Using the new concept, a classifier can be induced as shown in Figure 5.13.

```
if Asset Ownership==Tenement
   and Volume<=1300
   and Employment Status==Employee
   then -> No
else ->yes
```

Fig. 5.10   A Model for Deciding whether a Certain Insurer is Willing to Buy a Complementary Insurance.

```
if Employement == Self
   then -> Gold
if Ownership == House and Aggregation == Yes
   then -> Gold
if Employement == Employee
   then -> Silver
if Ownership == Tenement and Employement == None
   then -> Silver
if Ownership == None and Employement == None
   then -> Silver
```

Fig. 5.11   A Model for Deciding what Type of Complementary Insurance an Insurer is Willing to Buy.

$$Wealth = \begin{cases} RichOwnership = House \quad and \quad Volume \geq 2000 \\ PoorOwnership = None \quad and \quad Volume < 1000 \\ Else \end{cases}$$

Fig. 5.12   A Definition of a New Intermediate Concept.

5.3.2   *The Decomposer's Characteristics*

5.3.2.1   *Overview*

The following sub-sections present the main properties that characterize decomposers. These properties can be useful for differentiating between various decomposition frameworks.

```
if Wealth == Rich
   then -> Gold
if Wealth == Poor and Employment Status == Employee
   then -> Silver
if Wealth == Poor and Employment Status == None
   then -> None
if Wealth == Else
   then -> Silver
```

Fig. 5.13   A Classifier Using the New Intermediate Concept.

5.3.2.2   *The Structure Acquiring Method*

This important property indicates how the decomposition structure is obtained:

- Manually (explicitly) based on an expert's knowledge in a specific domain [Blum and Mitchell (1998); Michie (1995)]. If the origin of the dataset is a relational database, then the schema's structure may imply the decomposition structure.
- Predefined due to Some Restrictions (as in the case of distributed data mining)
- Arbitrarily [Domingos (1996); Chan and Stolfo (1995)] — The decomposition is performed without any profound thought. Usually after setting the size of the subsets, members are randomly assigned to the different subsets.
- Induced without human interaction by a suitable algorithm [Zupan *et al.* (1998)].

Ronco *et al.* (1996) suggest a different categorization in which the first two categories are referred as "Ad-hoc decomposition" and the last two categories as "Self-decomposition".

Usually in real-life applications the decomposition is performed manually by incorporating business information into the modeling process. For instance [Berry and Linoff (2000)] provide a practical example in their book saying:

It may be known that platinum cardholders behave differently from gold cardholders. Instead of having a data mining technique figure this out, give it the hint by building separate models for the platinum and gold cardholders.

Berry and Linoff (2000) state that decomposition can be also useful for handling missing data. In this case they do not refer to sporadic missing data but to the case where several attributes values are available for some tuples but not for all of them. For instance: "Historical data, such as billing information, is available only for customers who have been around for a sufficiently long time" or "Outside data, such as demographics, is available only for the subset of the customer base that matches"). In this case,one classifier can be trained for customers having all the information and a second classifier can be trained for the remaining customers.

5.3.2.3 *The Mutually Exclusive Property*

This property indicates whether the decomposition is mutually exclusive (*disjointed decomposition*) or partially overlapping (i.e. a certain value of a certain attribute in a certain tuple is utilized more than once). For instance, in the case of sample decomposition, "mutually exclusive" means that a certain tuple cannot belong to more than one subset [Domingos (1996); Chan and Stolfo (1995)]. [Bay (1999)], on the other hand, has used non-exclusive feature decomposition.

Similarly CART and MARS perform mutually exclusive decomposition of the input space, while HME allow subspaces to overlap.

Mutually exclusive decomposition can be deemed as a *pure* decomposition. While pure decomposition forms a restriction on the problem space, it has some important and helpful properties:

- A greater tendency in reduction of execution time than non-exclusive approaches. Since most learning algorithms have computational complexity that is greater than linear in the number of attributes or tuples, partitioning the problem dimensionality in a mutually exclusive manner means a decrease in computational complexity [Provost and Kolluri (1997)].
- Since mutual exclusiveness entails using smaller datasets, the models obtained for each sub-problem are smaller in size. Without the mutually exclusive restriction, each model can be as complicated as the model obtained for the original problem. Smaller models contribute to comprehensibility and ease in maintaining the solution.
- According to [Bay (1999)], mutually exclusive decomposition may help

avoid some error correlation problems that characterize non-mutually exclusive decompositions. However [Sharkey (1999)] argue that mutually exclusive training sets do not necessarily result in low error correlation. This point is true when each sub-problem is representative (i.e. represent the entire problem, like in sample decomposition).

- Reduced tendency to contradiction between sub-models. When mutually exclusive restriction is not enforced, different models might generate contradictive classifications using the same input. Reducing inter-models contraindications help us to grasp the results and to combine the sub-models into one model. [Ridgeway *et al.* (1999),], for instance, claim that the resulting predictions of ensemble methods are usually inscrutable to end-users, mainly due to the complexity of the generated models, as well as the obstacles in transforming theses models into a single model. Moreover, since these methods do not attempt to use all relevant features, the researcher will not obtain a complete picture of which attribute actually affects the target attribute, especially when, in some cases, there are many relevant attributes.

- Since the mutually exclusive approach encourages smaller datasets, they are more feasible. Some data mining tools can process only limited dataset size (for instance when the program requires that the entire dataset will be stored in the main memory). The mutually exclusive can make certain that data mining tools are fairly scalable to large data sets [Chan and Stolfo (1997); Provost and Kolluri (1997)].

- We claim that end-users can grasp mutually exclusive decomposition much easier than many other methods currently in use. For instance boosting, which is a well-known ensemble method, distorts the original distribution of instance space, a fact that non-professional users find hard to grasp or understand.

5.3.2.4 *The Inducer Usage*

This property indicates the relation between the decomposer and the inducer used. Some decomposition implementations are "inducer-free", namely they do not use intrinsic inducers at all. Usually the decomposition procedure needs to choose the best decomposition structure among several structures that it considers. In order to measure the performance of a certain decomposition structure there is a need to realize the structure by building a classifier for each component. However since "inducer-free" decomposition does not use any induction algorithm, it uses a frequency table of the Cartesian product of the feature values instead. Consider the following example. The training set consists of four binary input attributes (a_1, a_2, a_3, a_4) and one target attribute (y). Assume that an "inducer-free" decomposition procedure examines the following feature set decomposition: (a_1, a_3) and (a_2, a_4). In order to measure the classification performance of this structure, it is required to build two classifiers; one classifier for each subset. In the absence of induction algorithm, two frequency tables are built; each table has $2^2 = 4$ entries representing the Cartesian product of the attributes in each subset. For each entry in the table, we measure the frequency of the target attribute. Each one of the tables can be separately used to classify a new instance x: we search for the entry that corresponds to the instance x and select the target value with the highest frequency in that entry. This "inducer-free" strategy has been used in several places. For instance [Domingos and Pazzani (1997)] have investigated the extension of Naïve Bayes which can be considered as a feature set decomposition with no intrinsic inducer. [Zupan *et al.* (1998)] has developed the function decomposition by using sparse frequency tables.

Other implementations are considered as an "inducer-dependent" type, namely these decomposition methods use intrinsic inducers, and they have been developed specifically for a certain inducer. They do not guarantee effectiveness in any other induction methods. For instance the work of [Lu and Ito (1999)] was developed specifically for neural networks.

The third type of decomposition method is the "inducer-independent" type; these implementations can be performed on any given inducer. However, it uses the same inducer in all subsets. As opposed to the "inducer-free" implementation, which does not use any inducer for its execution, "inducer-independent" requires the use of an inducer. Nevertheless, it is not limited to a specific inducer like the "inducer-dependent".

The last type is the "inducer-chooser" type, which given a set of inducers, the system is capable of using the most appropriate inducer on each sub-problem.

5.3.2.5   *Exhaustiveness*

This property indicates whether all data elements should be used in the decomposition. For instance, an exhaustive feature set decomposition refers to the situation in which each feature participates in at least one subset.

5.3.2.6 *Combiner Usage*

This property specifies the relation between the decomposer and the combiner. Some decomposers are combiner-dependent: namely they have been developed specifically for a certain combination method like voting or Naïve Bayes (For additional combining methods see Chapter 4). Other decomposers are combiner-independent, namely the combination method is provided as input to the framework. Potentially there could be decomposers that, given a set of combiners, would be capable of choosing the best combiner in the current case.

5.3.2.7 *Sequentially or Concurrently*

This property indicates whether the various sub-classifiers are built sequentially or concurrently. In sequential framework the outcome of a certain classifier may effect the creation of the next classifier. On the other hand, in concurrent framework each classifier is built independently and their results are combined in some fashion. [Sharkey (1996)] refers to this property as "The relationship between modules" and distinguish between three different types: Successive, Cooperative and Supervisory. Roughly speaking the "Successive" refers to "Sequential" while "Cooperative" refers to "Concurrent". The last type applies to the case in which one model controls the other model. [Sharkey (1996)] provide an example in which one neural network is used to tune another neural network.

The original problem in *Intermediate Concept Decomposition* is usually converted to a sequential list of problems, where the last problem aims to solve the original one. On the other hand, in *Original Concept Decomposition* the problem is usually divided into several sub-problems which exist on their own. Nevertheless, there are some exceptions, for instance [Quinlan (1993)] proposed an Original Concept framework known as "windowing" that is considered to be sequential. For other examples the reader is referred to Chapter 4.

Naturally there might be other important properties which can be used to differentiate a decomposition scheme, however this book focuses on the properties presented above. Table 5.2 summarizes the most relevant research performed on each decomposition type.

Table 5.2   Summary of Decomposition Methods in the Literature.

Paper	Decomposition Type	Mutually Exclusive	Structure Acquiring Method
[Anand *et al.* (1995)]	Concept	No	Arbitrarily
[Buntine (1996)]	Concept	Yes	Manually
[Michie (1995)]	Function	Yes	Manually
[Zupan *et al.* (1998)]	Function	Yes	Induced
[Ali and Pazzani (1996)]	Sample	No	Arbitrarily
[Domingos (1996)]	Sample	Yes	Arbitrarily
[Ramamurti and Ghosh (1999)]	Space	No	Induced
[Kohavi *et al.* (1997)]	Space	Yes	Induced
[Bay (1999)]	Attribute	No	Arbitrarily
[Kusiak (2000)]	Attribute	Yes	Manually

5.3.3   *Distributed and Parallel Data Mining*

Distributed Data Mining (DDM) deals with mining data that might be inherently distributed among different, loosely coupled sites with slow connectivity, such as geographically distributed sites connected over the Internet [Kargupta and Chan (2000)]. Usually DDM is categorized according to data distribution:

- Homogeneous – In this case, the datasets in all the sites are built from the same common set of attributes. This state is equivalent to the sample decomposition discussed above, when the decomposition structure is set by the environment.
- Heterogeneous – In this case, the quality and quantity of data available to each site may vary substantially. Since each specific site may contain data for different attributes, leading to large discrepancies in their performance, integrating classification models derived from distinct and distributed databases is complex.

DDM can be useful also in the case of "mergers and acquisitions" of corporations. In this case each company involved may have its own IT legacy systems; consequently different sets of data are available.

In distributed data mining the different sources are given, namely the instances are pre-decomposed. As a result DDM is mainly focused on combining the various methods. Several researchers discuss ways of leveraging distributed techniques in knowledge discovery, such as data cleaning and preprocessing, transformation, and learning.

Prodromidis *et al* (1999) proposed a meta-learning approach for DDM under the name JAM system. The meta-learning approach is about combining several models (describing several sets of data from several sources of data) into one high-level model. [Guo and Sutiwaraphun (1998)] describe a meta-learning concept know as *Knowledge Probing* to DDM. In Knowledge Probing, supervised learning is organized into two stages. In the first stage, a set of base classifiers is constructed using the distributed data sets. In the second stage, the relationship between an attribute vector and the class predictions from all of the base classifiers is determined. [Grossman *et al.* (1999)] outline fundamental challenges for mining large-scale databases, one of them being the need to develop DDM algorithms.

A closely related field is *Parallel Data Mining* (PDM). PDM deals with mining data by using several tightly-coupled systems with fast interconnection, like in the case of a cluster of shared memory workstations [Zaki and Ho (2000)]. The main goal of PDM techniques is to scale-up the speed of the data mining on large datasets. It addresses the issue by using high performance, multi-processor computers. The increasing availability of such computers calls for extensive development of data analysis algorithms that can scale up as we attempt to analyze data sets measured in terabytes on parallel machines with thousands of processors. This technology is particularly suitable for applications that typically deal with large amounts of data, e.g. company transaction data, scientific simulation and observation data. [Zaki *et al.* (1999)] discuss a project called SPIDER that uses shared-memory multiprocessors systems (SMP's) to accomplish PDM on distributed data sets.

The above references indicate that DDM as well as PDM are emerging and active area of research.

5.3.4 *The Uniqueness of the Proposed Decomposition Framework*

The main distinction between existing approaches, such as ensemble methods and distributed data mining to decomposition methodology, focuses on the following fact: The assumption that each model has an access to comparable quality of data is not valid in decomposition approach. According to [Tumer and Ghosh (2000)]:

"A fundamental assumption in all the multi-classifier approaches is that the designer has access to the entire data set, which can be used in its entirety, resampled in a random (bagging) or weighted (boosting) way , or

randomly partitioned and distributed. Thus, except for boosting situations, each classifier sees training data of comparable quality. If the individual classifiers are then appropriately chosen and trained properly, their performances will be (relatively) comparable in any region of the problem space. So gains from combining are derived from the diversity among classifiers rather that by compensating for weak members of the pool. "

This assumption is clearly invalid for decomposition methodology, where classifiers may have significant variations in their overall performance. Furthermore, according to [Tumer and Ghosh (2000)], when individual classifiers have substantially different performances over different parts of the input space, combining is still desirable. Nevertheless neither simple combiners nor more sophisticated combiners are particularly well suited for the type of problems that arise. [Tumer and Ghosh (2000)] state that:

"The simplicity of averaging the classifier outputs is appealing, but the prospect of one poor classifier corrupting the combiner makes this a risky choice. Weighted averaging of classifier outputs appears to provide some flexibility. Unfortunately, the weights are still assigned on a per classifier basis rather than a per tuple basis. If a classifier is accurate only in certain areas of the input space, this scheme fails to take advantage of the variable accuracy of the classifier in question. Using a combiner that provides different weights for different patterns can potentially solve this problem, but at a considerable cost."

The uniqueness of the proposed decomposition framework compared to other decomposition frameworks can be summarized in the following points:

- No research in the literature has developed a decomposer that searches for the optimal mutually exclusive decomposition in decision trees. As described in the previous sections, enforcement of mutual exclusiveness has some important advantages. Ensemble methods do not try to find the best mutually exclusive structure. While some methods fulfill the mutually exclusive property, they do not try to find the best decomposition and decompose the problem in a random manner. Other methods (like boosting) that are not randomly based, do not enforce the mutually exclusive restriction. The "Mixture-Of-Experts" methodology developed in the neural network community almost fulfills the mutually exclusive property. Nevertheless, in many cases neural networks are not suitable to data mining as they are unintelligible.

- Although each elementary decomposition method has been extensively investigated separately, the potential contribution of the hybridization of these methods has not yet been investigated. Namely, no research has considered the ensemble methods in the light of the entire framework of decomposition methodology proposed here. For example, no one has concluded when to use each type of decomposition. Furthermore, there is no research that examines the relation of parallel decomposition methods with those of sequential decomposition.

Due to the issues presented above, we argue that even for the Original Concept decomposition methods, the need for new methods for inducing the best decomposition structure undoubtedly exists.

This book focuses on algorithms that search for the best decomposition structure. Some may justifiably claim that searching for the best decomposition might be time-consuming, namely prolonging the data mining process.

In order to avoid this disadvantage, the complexity of the decomposition algorithms should be kept as small as possible. However, even if this can not be accomplished, there are still important advantages, such as better comprehensibility and better performance that makes decomposition worth the additional time complexity.

Furthermore, it should be noted that in an ongoing data mining effort (like in churning application) searching for the best decomposition structure might be performed in wider time buckets (for instance once a year) than training the classifiers (for instance once a week). Moreover, for acquiring decomposition structure, only a relatively small sample of the training set may be required. Consequently, the execution time of the decomposer will be relatively small compared to the time needed to train the classifiers.

5.3.5 *Problems Formulation*

For each elementary decomposition, we mathematically formulate the problem of finding the optimal decomposition structure given a certain Inducer I. By stating optimal structure, we refer to the structure that minimizes the generalization error of the combined classifiers over the distribution D. It should be noted that the optimal structure is not necessarily unique.

This work makes the following assumptions:

• Null (missing) values are not allowed (unless they are encoded as a special value).
• All attributes have nominal domain.
• Mutually exclusive — Due to the reasons presented in the last section,

we search only for mutually exclusive decompositions.

- We assume that the same probabilistic inducer is used for all sub-problems. Furthermore, we assume that this inducer is given, i.e. this work does not discuss the issue of choosing the appropriate inducer for a given problem.

5.3.5.1 *Feature Set Decomposition*

We first add the following notation:

- $G_k = \{a_{\alpha_k(j)} \,|\, j = 1, \ldots, l_k\}$ —indicates the k'th subset that contains l_k input attributes where $\alpha_k : \{1, \ldots, l_k\} \to \{1, \ldots, n\}$ is a function that maps the attribute index j to the original attribute index in the set A.
- $R_k = \{i \,|\, \exists j \in \{1, \ldots, l_k\} \ s.t. \ \alpha_k(j) = i\}$ denotes the corresponding indexes of subset k in the complete attribute set A.
- $\pi_{G_k \cup y} S$ represents the corresponding projection of S.
- $Z = \{G_1, \ldots, G_k, \ldots, G_\omega\}$ represents a decomposition of the attribute set A into ω mutually exclusive subsets such that $\left(\bigcup_{k=1}^{\omega} G_k \right) \subseteq A$

Formally, the attribute decomposition problem can be phrased as described in [Maimon and Rokach (2001)]:

Given an inducer I, a combination method C, and a training set S with input feature set $A = \{a_1, a_2, \ldots, a_n\}$ and target feature y from a distribution D over the labeled instance space, the goal is to find an optimal decomposition Z_{opt} of the input feature set A into ω mutually exclusive subsets $G_k = \{a_{\alpha_k(j)} \,|\, j = 1, \ldots, l_k\}$; $k = 1, \ldots, \omega$ that are not necessarily exhaustive such that the generalization error of the induced classifiers $I(\pi_{G_k \cup y} S)$; $k = 1, \ldots, \omega$ combined using method C, will be minimized over the distribution D.

It should be noted that since it is not obligatory that all input attributes actually belong to one of the subsets, the problem can be treated as an extension of the feature selection problem, i.e. finding the optimal decomposition of the form $Z_{opt} = \{G_1\}$, as the non-relevant features are in fact $NR = A - G_1$. Feature selection is fundamental to machine learning. The aim of feature selection is to focus a learning algorithm on some subset of the given input attributes, while ignoring the rest. This goal is accomplished by identifying the most salient and useful features for learning. Moreover, when using a Simple Bayes for combining the classifiers as in this case, the Naïve Bayes method can be treated as a specific decomposition: $Z = \{G_1, G_2, \ldots, G_n\}$, where $G_i = \{a_i\}$.

5.3.5.2 *Space Decomposition*

The formal definition of Space Decomposition problem:

Given a learning method I, *and a training set* S *with input attribute set* $A = \{a_1, a_2, \ldots, a_n\}$ *and target attribute* y *from a distribution* D *over the labeled instance space, the goal is to find an optimal decomposition* W_{opt} *of the instance space* X *into* ψ *subspaces* $B_k \subseteq X$; $k = 1, \ldots, \psi$ *fulfilling* $(\bigcup_{k=1}^{\psi} B_k) = X$ *and* $B_i \cap B_j = \emptyset$; $i, j = 1, \ldots, \psi$; $i \neq j$ *such that the generalization error of the induced classifiers* $M_k = I(\sigma_{x \in B_k} S)$; $k = 1, \ldots, \psi$ *will be minimized over the distribution* D.

The generalization error in this case is defined as

$$\varepsilon(B_1, \ldots, B_\psi, M_1, \ldots, M_\psi) = \sum_{k=1}^{\psi} \sum_{x \in B_k} \sum_{c_j \in dom(y)} L(x, c_j, M_k) \cdot D(x, c_j)$$

(5.1)

where the loss function is defined as

$$L(x, c_j, M_k) = \begin{cases} 0 c_j = \underset{c_j^* \in dom(y)}{\operatorname{argmax}} \hat{P}_{M_k}(y = c_j^* | x) \\ 1 c_j \neq \underset{c_j^* \in dom(y)}{\operatorname{argmax}} \hat{P}_{M_k}(y = c_j^* | x) \end{cases}$$

(5.2)

where M_k is the corresponded classifier of subspace B_k.

It should be noticed that if the inducer is a decision tree, then the space decomposition problem formulated here can be related to multivariate decision trees. Decision tree induction algorithms partition the instance space in a top-down, divide and conquer manner. Most of the well known algorithms are univariate decision trees, i.e. they test only a single attribute in each node. Applying multivariate decision tree algorithms [Murthy *et al.* (1994)] may lead to the discovery of patterns that univariate can hardly reveal.

Most of the Multivariate Splitting Criteria are based on linear combination of the input attributes. Thus the split criterion will look like $\sum_i w_i \cdot a_i$ where w_i is the weight of attribute a_i in the criterion. Using the CART algorithm [Biermann *et al.* (1982)] it is possible to search for linear combination of numeric attributes. For example instead of a univariate split criterion such as: "IF INCOME $<= 100$ THEN ... ", CART will consider more general splits like: "IF 0.5*INCOME + 0.2*AGE $<= 70$ THEN ...". According to CART manual nominal attributes are not allowed in the linear combination, so to include them it is required to expand them into a set of dummy variables (as often used in classic regression). It should be noted that it is computationally expensive to gauge the value of a linear combination of many attributes per node, especially in large-scale training sets.

In fact, the space decomposition can be considered as a preliminary step before using regular univariate algorithm. The problem described here is also related to change the detection problem in classification models [Zeira *et al.* (2004)]. Consider a phenomenon that significantly changes over time. In this case, it is interesting to detect the time point at which the change takes place in order to decompose the instance space into two sub-spaces up to that point and afterward.

5.3.5.3 *Sample Decomposition*

The formal definition of Sample Decomposition problem is:

Given a learning method I, a combination method C, and a training set S with input attribute set $A = \{a_1, a_2, \ldots, a_n\}$ and target attribute y from a distribution D over the labeled instance space, the goal is to find an optimal decomposition T_{opt} of the training set S into ξ subsets $E_k \subseteq S$; $k = 1, \ldots, \xi$ fulfilling $(\bigcup_{k=1}^{\xi} E_k) \subseteq S$ and $E_i \cap E_j = \emptyset$; $i, j = 1, \ldots, \xi$; $i \neq j$ such that the generalization error of the C-combination of the induced classifiers of the induced classifiers $I(E_k), k = 1, \ldots, \xi$ will be minimized over the distribution D.

It should be noted that the sample selection problem [Vapnik (1995)] could be considered as a specific case of the sample decomposition problem defined here. The aim is to find the smallest sufficient subset of the dataset and that by using a superset of it will not improve accuracy. The rational of using the sampling idea is that having massive amounts of data does not necessary imply that induction algorithms must use the entire dataset. Samples often provide the same accuracy with far less computational cost.

5.3.5.4 *Concept Aggregation*

The formal definition of Concept Aggregation problem is:

Given a learning method I and a training set S with input attribute set $A = \{a_1, a_2, \ldots, a_n\}$ and target attribute y from a distribution D over the labeled instance space, the goal is to find an optimal decomposition of the target values set into ζ subsets $Y_k \subseteq V_y$ $k = 1, \ldots, \zeta$ fulfilling $(\bigcup_{k=1}^{\zeta} Y_k) = V_y$ and $Y_i \cap Y_j = \emptyset$; $i, j = 1, \ldots, \zeta$; $i \neq j$ such that the *generalization error of the two steps classification made first by the classifier* $I(\{\langle x_i, k \rangle \, | \forall \langle x_i, y_i \rangle \in S; y_i \in Y_k\})$ *and then by appropriate classifier* $I_k(\{\langle x_i, y_i \rangle \, | \forall \langle x_i, y_i \rangle \in S; y_i \in Y_k\})$ *will be minimized over the distribution* D.

5.3.5.5 *Function Decomposition*

For function decomposition we extend the single-step function decomposition defined in [Zupan *et al.* (1998)].

We first add the following notation:

- $H = \{a_{\alpha(j)} \, | j = 1, \ldots, l\}$ −indicates a subset of A that contains l input attributes where i is the original attribute index in the set A.
- Intermediate concept F maps the space defined by the Cartesian product of the attributes in H into a single discrete attribute with ψ different values.
- We denote in x^1 the corresponding values of the attributes in H and in x^2 the values of the other attributes in A.

Consequently the function decomposition problem can be formally phrased as:

Given a learning method I *and a training set* S *with input attribute set* $A = \{a_1, a_2, \ldots, a_n\}$ *and target attribute* y *from a distribution* D *over the labeled instance space, the goal is to find an optimal intermediate concept* F *over* A *such that the generalization error of the classifier* $I(\{\langle F(x_i^1), x_i^2, y_i \rangle \, | i = 1, \ldots, m\})$ *will be minimized over the distribution* D.

Chapter 6

Feature Set Decomposition

6.1 Overview

This chapter presents theoretical aspects of feature set decomposition in classification problems. Feature set decomposition generalizes the task of feature selection which is extensively used in data mining. Feature selection aims to provide a representative set of features from which a classifier is constructed. On the other hand, in feature set decomposition, the original feature set is decomposed into several subsets. An inducer is trained upon the training data for each subset independently, and generates a classifier for each one. Subsequently, an unlabeled instance is classified by combining the classifications of all classifiers. This method potentially facilitates the creation of a classifier for high dimensionality data sets because each sub-classifier copes with only a projection of the original space.

Figure 6.1 illustrates the general framework of feature set decomposition. The grey boxes depict various components in the decomposition framework, while the transparent boxes are considered as input/output. In this general framework, a different inducer can be used for each subset. Nevertheless, one may use the same inducer for each subset and still obtain different classifiers.

In the literature there are several works that fit the feature set decomposition framework. However, in most of the papers the decomposition structure was obtained ad-hoc using prior knowledge. Moreover, as a result of a literature review, [Ronco *et al.* (1996)] have concluded that "*There exists no algorithm or method susceptible to perform a vertical self-decomposition without* a-priori *knowledge on the task!*". [Bay (1999)] presented a feature set decomposition algorithm known as MFS which combines multiple Nearest Neighbor classifiers, each using only a subset of

151

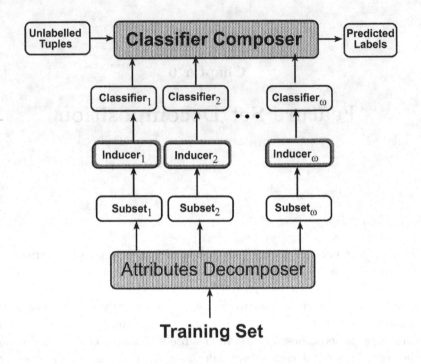

Fig. 6.1   General Framework of Feature Set Decomposition.

random features. Experiments show MFS can improve the standard Nearest Neighbor classifiers. This procedure resembles the well known bagging algorithm [Breiman (1996)], however, instead of sampling instances with replacement, it samples features without replacement.

Another feature set decomposition was proposed by [Kusiak (2000)]. In this case the features are grouped according to the attribute type: nominal value features, numeric value features and text value features. A similar approach was used by [Gama (2000)] for developing the Linear-Bayes classifier. The basic idea consists of aggregating the features into two subsets: the first subset containing only the nominal features and the second subset only the continuous features.

An approach for constructing an ensemble of classifiers using rough set theory was presented by [Hu (2001)]. Although Hu's work refers to ensemble methodology and not decomposition methodology, it is still relevant for this case, especially as the declared goal was to construct an ensemble such that different classifiers use different attributes as much as possible.

According to Hu, diversified classifiers lead to uncorrelated errors, which in turn improve classification accuracy. The method searches for a set of reducts, which include all the indispensable attributes. A reduct represents the minimal set of attributes which has the same classification power as the entire attribute set.

In another research, [Tumer and Ghosh (1996)] proposed to decompose the feature set according to the target class. For each class the features with low correlation relating to that class have been removed. This method has been applied on a feature set of 25 sonar signals where the target was to identify the meaning of the sound (whale, cracking ice, etc.). [Cherkauer (1996)] used feature set decomposition for radar volcanoes recognition. Cherkauer manually decomposed a feature set of 119 into 8 subsets. Features that are based on different image processing operations were grouped together. As a consequence, for each subset, four neural networks with different sizes were built. Combining the classifications of these networks has reached the performance of human expert. [Chen *et al.* (1997)] proposed a new combining framework for feature set decomposition and demonstrate its applicability in text-independent speaker identification. [Jenkins and Yuhas (1993)] manually decomposed the features set of a certain truck backer-upper problem and reported that this strategy has important advantages.

A paradigm, termed Co-Training, for learning with labeled and unlabeled data was proposed by [Blum and Mitchell (1998)]. This paradigm can be considered as a feature set decomposition for classifying Web pages, which is usseful when there is a large sample of data, of which only a small part is labeled. In many applications unlabeled examples are significantly easier to collect than labeled ones. This is especially true when the labeling process is time-consuming or expensive, such as in medical applications. According to the Co-Training paradigm, the input space is divided into two different views (i.e. two independent and redundant sets of features). For each view Blum and Mitchell built a different classifier to classify unlabeled data. The newly labeled data of each classifier is then used to retrain the other classifier. Blum and Mitchell have shown both empirically and theoretically that unlabeled data can be used to augment labeled data.

More recently [Liao and Moody (2000)] presented another option to a decomposition technique whereby initially all input features are grouped by using a hierarchical clustering algorithm based on pairwise mutual information, such that statistically similar features are assigned to the same group. As a consequence, several feature subsets are constructed by selecting one feature from each group. Subsequently for each subset a neural network is constructed, all of which are then combined.

In the statistics literature, [Friedman (1991)] proposed the MARS algorithm. In this algorithm a multiple regression function is approximated using linear splines and their tensor products. It has been shown that the algorithm performs ANOVA decomposition, namely the regression function is represented as a grand total of several sums. The first sum is over all basic functions that involve only a single attribute. The second sum is over all basic functions that involve exactly two attributes, representing (if present) two-variable interactions. Similarly, the third sum represents (if present) the contributions from three-variable interactions, and so on.

Other works on feature set decomposition have been developed by extending the Naïve Bayes classifier. The Naïve Bayes classifier [Domingos and Pazzani (1997)] uses the Bayes rule to compute the conditional probability of each possible class, assuming the input features are conditionally independent given the target feature. Due to the conditional independence assumption, this method is called "Naïve". Nevertheless, a variety of empirical researches show surprisingly that the Naïve Bayes classifier can perform quite well compared to other methods, even in domains where clear feature dependencies exist [Domingos and Pazzani (1997)]. Furthermore, Naïve Bayes classifiers are also very simple and easy to understand [Kononenko (1990)].

Both [Kononenko (1991)] and [Domingos and Pazzani (1997)], suggested to extend the Naïve Bayes classifier by finding the single best pair of features to join by considering all possible joins. [Kononenko (1991)] described the Semi-Naïve Bayes Classifier that uses a conditional independence test for joining features. [Domingos and Pazzani (1997)] used estimated accuracy (as determined by leaveoneout cross validation on the training set). [Friedman et al. (1997)] have suggested the Tree Augmented Naïve Bayes classifier (TAN) which extends the Naïve Bayes, taking into account dependencies among input features. The Selective Bayes Classifier [Langley and Sage (1994)] preprocesses data using a form of feature selection to delete redundant features. [Meretakis and Wthrich (1999)] introduced the Large Bayes algorithm. This algorithm employs an *a-priori*-like frequent pattern mining algorithm to discover frequent and interesting features subsets of arbitrary size, together with their class probability estimation.

Recall from Chapter 1, [Duda and Hart (1973)] showed that the Bayesian classifier has the highest possible accuracy (i.e. the Bayesian classifier predicts the most probable class of a given instance based on the complete distribution). However, in practical induction scenarios, where the training set is very small compared to the whole space, the complete distribution can hardly be estimated directly.

6.2 Problem Formulation

The problem of decomposing an input feature set is that of finding the best decomposition, such that if a specific inducer is run on each feature subset data, then the combination of the generated classifiers will have the highest possible accuracy. Recall from Chapter 5 the formal definition of feature set decomposition problem:

Given an inducer I, a combination method C, and a training set S with input feature set $A = \{a_1, a_2, \ldots, a_n\}$ and target feature y from a distribution D over the labeled instance space, the goal is to find an optimal decomposition Z_{opt} of the input feature set A into ω mutually exclusive subsets $G_k = \{a_{\alpha_k(j)} \, | \, j = 1, \ldots, l_k\} \quad ; \; k = 1, \ldots, \omega$ that are not necessarily exhaustive such that the generalization error of the induced classifiers $I(\pi_{G_k \cup y} S) \; ; \; k = 1, \ldots, \omega$ combined using method C, will be minimized over the distribution D.

The notation a_i denotes the i-th feature whose values are drawn from $dom(a_i)$. The notation y represents the target feature whose values are drawn from a discrete set of classes: $dom(y)$. The notation $I(\pi_{G_k \cup y} S)$ represents a probabilistic classifier which was induced by activating the induction method I on the projection of S on the features of G_k. Using $I(\pi_{G_k \cup y} S)$ one can estimate the probability $\hat{P}_{I(\pi_{G_k \cup y} S)}(y = c_j \, | \, a_i = x_{q,i} \; i \in R_k)$ of an observation x_q. Note that the hat above the conditional probability distinguishes the probability estimation from the actual conditional probability.

This chapter focuses on feature set decomposition designed for decision trees which are combined using the Naïve Bayes combination, namely I is any decision tree inducer and C is the Naïve Bayes combination.

In the Naïve Bayes combination, a classification of a new instance is based on the product of the conditional probability of the target feature, given the values of the input features in each subset. Mathematically it can be formulated as follows:

$$v_{MAP}(x_q) = \underset{\substack{c_j \in dom(y) \\ \hat{P}_{I(S)}(y = c_j) > 0}}{\arg\max} \frac{\prod_{k=1}^{\omega} \hat{P}_{I(\pi_{G_k \cup y} S)}(y = c_j \, | \, a_i = x_{q,i} \; i \in R_k)}{\hat{P}_{I(S)}(y = c_j)^{\omega - 1}}$$

(6.1)

Recall that R_k denotes the correspondence indexes of subset k in the complete feature set A.

In case of decision trees, $\hat{P}_{I(\pi_{G_k \cup y}S)}(y = c_j \,|a_i = x_{q,i} \ i \in R_k)$ can be estimated by using the appropriate frequencies in the relevant leaf. However, using the frequency as is, will typically over-estimate the probability. In order to avoid this phenomenon it is useful to perform the Laplace correction presented in Chapter 1.

It should be noted that the optimal is not necessarily unique. Furthermore, it is not obligatory that all input features actually belong to one of the subsets. Consequently, the problem can be treated as an extension of the feature selection problem, i.e. finding the optimal decomposition of the form $Z_{opt} = \{G_1\}$, as the non-relevant features are in fact $NR = A - G_1$. Feature selection is fundamental to machine learning. The aim of feature selection is to focus an inducer's attention on some subset of the given input features, while ignoring the rest. This goal is accomplished by identifying the most salient and useful features for induction.

Moreover, when using the Naïve Bayes for combining the classifiers as in this case, the Naïve Bayes method can be treated as specific decomposition: $Z = \{G_1, G_2, \ldots, G_n\}$, where $G_i = \{a_i\}$.

According to the above feature set decomposition concept, the complete distribution is estimated by combining several partial distributions. On the one hand, using partial distribution may ignore the important relationship between the input attributes. On the other hand, estimating partial distribution is more reliable when the number of training instances is limited.

This problem can be related to the bias-variance tradeoff. The bias of an inducer for a given classification problem is the persistent or systematic error that the inducer is expected to make. A closely related concept to bias is variance. The variance captures random variation in the algorithm from one training set to another. As the subset becomes smaller, fewer probabilities are required to be estimated and potentially the variance in the estimation of each one of them is smaller. On the other hand, when there are more subsets, it is expected that the approximation of the full distribution using the partial distributions would become less accurate (i.e. higher bias error).

6.3 Definitions and Properties

Definition 6.1 The decompositions $Z^1 = \{G_1^1, \ldots, G_k^1, \ldots, G_{\omega_1}^1\}$ and $Z^2 = \{G_1^2, \ldots, G_k^2, \ldots, G_{\omega_2}^2\}$ are said to be *equivalent* if for each instance with positive probability $(\forall x_q \in X; P(x_q) = \sum_{c \in dom(y)} D(x_q, c) > 0)$, the following is satisfied:

$$
\underset{\substack{c_j \in dom(y) \\ P(y=c_j) > 0}}{\arg\max} \quad \frac{\prod_{k=1}^{\omega_1} P(y = c_j \,|\, a_i = x_{q,i} \; i \in R_k^1)}{P(y = c_j)^{\omega_1 - 1}} = \tag{6.2}
$$

$$
\underset{\substack{c_j \in dom(y) \\ P(y=c_j) > 0}}{\arg\max} \quad \frac{\prod_{k=1}^{\omega_2} P(y = c_j \,|\, a_i = x_{q,i} \; i \in R_k^2)}{P(y = c_j)^{\omega_2 - 1}}
$$

Definition 6.2 The decomposition $Z = \{G_1, \ldots, G_k, \ldots, G_\omega\}$ is said to be *completely equivalent* if for each instance with positive probability $(\forall x_q \in X; P(x_q) = \sum_{c \in dom(y)} D(x_q, c) > 0)$, the following is satisfied:

$$
\underset{\substack{c_j \in dom(y) \\ P(y=c_j) > 0}}{\arg\max} \quad \frac{\prod_{k=1}^{\omega} P(y = c_j \,|\, a_i = x_{q,i} \; i \in R_k)}{P(y = c_j)^{\omega - 1}} = \tag{6.3}
$$

$$
\underset{\substack{c_j \in dom(y) \\ P(y=c_j) > 0}}{\arg\max} \quad P(y = c_j \,|\, a_i = x_{q,i} \; i = 1, \ldots, n)
$$

Since [Duda and Hart (1973)] showed that the right term of Equation 6.3 is optimal, it follows that a completely equivalent decomposition is also optimal. The importance of finding a completely equivalent decomposition is derived from the fact that in real problems with limited training sets, it is easier to approximate probabilities with fewer dimensions.

Definition 6.3   The decompositions $Z^1 = \{G_1^1, \ldots, G_k^1, \ldots, G_{\omega_1}^1\}$ and $Z^2 = \{G_1^2, \ldots, G_k^2, \ldots, G_{\omega_2}^2\}$ are said to be *identical*, and is written as $Z^1 = Z^2$ if $\forall G_i^1 \in Z^1; \exists G_j^2 \in Z^2; G_i^1 = G_j^2$ and $\forall G_j^2 \in Z^2; \exists G_i^1 \in Z^1; G_i^1 = G_j^2$

Definition 6.4   The *Structural Similarity Measure* of two decomposition structures is defined as:

$$\delta(Z^1, Z^2) = \sum_{i=1}^{n-1} \sum_{j=i+1}^{n} \frac{2 \cdot \eta(a_i, a_j, Z^1, Z^2)}{n \cdot (n-1)} \qquad (6.4)$$

where $\eta(a_i, a_j, Z^1, Z^2)$ is a binary function that returns the value 1 if the features a_i, a_j belong to the same subset in both decompositions Z^1, Z^2 or if a_i, a_j belong to different subsets in both decompositions.

For example, given that $A = \{a_1, a_2, a_3, a_4, a_5, a_6\}$, $Z^1 = \{\{a_4, a_2\}; \{a_5, a_3\}\}$ and $Z^2 = \{\{a_1, a_3, a_5\}; \{a_2, a_4\}\}$ then:

$$\delta(Z^1, Z^2) = \sum_{i=1}^{n-1} \sum_{j=i+1}^{n} \frac{2 \cdot \eta(a_i, a_j, Z^1, Z^2)}{n \cdot (n-1)} = \qquad (6.5)$$

$$\frac{2}{5 \cdot 6}(\eta(a_1, a_2, Z^1, Z^2) + \eta(a_1, a_3, Z^1, Z^2)$$

$$+\eta(a_1, a_4, Z^1, Z^2) + \eta(a_1, a_5, Z^1, Z^2) + \eta(a_1, a_6, Z^1, Z^2) + \eta(a_2, a_3, Z^1, Z^2)$$

$$+\eta(a_2, a_4, Z^1, Z^2) + \eta(a_2, a_5, Z^1, Z^2) + \eta(a_2, a_6, Z^1, Z^2) + \eta(a_3, a_4, Z^1, Z^2)$$

$$+\eta(a_3, a_5, Z^1, Z^2) + \eta(a_3, a_6, Z^1, Z^2) + \eta(a_4, a_5, Z^1, Z^2) + \eta(a_4, a_6, Z^1, Z^2)$$

$$+\eta(a_5, a_6, Z^1, Z^2)) = \frac{2}{30}(0 + 0 + 0 + 0 + 0 + 1 +$$

$$1 + 1 + 1 + 1 + 1 + 1 + 1 + 1 + 1) = \frac{10}{15}$$

The *Structural Similarity Measure* can be used for comparing any two decomposition structures and it lies between 0 and 1. Furthermore, this measure is useful for evaluating the quality of a certain decomposition by comparing its structure to the structure of a completely equivalent decomposition. When the two structures agree perfectly, this measure obtains the value 1.

It is important to note that the Structural Similarity Measure is an extension of the *Rand index* [Rand (1971)] developed for evaluating clustering methods

Lemma 6.1 *The Structural Similarity Measure has the following properties:*

(1) *Symmetry:* $\delta(Z^1, Z^2) = \delta(Z^2, Z^1)$
(2) *Positivity:* $\delta(Z^1, Z^2) = 1$ *IIf* $Z^1 = Z^2$
(3) *Triangular Inequality:* $(1 - \delta(Z^1, Z^2)) \leq (1 - \delta(Z^1, Z^3)) + (1 - \delta(Z^2, Z^3))$

The proof of the first property of Lemma 6.1 results explicitly from the definition. The proof of the first direction of property 2 of Lemma 6.1 is also true, namely if $Z^1 = Z^2$ then $\delta(Z^1, Z^2) = 1$.

The opposite direction, namely if $\delta(Z^1, Z^2) = 1$ then $Z^1 = Z^2$, is proved by contradiction. We assume that there are cases where $\delta(Z^1, Z^2) = 1$ but $Z^1 \neq Z^2$. If $Z^1 \neq Z^2$ then without loss of generality $\exists G_i^1 \in Z^1$ such that there is no $G_j^2 \in Z^2$ which fulfill $G_i^1 = G_j^2$. Consequently $\exists a_i, a_j$ such that $\eta(a_i, a_j, Z^1, Z^2) = 0$, which contradict the assumption and therefore our original assumption that $\delta(Z^1, Z^2) = 1$ but $Z^1 \neq Z^2$ must be false.

In order to prove property 3 of Lemma 6.1, we simply have to rewrite the triangular inequality as follows:

$$\delta(Z^1, Z^2) \geq \delta(Z^1, Z^3) + \delta(Z^2, Z^3) - 1$$

Note that:

$$\delta(Z^1, Z^3) + \delta(Z^2, Z^3) = \sum_{i=1}^{n-1} \sum_{j=i+1}^{n} 2 \cdot \frac{\eta(a_i, a_j, Z^1, Z^3) + \eta(a_i, a_j, Z^2, Z^3)}{n \cdot (n-1)}$$

Due to the fact that if $\eta(a_i, a_j, Z^1, Z^3) + \eta(a_i, a_j, Z^2, Z^3) = 2$ then $\eta(a_i, a_j, Z^1, Z^2) = 1$ the Triangular Inequality is true.

Definition 6.5 Let $Z = \{G_1, \ldots, G_k, \ldots, G_\omega\}$. The "degree of mutual exclusiveness" is defined as:

$$\mu(Z) = 1 - \frac{4}{\omega \cdot (\omega - 1)} \sum_{i=1}^{\omega-1} \sum_{j=i+1}^{\omega} \frac{|G_i \cap G_j|}{(|G_i| + |G_j|)} \tag{6.6}$$

Note that $0 \leq \mu(Z) \leq 1$ where $\mu(Z) = 0$ when $G_i = G_j \, \forall i \neq j$ and $\mu(Z) = 1$ when $G_i \cap G_j = \emptyset \, \forall i \neq j$.

Definition 6.6 The *Error Correlation* of a given decomposition $Z = \{G_1, \ldots, G_k, \ldots, G_\omega\}$, using inducer I on training set S is defined as the probability of two classifiers $I(\pi_{G_i \cup y} S), I(\pi_{G_j \cup y} S)$ making the same misclassification.

$$\phi(Z, I, S, D) = \frac{1}{\omega \cdot (\omega - 1)} \sum_{x_q \in X} \sum_{i=1}^{\omega-1} \sum_{j=i+1}^{\omega} P_D(x_q) \cdot \varsigma(I, S, G_i, G_j, x_q, D)$$

(6.7)

where:

$$\varsigma(I, S, G_i, G_j, x_q, D) = \begin{cases} 1 \; y_{I(\pi_{G_i \cup y} S)}(x_q) = y_{I(\pi_{G_j \cup y} S)}(x_q) \neq y_D(x_q) \\ 0 \; Otherwise \end{cases}$$

$$y_{I(\pi_{G_k \cup y} S)}(x_q) = \underset{c_j \in dom(y)}{\arg\max} \; \hat{P}_{I(\pi_{G_k \cup y} S)}(y = c_j \,|a_i = x_{q,i} \; i \in R_k)$$

$$y_D(x_q) = \underset{c_j \in dom(y)}{\arg\max} \; P_D(y = c_j \,|a_i = x_{q,i} \; i = 1, \ldots, n)$$

As decompositions with greater error rate tend to higher error correlation rate, it might be biased to compare decompositions with different error rates. As a result, it is more desirable to compare the portion of the error rate that can be explained by error correlation. This can be estimated by normalizing the error correlation, namely by dividing it by the error rate.

6.4   Conditions for Complete Equivalence

Four Lemmas are presented in order to shed light on the suggested problem. These Lemmas show that the Naïve Bayes combination can be useful in various cases of separable functions even when the Naïve assumption of conditional independence is not necessarily fulfilled. Furthermore, because these Lemmas provide the optimal decomposition structures they can be used for evaluating the performance of the algorithms proposed in the following chapter. The proofs of these Lemmas are straightforward and are provided below.

Lemma 6.2 *Decomposition Z is completely equivalent if it satisfies the following conditions:*

(1) The subsets $G_k, k = 1, \ldots, \omega$ and the $NR = A - \bigcup_{k=1}^{\omega} G_k$ are conditionally independent given the target feature;
(2) The NR set and the target feature are independent.

The proof of Lemma 6.2 begins by writing the following equation:

$$P(y = c_j \,|a_i = x_{q,i} \ i = 1, \ldots, n) = P(y = c_j \,\Big|a_i = x_{q,i} \ i \in R_{NR} \cup \bigcup_{k=1}^{\omega} R_k)$$

$$(6.8)$$

According to the Bayes Theorem:

$$= \frac{P(a_i = x_{q,i} \ i \in R_{NR} \cup \bigcup_{k=1}^{\omega} R_k \,|y = c_j)P(y = c_j)}{P(a_i = x_{q,i} \ i \in R_{NR} \cup \bigcup_{k=1}^{\omega} R_k)} \qquad (6.9)$$

Using the independence assumption Equation 6.9 can be rewritten as:

$$\frac{P(a_i = x_{q,i} \ i \in R_{NR} \,|y = c_j) \cdot \prod_{k=1}^{\omega} P(a_i = x_{q,i} \ i \in R_k \,|y = c_j) \, P(y = c_j)}{P(a_i = x_{q,i} \ i \in R_{NR} \cup \bigcup_{k=1}^{\omega} R_k)}$$

$$(6.10)$$

Using the Bayes Theorem again, Equation 6.10 becomes:

$$\frac{P(y=c_j|a_i=x_{q,i} \ i\in R_{NR})P(a_i=x_{q,i} \ i\in R_{NR})}{P(y=c_j)^{\omega} \cdot P(a_i=x_{q,i} \ i\in R_{NR}\cup \bigcup_{k=1}^{\omega} R_k)} \cdot$$
$$\cdot \prod_{k=1}^{\omega} P(y = c_j \,|a_i = x_{q,i} \ i \in R_k)P(a_i = x_{q,i} \ i \in R_k) \qquad (6.11)$$

Due to the fact that the NR set and the target feature are independent:

$$= \frac{P(a_i=x_{q,i} \ i\in R_{NR}) \cdot \prod_{k=1}^{\omega} P(y=c_j|a_i=x_{q,i} \ i\in R_k) \cdot P(a_i=x_{q,i} \ i\in R_k)}{P(y=c_j)^{\omega-1} \cdot P(a_i=x_{q,i} \ i\in R_{NR}\cup \bigcup_{k=1}^{\omega} R_k)} \qquad (6.12)$$

As the value of the following expression:

$$\frac{P(a_i = x_{q,i} \; i \in R_{NR}) \cdot \prod_{k=1}^{\omega} P(a_i = x_{q,i} \; i \in R_k)}{P(a_i = x_{q,i} \; i \in R_{NR} \cup \bigcup_{k=1}^{\omega} R_k)} \tag{6.13}$$

is constant given specific values of the input features, the result is:

$$\underset{\substack{c_j \in dom(y) \\ P(y = c_j) > 0}}{\arg\max} \; \prod_{k=1}^{\omega} \frac{P(y = c_j | a_i = x_{q,i} \; i \in R_k)}{P(y = c_j)^{\omega - 1}} = \tag{6.14}$$

$$\underset{\substack{c_j \in dom(y) \\ P(y = c_j) > 0}}{\arg\max} \; P(y = c_j | a_i = x_{q,i} \; i = 1, \ldots, n)$$

namely Z is *completely equivalent*.

Lemma 6.2 represents a sufficient condition for complete equivalence. It is important to note that it does not represent a necessary condition, as illustrated in Lemma 6.3.

Lemma 6.3

Let $A = \{a_1, \ldots, a_l, \ldots, a_N\}$ *denote a group of n independent input binary features and let $Z = \{G_1, \ldots, G_\omega\}$ denote a decomposition, then if the target feature follows the function:*

$$y = f_1(a_i, i \in R_1) \vee f_2(a_i, i \in R_2) \vee \ldots \vee f_\omega(a_i, i \in R_\omega)$$

or:

$$y = f_1(a_i, i \in R_1) \wedge f_2(a_i, i \in R_2) \wedge \ldots \wedge f_\omega(a_i, i \in R_\omega)$$

where $f_1, \ldots, f_\omega$ are Boolean functions and $R_1, \ldots, R_\omega$ are mutually exclusive, then Z is completely equivalent.

It is obvious that all input features which do not belong to any of the sets $R_1, \ldots, R_\omega$ can be ignored. The proof of Lemma 6.3 begins by showing that if y fulfills $y = f_1(a_i, i \in R_1) \vee \ldots \vee f_\omega(a_i, i \in R_\omega)$ and the values of the functions are independent then the decomposition $Z = \{G_1, \ldots, G_\omega\}$ where $G_k = \{a_i, i \in R_k\}$ is completely equivalent.

Case 1: At least one of the functions of the instance to be classified gets the value 1, because such a function also fulfills $P(y = 0 \,|\, f_k = 1) = 0$:

$$\underset{c_j \in \{0,1\}}{\arg\max} \frac{\prod\limits_{k=1}^{\omega} P(y = c_j | f_k)}{P(y = c_j)^{\omega - 1}} = 1 = \underset{c_j \in \{0,1\}}{\arg\max} P(y = c_j \,|\, f_k, k = 1, \ldots, \omega) \quad (6.15)$$

Case 2: The values of the functions of the instance to be classified are all zeros.

In this case $P(y = 0) = P(f_1(a_j; j \in R_1) = 0 \cap \ldots \cap f_\omega(a_j; j \in R_\omega) = 0)$. Due to the fact that the input features are independent:

$$P(y = 0) = \prod_{i=1}^{\omega} P(f_i(a_j; j \in R_i) = 0)$$

furthermore:

$$P(y = 0 \,|\, f_i(a_j; j \in R_i) = 0) = \prod_{k \neq i}^{P(f_k(a_j; j \in R_k) = 0)}$$

according to the complete probability theorem:

$$P(y = 1) = 1 - \prod_{i=1}^{\omega} P(f_i(a_j; j \in R_i) = 0)$$

and:

$$P(y = 1 \,|\, f_i(a_j; j \in R_i) = 0) = 1 - \prod_{k \neq i}^{P(f_k(a_j; j \in R_k) = 0)}$$

what is left to prove is:

$$\arg\max_{c_j \in \{0,1\}} \left(\frac{\prod\limits_{i=1}^{\omega} \prod\limits_{k\neq i}^{P(f_k(a_j; j \in R_k)=0)}}{(\prod\limits_{i=1}^{\omega} P(f_i(a_j; j \in R_i) = 0))^{\omega-1}} \right), \tag{6.16}$$

$$\frac{\prod\limits_{i=1}^{\omega} (1 - \prod\limits_{k\neq i}^{P(f_k(a_j;j\in R_k)=0)})}{(1 - \prod\limits_{i=1}^{\omega} P(f_i(a_j; j \in R_i) = 0))^{\omega-1}}) = 0$$

As the first argument of the argmax function equals one, it is required to show that:

$$\frac{\prod\limits_{i=1}^{\omega} (1 - \prod\limits_{k\neq i}^{P(f_k(a_j;j\in R_k)=0)})}{(1 - \prod\limits_{i=1}^{\omega} P(f_i(a_j; j \in R_i) = 0))^{\omega-1}} < 1 \tag{6.17}$$

The last inequality can be validated by multiplying the numerator and denominator by $(1 - \prod_{i=1}^{\omega} P(f_i(a_j; j \in R_i) = 0))$ with the assumption that $1 > (1 - \prod_{i=1}^{\omega} P(f_i(a_j; j \in R_i) = 0)) > 0$.

It should be noted that if the term is equal to 0, then $P(y = 1) = 0$ and if the term is equal to 1 then $P(y = 1) = 1$. In both cases the decomposition Z is completely equivalent.

$$\frac{(1 - \prod\limits_{i=1}^{\omega} P(f_i(a_j; j \in R_i) = 0)) \cdot \prod\limits_{i=1}^{\omega} (1 - \prod\limits_{k\neq i}^{P(f_k(a_j;j\in R_k)=0)})}{(1 - \prod\limits_{i=1}^{\omega} P(f_i(a_j; j \in R_i) = 0)) \cdot (1 - \prod\limits_{i=1}^{\omega} P(f_i(a_j; j \in R_i) = 0))^{\omega-1}} =$$

$$(1 - \prod\limits_{i=1}^{\omega} P(f_i(a_j; j \in R_i) = 0)) \cdot \prod\limits_{i=1}^{\omega} \frac{(1 - \prod\limits_{k\neq i}^{P(f_k(a_j;j\in R_k)=0)})}{(1 - \prod\limits_{i=1}^{\omega} P(f_i(a_j; j \in R_i) = 0))}$$

However because the following inequality is true:

$$\prod_{k\neq i}^{P(f_k(a_j;j\in R_k)=0)} \geq \prod_{i=1}^{\omega} P(f_i(a_j;j\in R_i)=0)$$

thus, we obtain:

$$\prod_{i=1}^{\omega} \frac{(1 - \prod_{k\neq i}^{P(f_k(a_j;j\in R_k)=0)})}{(1 - \prod_{i=1}^{\omega} P(f_i(a_j;j\in R_i)=0))} \leq 1$$

or:

$$(1 - \prod_{i=1}^{\omega} P(f_i(a_j;j\in R_i)=0)) \cdot \prod_{i=1}^{\omega} \frac{(1 - \prod_{k\neq i}^{P(f_k(a_j;j\in R_k)=0)})}{(1 - \prod_{i=1}^{\omega} P(f_i(a_j;j\in R_i)=0))} < 1$$

$$(6.18)$$

For completing the proof, it is required to show that it is true also for the case:

$$y = f_1(a_j, j \in R_1) \wedge f_2(a_j, j \in R_2) \wedge \ldots \wedge f_\omega(a_j, j \in R_\omega)$$

For this purpose it is sufficient to show that it is true for the opposite target feature $\overline{y}$. According to de Morgan's law:

$$y = \overline{f_1(a_j, j \in R_1)} \vee \overline{f_2(a_j, i \in R_2)} \vee \ldots \vee \overline{f_\omega(a_j, j \in R_\omega)} \qquad (6.19)$$

$$\overline{y} = \overline{f_1(a_j, j \in R_1)} \vee \overline{f_2(a_j, j \in R_2)} \vee \ldots \vee \overline{f_\omega(a_j, j \in R_\omega)} =$$
$$f_1^*(a_j, j \in R_1) \vee f_2^*(a_j, j \in R_2) \vee \ldots \vee f_\omega^*(a_j, j \in R_\omega)$$

Because Z is completely equivalent for $\overline{y}$ it is also completely equivalent for y.

Lemma 6.4

Let $A = \{a_1, \ldots, a_l, \ldots, a_N\}$ be a group of n independent input binary features and let $Z = \{G_1, \ldots, G_\omega\}$ be a decomposition, then if the target feature follows the function:

$$y = 2^0 \cdot f_1(a_i, i \in R_1) + 2^1 \cdot f_2(a_i, i \in R_2) + \cdots + 2^{\omega-1} f_\omega(a_i, i \in R_\omega)$$

where $f_1, \ldots, f_\omega$ are Boolean functions and $R_1, \ldots, R_\omega$ are mutually exclusive then Z is completely equivalent.

In order to prove Lemma it is useful to define the following functions:

$$bit(i, x) = The\,ith\,bit\,of\,x = \left\lfloor (x - 2^i \cdot \lfloor x/2^i \rfloor)/2^{i-1} \right\rfloor$$

$$XNOR(x, y) = x \cdot y + (1 - x) \cdot (1 - y)$$

In this case Equation 6.1 can be rewritten as:

$$= \underset{c_j \in dom(y)}{\arg\max} \frac{\prod_{k=1}^{\omega} \{XNOR(f_k, bit(k,c_j)) \cdot P(f_j = bit(j,c_j) \, \forall j \neq k)\}}{P(y=c_j)^{\omega-1}}$$

as the input features are independent:

$$\underset{c_j \in dom(y)}{\arg\max} \frac{\prod_{k=1}^{\omega} \{XNOR(f_k, bit(k,c_j)) \cdot \prod_{j \neq k}^{P(f_j=bit(j,c_j))} \}}{P(y = c_j)^{\omega-1}} = \qquad (6.20)$$

$$\underset{c_j \in dom(y)}{\arg\max} \frac{\prod_{k=1}^{\omega} P(f_j = bit(j,c_j))^{\omega-1} \cdot \prod_{k=1}^{\omega} XNOR(f_k, bit(k,c_j))}{P(y = c_j)^{\omega-1}} =$$

$$\underset{c_j \in dom(y)}{\arg\max} \frac{P(y = c_j)^{\omega-1} \cdot \prod_{k=1}^{\omega} XNOR(f_k, bit(k,c_j))}{P(y = c_j)^{\omega-1}} =$$

$$\underset{c_j \in dom(y)}{\arg\max} \prod_{k=1}^{\omega} XNOR(f_k, bit(k,c_j)) =$$

$$\underset{c_j \in dom(y)}{\arg\max} P(y = c_j \, | a_i = x_{q,i} \; i = 1, \ldots, n)$$

The last Lemma illustrates that although the conditionally independent requirement is not fulfilled, it is still possible to find a completely equivalent decomposition.

Lemma 6.5

Let $A = \{a_1, \ldots, a_i, \ldots, a_n\}$ be a group of n input binary features distributed uniformly. If the target feature behaves as $y = a_1 \oplus a_2 \oplus \ldots \oplus a_n$ then there is no decomposition besides $Z = \{A\}$ which is completely equivalent.

Proof of Lemma 6.5: Obviously if $Z \neq \{A\}$ then Z contains at least one subset. If there is an odd number of input features with the value "1", then the target feature should also get the value "1". For that reason the posteriori probability for the target feature to get "1" given only the subset of the input feature set is $1/2$.

$$P(y = 1/S \subset A) = \frac{1}{2}$$

hence:

$$\frac{\prod_{k=1}^{\omega} P(y = 1 \,|a_i \; i \in R_k \,)}{P(y = 1)^{\omega - 1}} = \frac{\prod_{k=1}^{\omega} P(y = 0 \,|a_i \; i \in R_k \,)}{P(y = 0)^{\omega - 1}} = 1 \qquad (6.21)$$

Lemma 6.5 shows that there are problems such that no completely equivalent decomposition can be found, besides the obvious one.

6.5 Algorithmic Framework for Feature Set Decomposition

6.5.1 *Overview*

This section presents an algorithmic framework that implements the idea of feature set decomposition by searching for the optimal Feature Set Decomposition Structure (Z_{opt}). This framework nests many algorithms, three of which are described in details. The first algorithm performs a serial search while using a new Vapnik–Chervonenkis dimension bound for multiple oblivious trees as an evaluating schema. The second algorithm performs a multi search while using wrapper evaluating schema. The third algorithm performs a serial first search using information gain and a statistical independence test as an evaluating schema.

Although the following framework can be easily adjusted to any inducer, this section focuses on classifiers that are represented by decision trees, namely each subset in the decomposition is represented by a different decision tree. Because this work considers only mutually exclusive decomposition, the procedure can construct up to n decision trees (in the extreme case where each tree represents one input feature) and up to n features in a single tree (in the case where a single tree includes all input features). Each valid instance (an instance that belongs to the instance space), is associated in each tree with exactly one path between the root and the leaf. The following assumptions have been made:

- There are no missing values. Either missing values are replaced with a valid value or the missing observation has been removed.
- All features have discretely valued domains. Continuous features should be made discrete before using them in the algorithm.
- Both assumptions can be relaxed by employing suitable methods described in the literature.

The following sections discuss various aspects of the suggested framework, namely: how the space of all decomposition structures is being sort after, how a certain structure is evaluated, how the decision tree classifier for each subset is obtained, how a classification of an unlabeled instance is performed, and what is the computational complexity of the proposed algorithmic framework.

6.5.2   *Searching Methods*

Naturally a good decomposition can be found by performing exhaustive enumerations over all possible decomposition structures. Each decomposition structure is evaluated and the best one is selected. Obviously, this exhaustive search procedure is feasible only for small data sets. However, this procedure can be used as a "gold standard" for analyzing the performance of other algorithms, as it is the best approximation to the optimal decomposition structure. Note that this exhaustive search does not necessarily lead to the optimal decomposition structure (namely with the minimum generalization error). This results from the fact that the selection of the best decomposition structure is not based on the actual value of the generalization error, but on an approximation of this value. For instance,if the wrapper approach is employed, then the generalization error of a certain decomposition structure is approximated by averaging the errors obtained by repeatedly performing the following steps:

(1) Sample a subset of the training set.
(2) Use this sample for inducing sub classifiers according to the decom-

position structure that is examined.

(3) Measure the error on the unused portion of the training set by comparing the combined classifications with the actual target value.

A feasible alternative to the exhaustive search is to use a hill climbing algorithm procedure. In this section we consider two different hill climbing search methods: "Multi-Search" and "Serial Search". Both methods begin with a single empty subset and add one attribute per iteration to the decomposition structure.

Each iteration in the Multi-Search method considers changing the current decomposition structure by adding one of the unused features to one of the existing subsets or to a newly created subset. The change which most improves the evaluation criterion is selected for the next iteration. The next subsection discusses various evaluation methods.

In order to avoid a local optimum, the search continues to the next iteration with the best addition, even if the selected addition does not improve the evaluation criterion or even makes it worse. The output of the search is the structure with the highest performance found during the search and not necessarily the last structure. The search stops when there is no feature left.

Figure 6.2 specifies the pseudo-code of the multi search. Note that the procedure gets the references to the following sub-procedures: Evaluation, Induction, Updating (Not a mandatory parameter, can be empty if there is no support for classifier's updating) and Combining. The Multi-Search-Feature-Set-Decomposition calls the Evaluate function which is responsible to evaluate the performance of the proposed decomposition. Figure 6.3 specifies the pseudo-code for evaluating a certain decomposition.

The above pseudo-code does not explicitly specify how the caching is updated as various caching mechanisms may be suggested. A simple caching mechanism can hold only the classifiers of the basic decomposition (denoted as Z in the pseudo-code). A more extended caching mechanism can keep all classifiers that have been induced and that might be used in the upcoming iterations.

An alternative to the Multi-Search is the Serial-Search presented in Figure 6.4. This search begins with a single empty subset of input features. In each iteration the algorithm enumerates over all available features (which have not been allocated to previous subsets) and determines the evaluation measure obtained by adding each feature to the current subset.

The feature that most improves the evaluation score is selected, on condition that no similar (or even greater) improvement could be obtained by adding this feature to a newly created subset. If no input feature was selected, an attempt is made to construct a new subset with the input features that were not used by previous subsets. This procedure continues until there are no more unused features or until the current subset is left empty (namely there are no more relevant features left).

Many other search strategies can be suggested here (for instance genetic algorithms). However, this book focuses on simple cost effective procedures.

6.5.3 *Induction Methods*

Any inducer can be used in the proposed framework, particularly any decision tree inducer. Preferably the selected inducer is capable of adding features incrementally; otherwise each iteration of the search may require generating the decision tree from scratch. This difficulty can be resolved by using Oblivious Decision Trees. Oblivious Decision Trees are found to be effective for feature selection which is a simplified case of the problem solved here. In the case of feature set decomposition, each subset is represented by an oblivious decision tree and each feature is located on a different layer. As a result, adding a new feature to a subset is performed by adding a new layer and connecting it to the nodes of the last layer. The nodes of a new layer are defined as the Cartesian product combinations of the previous layer's nodes with the values of the new added feature. In order to avoid unnecessary splitting, the algorithm splits a node only if it is useful (for example if the information gain of the new feature in this node is strictly positive).

Multi-Search-Feature-Set-Decomposition(S,A,E,C,I,U)
S - the training set.
A - the set of input features.
E - a method for evaluating the decomposition performance.
C - a method for combining the classifiers.
I - a method for building a classifier.
U - a method for adding an attribute to a classifier.

$Z, Z^{Best}, Cache \leftarrow \emptyset$; $BestEvaluation \leftarrow \infty; CandidateSet \leftarrow A$
WHILE ($CandidateSet \neq \emptyset$) DO
  $CurrentBestEvaluation \leftarrow \infty$; $SelectedAttribute, Z^{CurrentBest} \leftarrow \emptyset$
  DO $\forall a \in CandidateSet$
    DO $\forall G \in Z$
      $Evaluation^* = Evaluate(S, Z, E, C, I, U, G, a, Cache)$
      IF $Evaluation^* < CurrentBestEvaluation$ THEN
        $SelectedAttribute \leftarrow a; G^* \leftarrow G \cup \{a\}; Z^* \leftarrow Z \cup \{G^*\}/\{G\}$
        $Z^{CurrentBest} \leftarrow Z^*; CurrentBestEvaluation \leftarrow Evaluation^*$
      END IF
    END DO
    $Evaluation^* = Evaluate(S, Z, E, C, I, U, \emptyset, a, Cache)$
    IF $Evaluation^* < CurrentBestEvaluation$ THEN
      $SelectedAttribute \leftarrow a$; $Z^{CurrentBest} \leftarrow Z^*$
      $CurrentBestEvaluation \leftarrow Evaluation^*$
    END IF
  END DO
  $CandidateSet \leftarrow CandidateSet/\{SelectedAttribute\}$
  $Z \leftarrow Z^{CurrentBest}$
  Update Cache For Next Iterations
  IF $CurrentBestEvaluation < BestEvaluation$ THEN
    $G^* \leftarrow \{a\}$; $Z^* \leftarrow Z \cup \{G^*\}$; $Z^{Best} \leftarrow Z^{CurrentBest}$
    $BestEvaluation \leftarrow CurrentBestEvaluation$
  END IF
END WHILE
RETURN Z^{Best}

Fig. 6.2   Pseudo-Code of the Multi Search Algorithm.

Evaluate($S,Z,E,C,I,U,G,a,Cache$)

S - the training set.

Z - the decomposition structure

E - an evaluation method for the decomposition performance.

C - a method for combining the classifiers.

I - a method for building a classifier.

U - a method for adding an attribute to a classifier.

G - the subset to be updated

a - the attribute to be added to G.

$Cache$ - the classifiers cache.

$Classifiers = \emptyset$

$G^* \leftarrow G \cup \{a\}$

$Z^* \leftarrow Z \cup \{G^*\}/\{G\}$

DO $\forall G_i \in Z^*$

  IF ($Cache$ contains a classifier for G_i) THEN

    $Classifier \leftarrow$ Get from cache the classifier of G_i

  ELSE

    IF $G_i \neq G^*$ OR

       no method U is provided OR

       $Cache$ does not contain $I(G)$ THEN

     $Classifier \leftarrow I(\pi_{G_i}S)$

    ELSE

     $Classifier \leftarrow$ Get classifier that corresponds to G.

     $Classifier \leftarrow U(Classifier, a, \pi_{G_i}S)$

    END IF

  END IF

  Add $Classifier$ to $Classifiers$

  Update $Cache$ if required

END DO

RETURN E(C(Classifiers))

Fig. 6.3   Pseudo-Code for Evaluating a Decomposition.

Serial-First-Feature-Set-Decomposition(S,A,E,C,I,U)

S - the training set.

A - the set of input features.

E - an evaluation method for the decomposition performance.

C - a method for combining the classifiers.

I - a method for building the classifier.

U - a method for adding an attribute to a classifier.

$Z, Cache \leftarrow \emptyset; CandidateSet \leftarrow A; i \leftarrow 0; BestEvaluation \leftarrow \infty$

DO

   $i \leftarrow i + 1$

   $G_i = \emptyset$

   DO

      $SelectedAttribute \leftarrow \emptyset$

      $CurrentBestEvaluation \leftarrow BestEvaluation$

      DO $\forall a \in CandidateSet$

         $Evaluation^* = Evaluate(S, Z, E, C, I, U, Gi, a, Cache)$

         IF $Evaluation^* < CurrentBestEvaluation$ THEN

            $SelectedAttribute \leftarrow a$

            $CurrentBestEvaluation \leftarrow Evaluation*$

         END IF

      END DO

      IF $SelectedAttribute \neq \emptyset$ THEN

         $CandidateSet \leftarrow CandidateSet/\{SelectedAttribute\}$

         $Z \leftarrow Z/\{G_i\}$

         $G_i \leftarrow G_i \cup SelectedAttribute$

         $Z \leftarrow Z \cup \{G_i\}$

         $BestEvaluation \leftarrow CurrentBestEvaluation$

      END IF

   UNTIL $SelectedAttribute \neq \emptyset$ OR $CandidateSet = \emptyset$

UNTIL $G_i = \emptyset$

RETURN Z

Fig. 6.4   Pseudo-Code for of the Serial Search.

6.5.4   *Accuracy Evaluation Methods*

6.5.4.1   *The Wrapper Method*

Over-fitting and under-fitting are well known problems in machine learning. According to the Occam's-razor one should prefer the simplest classifier that fits the data. One reasonable explanation for this principle is that because there are fewer simple classifiers than complicated classifiers, it is less likely that one will find a simple classifier that coincidentally fits the training set. On the other hand, there are many complicated classifiers that overfit the training set. As a result, if one uses the training error as the sole criterion for choosing the best classifier, then there will be a tendency to select a complicated classifier that just overfits the training set.

The most straightforward approach to overcome this problem is to use the wrapper procedure. In this approach the decomposition structure is evaluated by repeatedly sampling the training set and measuring the accuracy of the inducers obtained for this decomposition on an unused portion of the training set. At the last stage,the inducer is executed again for each feature subset, this time by using the entire training set. The fact that it repeatedly executes the inducer is considered a major drawback. For this reason, wrappers may not scale well to large datasets containing many features.

6.5.4.2   *Conditional Entropy*

Information Gain is a well-known splitting criterion in decision trees literature. Algorithms like IFN use it for selecting the best feature according to which the current node is split.

A similar idea can be used to evaluate a certain decomposition structure. Let $P(y = y_q | x_q, I, S, Z)$ denote the conditional distribution of the target attribute y, given the input attributes obtained by performing the following steps:

- Given an Inducer I, a feature set decomposition $Z = \{G_1, \ldots, G_k, \ldots, G_\omega\}$ and a dataset S, the following crisp sub-classifiers are induced: $I(\pi_{G_k \cup y} S); k = 1, \ldots, \omega$
- The crisp classification of the sub-classifiers are combined using the Naïve Bayesian combination to create the conditional distribution of y given the input attributes.

Let $Entropy(y | S, I, Z)$ denote the entropy of the target attribute y on the dataset S, thus:

$$Entropy(y\,|S,I,Z\,) = \frac{\sum\limits_{x_i \in S} \log P(y=y_q|x_q\,,I,S,Z)}{|S|} \qquad (6.22)$$

Consequently the total information gain obtained by changing a decomposition structure from Z_1 to Z_2 (particularly by adding a certain attribute to a certain subset) is:

$$IG(y\,|S,I,\,Z_1,Z_2) = Entropy(y\,|S,I,Z_1\,) - Entropy(y\,|S,I,Z_2) \qquad (6.23)$$

6.5.4.3 VC-Dimension

An alternative approach for evaluating performance is to use the generalization error bound in terms of the training error and concept size. As stated before, using an oblivious decision tree may be attractive in this case as it adds features to a classifier in an incremental manner. Oblivious decision trees can be considered as restricted decision trees. For that reason, any generalization error bound that has been developed for decision trees in the literature [Mansour and McAllester (2000)] can be used in this case also. However, there are several reasons to develop a specific bound. First, by utilizing the fact that the oblivious structure is more restricted, it might be possible to develop a tighter bound. Second, in this case it is required to extend the bound for several oblivious trees combined using the Naïve Bayes combination.

In this chapter we are using the VC theory for evaluating the generalization error bound. Alternatively we could use other theories. In order to use the VC-bound presented in Theorem 1.1, we need to measure the VC-Dimension. Recall that the VC dimension for a set of indicator functions is defined as the maximum number of data points that can be shattered by the set of admissible functions. By definition, a set of m points is shattered by a concept class if there are concepts (functions) in the class that split the points into two classes in all of the 2^m possible ways. The VC dimension might be difficult to compute accurately. For that reason this book introduces an upper bound and a lower bound of the VC dimension. The hypothesis class of multiple mutually exclusive oblivious decision trees can be characterized by two vectors and one scalar: $\vec{L} = (l_1, \ldots, l_\omega)$, $\vec{T} = (t_1, \ldots, t_\omega)$ and n, where l_k is the number of layers (not including the root and target layers) in the tree k, t_k is the number of terminal nodes in the tree k, and n is the number of input features.

For the sake of simplicity, the bound described in this section is developed assuming that the input features and the target feature are both binary. This bound can be extended for other cases in a straightforward manner. Note that each oblivious decision tree with non-binary input features can be converted to a corresponding binary oblivious decision tree by using appropriate artificial features.

Theorem 6.1 *The VC-Dimension of ω mutually exclusive oblivious decision trees on n binary input features that are combined using the Naïve Bayes combination and that have $\vec{L} = (l_1, \ldots, l_\omega)$ layers and $\vec{T} = (t_1, \ldots, t_\omega)$ terminal nodes is not greater than:*

$$\begin{cases} F + \log U & \omega = 1 \\ 2(F+1)\log(2e) + 2\log U & \omega > 1 \end{cases} \tag{6.24}$$

and at least:

$$F - \omega + 1$$

where:

$$F = \sum_{i=1}^{\omega} t_i \quad U = \frac{n!}{\omega! \cdot (n - \sum_{i=1}^{\omega} l_i)!} \cdot \prod_{i=1}^{\omega} \frac{(2t_i - 4)!}{(t_i - 2)! \cdot (t_i - 2)!}.$$

In order to prove Theorem 6.1 it is useful to consider Lemma 6.6 and Lemma 6.7 first.

Lemma 6.6 *The VC dimension of the oblivious decision tree on n binary input features with l layers and t terminal nodes is not greater than:*

$$t + \log_2 \left(\frac{n!}{(n-l)!} \cdot \frac{(2t-4)!}{(t-2)! \cdot (t-2)!} \right) \tag{6.25}$$

In this book the probabilistic classifications of the oblivious decision trees are combined in order to create a crisp classification. Thus we need to estimate the VC dimension of the set of all combined crisp classifiers considered by the inducer.

It should be noted that this estimation also fits the VC dimension definition of a set of real functions presented by Vapnik: Let H^* be a set of real functions such that $h^* \in H^*$; $h^* : X \to (b_1, b_2)$ where b_1, b_2 are numeric constants. Let us consider along with H^* the set of binary crisp classifiers: $h \in H(\beta)$; $h(x) = \theta\{h^*(x) - \beta\}$; $h^* \in H^*$ where $\theta(z)$ is the step function ($\theta(z)$ obtains the value 0 if $z < 0$ and 1 otherwise). The VC dimension of H^* is defined to be the VC dimension of the set of corresponding binary classifiers $H(\beta)$ with $\beta \in (b_1, b_2)$.

In the case discussed here, a combined probabilistic classifier is obtained by combining the probabilistic classifications of the sub-classifiers. Assuming that the target attribute is binary (i.e. $y \in (c_1, c_2)$), then the combined probabilistic classifier can be represented as a real function whose target value is the conditional probability to have the class c_1 given the input attributes (alternatively we could use c_2). More specifically, the set of the combined probabilistic classifiers considered by the inducer is denoted by: $h^* \in H^*$; $h^* : X \to (0, 1)$. Consequently, we look for the VC dimension of the corresponded set of crisp classifiers $H(\beta)$, in which $\beta = 1/2$ (namely an instance x is classified as c_1 if the conditional probability is greater than $1/2$).

The hypothesis space size of a crisp oblivious decision tree with l layers, t terminal nodes and n input features to choose from is not greater than:

$$\frac{n!}{(n-l)!} \cdot 2^t \cdot \frac{(2t-4)!}{(t-2)! \cdot (t-2)!} \tag{6.26}$$

The first multiplier indicates the number of combinations for selecting with order l features from n. The second multiplier corresponds to the different classification options of the terminal nodes. The third multiplier represents the number of different binary tree structures that contains t leaves. The last multiplier is calculated using the Wallace tree structure (Wallace, 1996) which represents the tree as a string of the characters "F" (fork) and "L" (leaf). For instance the oblivious decision tree in Figure 1.5 can be represented as the following string: FFLFLLFLFLFLL. Note that in the case of the binary tree there is exactly one more leaf than in the inner nodes. Furthermore, the tree string always begins with an inner node (when $l \geq 1$) and ends with at least two leaf nodes.

Based on the familiar relation $VC(H) \leq \log_2(|H|)$ for finite H, the Lemma has been proved.

Lemma 6.7   *Consider ω mutually exclusive oblivious decision trees that* *are combined with the Naïve Bayes and that have a fixed structure contain-ing $\vec{T} = (t_1, \ldots, t_\omega)$ terminal nodes. The number of dichotomies it induces on a set of cardinality m is at most:*

$$2 \left(\frac{em}{1 + \sum\limits_{i=1}^{\omega} t_i} \right)^{1 + \sum\limits_{i=1}^{\omega} t_i} \tag{6.27}$$

In order to prove Lemman 6.7 one can use a similar Lemma introduced by [Schmitt (2002)]. The number of dichotomies that a higher order thresh-old neuron with k monomials induces on a set of cardinality m is at most:

$$2 \sum_{i=0}^{k} \binom{m-1}{i} < 2 \left(\frac{em}{k} \right)^k ; m > k \geq 1 \tag{6.28}$$

A definition of a higher-order threshold neuron has the form:

$$w_1 M_1 + w_2 M_2 + \cdots + w_k M_k - t_r \tag{6.29}$$

where $M_1, M_2, \ldots, M_k$ are monomials.

In fact ω oblivious decision trees which are combined with Naïve Bayes, can be converted to a higher order threshold neuron, where the set of ter-minal nodes constitutes the neuron's monomials and the log-odds in favor of $y = 1$ in each terminal node is the corresponding neuron's weight. Fur-thermore, in order to use the sign activation function, the threshold has been set to the sum of all other monomials.

Now it is possible to prove Theorem 6.1. The proof of the upper bound is discussed first. If $\omega = 1$ then Lemma 6.6 can be used directly. For the case $\omega > 1$ the bound of the number of dichotomies induced by ω mutually exclusive oblivious decision trees on an arbitrary set of cardinality m is first introduced. Because the biggest shattered set follows this bound as well, the statement of the theorem is derived. There are at most:

$$\frac{n!}{\omega! \cdot (n - \sum\limits_{i=1}^{\omega} l_i)!} \cdot \prod_{i=1}^{\omega} \frac{(2t_i - 4)!}{(t_i - 2)! \cdot (t_i - 2)!} \tag{6.30}$$

different structures for ω mutually exclusive oblivious trees on n binary input features with $\vec{L} = (l_1, \ldots, l_\omega)$ layers and $\vec{T} = (t_1, \ldots, t_\omega)$ terminal nodes. Notice that the division by $\omega!$ is required as there is no relevance to the order of the trees. According to Lemma 6.7 a fixed structure and variable weights can induce at most:

$$2 \left(\frac{em}{1 + \sum\limits_{i=1}^{\omega} t_i} \right)^{1 + \sum\limits_{i=1}^{\omega} t_i} \tag{6.31}$$

dichotomies on a given set of cardinality m. Enumerating over all structures, it is concluded that there are at most:

$$\frac{n!}{\omega! \cdot (n - \sum\limits_{i=1}^{\omega} l_i)!} \cdot \prod_{i=1}^{\omega} \frac{(2t_i - 4)!}{(t_i - 2)! \cdot (t_i - 2)!} \cdot 2 \left(\frac{em}{1 + \sum\limits_{i=1}^{\omega} t_i} \right)^{\sum\limits_{i=1}^{\omega} t_i} \tag{6.32}$$

dichotomies on a given set of cardinality m that are induced by the class considered. If the above class shatters the given set, then:

$$2^m \leq \frac{n!}{\omega! \cdot (n - \sum\limits_{i=1}^{\omega} l_i)!} \cdot \prod_{i=1}^{\omega} \frac{(2t_i - 4)!}{(t_i - 2)! \cdot (t_i - 2)!} \cdot 2 \left(\frac{em}{1 + \sum\limits_{i=1}^{\omega} t_i} \right)^{1 + \sum\limits_{i=1}^{\omega} t_i} \tag{6.33}$$

However the last inequality will not be true if:

$$m \geq 2(F + 1) \log(2e) + 2 \log U \tag{6.34}$$

where:

$$F = \sum_{i=1}^{\omega} t_i \tag{6.35}$$

$$U = \frac{n!}{\omega! \cdot (n - \sum\limits_{i=1}^{\omega} l_i)!} \cdot \prod_{i=1}^{\omega} \frac{(2t_i - 4)!}{(t_i - 2)! \cdot (t_i - 2)!}. \tag{6.36}$$

This concludes the proof. The lower bound is true due to the fact that any set of ω trees with a fixed structure has the above VC dimension. The result can be achieved by setting in each tree (besides one) a neutralized terminal node (i.e. a terminal node with posteriori probabilities that are equal to the *a-priori* probabilities).

Corollary 6.1   *In domains composed of n binary features, the VC dimension of the Naïve Bayes inducer is $O(n)$.*

The proof of Corollary 6.1 results immediately from the Theorem 6.1 by letting:

$$\omega = n$$
$$l_1, \ldots, l_n = 1$$
$$t_1, \ldots, t_n = 2$$

The VC dimension is at least $n+1$ and at most $2(2n+1)\log 2e$ concluding that the VC dimension is $o(n)$. This corollary was originally introduced by [Domingos and Pazzani (1997)]. However, here we present a new direction to prove it. This corollary illustrates that Naïve Bayes can be considered as an extreme point in the feature set decomposition search space.

Preliminary experiments have shown that estimating the generalization error by using the lower bound of the VC Dimension provides better performance.

Corollary 6.2   *Given a set of input features A^*, a training set S, an oblivious decision tree constructed using the projection of the features A^* onto S denoted as $ODT(S, A^*)$ and a single feature a_i such that $a_i \notin A^*$, if A^* and a_i are conditionally independent given the target attribute, then the generalization error bound calculated using Theorem 1.1 and Theorem 6.1 of the oblivious decision tree obtained by adding a_i as an additional layer to $ODT(S, A^*)$ is not less than the similar bound obtained by the Naïve Bayes combination of $ODT(S, A^*)$ and additional oblivious decision trees containing only a_i.*

Let $\hat{\varepsilon}(h_1, S)$, d_1 and t_1^1 represent respectively the training error, the lower VC-Dimension bound and the terminal nodes of an oblivious decision tree obtained by adding a_i as additional layer to $ODT(S, A^*)$ (referred to as the first case). Let $\hat{\varepsilon}(h_2, S)$, d_2 and (t_1^2, t_2^2) represent the training error, the lower VC-Dimension bound and the terminal nodes of a Naïve Bayes combination of $ODT(S, A^*)$ and an additional oblivious decision tree containing a_i (referred to as the second case).

Because A^* and a_i are conditionally independent given the target attribute, then on average: $\hat{\varepsilon}(h_2, S) \leq \hat{\varepsilon}(h_1, S)$.

Furthermore, as in the first case, at least one node in $ODT(S, A^*)$ is divided according the values of the feature a_i then: $t_1^1 \geq t_1^2 + t_2^2 - 1$. Using Theorem 6.1, it is concluded that $d_1 \geq d_2$. Consequently, according to Theorem 1.1 the corollary is proven.

Corollary 6.2 indicates that the proposed generalization error bound implicitly prefers to place conditionally independent features on different subsets, as Lemma 6.2 suggests.

6.5.5 Classification of an Unlabeled Instance

In order to classify an unlabeled instance, the following steps should be performed

(1) For each tree:

    (a) Locate the appropriate leaf for the unseen instance.

    (b) Extract the frequency vector (how many instances relate to each possible value of the target feature.)

    (c) Transform the frequency vector to a probability vector according to Laplace's law of succession, as described in the Introduction.

(2) Combine the probability vectors using the Naïve Bayes combination.

(3) Select the target value maximizing the Naïve Bayes combination.

6.5.6 Computational Complexity

Corollary 6.3 *Given an Inducer I, and a training set S containing m instances each of which has n input features, then the computational complexity of:*

- *Exhaustive search is: $O(n^n \cdot (g(I, S) + m \cdot h(I, S)))$*
- *Multi-search with simple caching is: $O(n^3 \cdot (g(I, S) + m \cdot h(I, S)))$*
- *Multi-search with extended caching is: $O(n^2 \cdot (g(I, S)) + n^3 m \cdot h(I, S))$*
- *Serial search is: $O(n^2 \cdot (g(I, S) + m \cdot h(I, S)))$*

where $g(I, S)$ indicates the computational complexity of adding a new feature to an existing classifier using inducer I. $h(I, S)$ indicates the computational complexity required to get the conditional probability vector of a certain instance from one classifier generated by Inducer I using training set S. m denotes the training set size, namely: $m = |S|$.

It is assumed that before starting a new search iteration the conditional probability vector of each instance in the training set based on each classifier is kept in memory. Furthermore, the Naïve Bayes combination of these probabilities vectors is also kept in the main memory (namely a total of $(n+1) \cdot m \cdot |V_y|$ cells are required at maximum).

Consequently, in order to evaluate the contribution of a changed structure (the original structure with one feature added to one of its subsets) it is required to enumerate over all instances as follows:

(1) Take the combined probability vector of the current instance.
(2) Divide the vector obtained in step 1 in the probability vector obtained by the classifier that has been changed but before the change has been made. In this case vector division is referred to as dividing item i in the first vector by the corresponding item i in the second vector.
(3) Multiply the last vector by the probability vector obtained by the new classifier for this instance.

Note that this procedure requires $O(m \cdot h(I, S))$ operations. In summary, adding a new feature to one of the existing classifiers and evaluating its performance requires $O(g(I, S) + m \cdot h(I, S))$ operations.

Because the Serial Search has up to n iterations and on each iteration the algorithm test up to n features add separately to the last subset, the computational complexity of this search method is: $O(n^2 \cdot (g(I, S) + m \cdot h(I, S))$. The Multi Search with simple caching (hold only classifiers of the basic decomposition) has similar behavior. However because each feature is tested not only on the current subset but on all currently available subsets (up to n), the computational complexity is $O(n^3 \cdot (g(I, S) + m \cdot h(I, S)))$. The extended caching mechanism keeps all classifiers that have been induced and that might be used in the upcoming iterations. Thus, the Multi Search with extended caching mechanism creates only n new classifiers in each iteration. Consequently its complexity is $O(n^2 \cdot (g(I, S)) + n^3 m \cdot h(I, S))$.

Regarding the exhaustive search, the number of combinations that n^* input features may be decomposed into exactly ω relevant subsets is:

$$P(n^*, \omega) = \frac{1}{\omega!} \sum_{j=0}^{\omega} \binom{\omega}{j} (-1)^j (\omega - j)^{n^*} \tag{6.37}$$

If n^* is big enough the above expression can be approximated to [Dietterich and Michalski (1983)]:

$$P(n^*, \omega) \approx \frac{\omega^{n^*}}{o!} \approx \omega^{n^* - \omega} e^{\omega} \sqrt{2 \cdot \pi \cdot \omega} \tag{6.38}$$

Evidently the number combinations that n^* input features may be decomposed into up to n^* subsets is:

$$C(n^*) = \sum_{\omega=1}^{n^*} P(n^*, \omega) = \sum_{\omega=1}^{n^*} \frac{1}{\omega!} \sum_{j=0}^{\omega} \binom{\omega}{j} (-1)^j (\omega - j)^{n^*} \tag{6.39}$$

Due to the fact that in the Feature Set Decomposition problem defined above, it is possible that part of the input feature will not be used by the inducers (the irrelevant set) then the total search space is:

$$T(n) = \sum_{n^*=0}^{n} \binom{n}{n^*} C(n^*) = \sum_{n^*=0}^{n} \binom{n}{n^*} \sum_{\omega=1}^{n^*} \frac{1}{\omega!} \sum_{j=0}^{\omega} \binom{\omega}{j} (-1)^j (\omega - j)^{n^*} \tag{6.40}$$

Corollary 6.3 indicates that the number of possible decompositions (i.e. the size of the search exhaustive space) increases in a strong exponential manner as the number of input features increase. The conclusion is that the Exhaustive Search is practical only for a small number of input features. Furthermore, the Serial Search required less computation then the Multi Search.

6.5.7 *Specific Algorithms Implementations*

6.5.7.1 *DOG*

The DOG (D-Oblivious-Generalization) algorithm performs a serial search, uses incremental oblivious decision trees (with gain ratio splitting criteria) for generating the classifiers, and evaluates the performance using the generalization error bound, described in Theorem 6.1. Consequently, the attribute which most improves the generalization error is selected on condition that no similar (or even better) generalization error can be obtained by adding this feature to a newly created subset.

6.5.7.2 *BCW*

The BCW (B-C4.5-Wrapper) algorithm performs a Multi search, uses the C4.5 algorithm [Quinlan (1993)] as an intrinsic inducer for generating the decision trees and evaluates the performance using the wrapper approach with five folds.

6.6   Experimental Study

6.6.1   *Overview*

In order to illustrate the potential of feature set decomposition approach in classification problems and to evaluate the performance of the proposed algorithmic framework, a profound comparative experiment has been conducted on benchmark data sets. The following subsections describe the experimental set-up and the obtained results.

6.6.2   *Algorithms Used*

This experiment starts by comparing two implementations of the framework described in this Chapter: The DOG algorithm and the BCW algorithm. These algorithms are also compared to the following single-model algorithms: IFN (A greedy Oblivious Decision Tree inducer that uses gain ratio as the splitting criteria), Naïve Bayes and C4.5. The first two unary-model algorithms were chosen as they represent specific points in the search space of the DOG algorithm. The C4.5 algorithm was chosen because it represents a specific point for the BCW search space and because it is considered as the state-of-the-art decision tree algorithm which is widely used in many other comparative studies.

In the second part of the experiment, the suggested algorithms are also compared to Bagging [Breiman (1996)] and AdaBoost [Freund and Schapire (1996)], all of which are non-mutually exclusive ensemble algorithms, i.e. algorithms that may use the same attribute in several classifiers of the ensemble.

Bagging employs bootstrap sampling to generate several training sets from the original training set, and then trains a component learner from each generated training set. The component predictions are often combined via majority voting.

Recall that AdaBoost sequentially constructs a series of component learners, where the training instances that are wrongly predicted by a learner will obtain higher weight in the training set of its subsequent learner. The component predictions are combined via weighted voting where the weights are determined by the algorithm itself.

6.6.3 *Data Sets Used*

The selected algorithms were examined on 33 datasets, 23 of which have been selected manually from the UCI Machine Learning Repository [Merz and Murphy (1998)]. The datasets chosen vary across a number of dimensions such as: the number of target classes, the number of instances, the number of input features and their type (nominal, numeric). Although many researchers recognize the limitations of using the UCI repository for comparing algorithms, this book uses it because it is considered as an objective method for comparing algorithms since the published results can be validated.

Some of the UCI databases passed a simple preprocessing stage. In this stage missing values were replaced by a distinctive value, and numeric features were discretized by dividing their original range to ten equal-size intervals (or one per observed value, whichever was the least). The results may be improved by using more sophisticated discretization methods [Dougherty *et al.* (1995)] or a more robust way to treat missing values (as performed by C4.5). However, since the main purposes of this trial were to assess the potential of feature set decomposition and to verify whether the proposed algorithms are capable of approximating optimal Feature Set Decomposition, any non-relevant differences between the algorithms have been disabled. Three datasets have been chosen from the NIPS2003 feature selection challenge (see http://clopinet.com/isabelle/Projects/NIPS2003/). These datasets consist of many input features.

The rest of the datasets were synthetically fabricated. The idea of using synthetic data with known properties to explore modeling techniques is appealing for a number of reasons. First, it provides the researcher with a greater control over the characteristics of the dataset. In particular, it enables the researcher to vary one property at a time, thereby allowing a more systematic examination of the relationship between dataset characteristics, inducer parameters, and accuracy. Furthermore, with artificial data it is possible to have both a small training set, a common real world occurrence, and a large validation set with which to assess the findings. Although the synthetic datasets used in this experiment are relatively simple, they still pose a tough challenge for the conventional algorithms, as the results illustrate.

The synthetic datasets were created using two different core functions: The first group of datasets is based on the k-DNF functions. Its purpose was to analyze the ability of feature set decomposition and more specifically the proposed algorithm to cope successfully with synthetic k-DNF problems. This database demonstrated the replication problem of decision trees. Since most decision trees (like C4.5) divide an instance space into mutually exclusive regions to represent a concept, in some cases a tree may contain several duplications of the same sub tree. The target feature was generated using three disjunctions, each of which contains three different features as follows:

$$y = (a_1 \cap a_2 \cap a_3) \cup (a_4 \cap a_5 \cap a_6) \cup (a_7 \cap a_8 \cap a_9) \qquad (6.41)$$

This experiment examined 5 datasets. Each dataset is denoted by $DNF(k, l)$, where k indicates the number of disjunctions and l indicates the number of features in each disjunction. The input features values were drawn from a uniform distribution. It it to be noted that in this case, by using Lemma 6.3, the optimal decomposition structure is known in advance.

The DNF learning problem is considered as one of the most important issues in computational learning theory [Servedio (2004)]. Many researchers studied a restricted version of this problem, such as:

- The SAT-k DNF problem (a DNF in which each truth assignment statisfies at most k terms).
- Learning arbitrary polynomial-size DNF under the uniform distribution in time $n^{O(logn)}$.
- A polynomial time algorithm for $O(logn)$-term DNF.
- A polynomial time algorithm for read-once DNF (each variable appears at most once).
- The read-k DNF (a DNF in which each variable appears at most k times) with constant k.
- A polynomial time algorithm for learning monotone (i.e. with no negated variables) read-k DNF under constantbounded product distributions (a distribution over the binary space in which there is constant $c \in (0, 1)$ such that $P(a_i = 1) \in [c, 1 - c]$ for all $i = 1, \ldots n$).
- A polynomial-time algorithm for learning polynomial-size DNF under constant-bounded product distributions.

- A polynomial time algorithm for learning monotone $2^{O(\sqrt{\log n})}$-term DNF under constantbounded product distribution.

Although these algorithms are very efficient in learning specific Boolean functions structures, they are limited in their capability to learn general domain problems as required in practice. More specifically, if these kind of algorithms are employed on the problem discussed in this section, it will most probably outperform other algorithms. At the same time it will most likely achieve less satisfactory results when it is used on different classification problems that can not be represented as read-once DNF functions. Thus, we decided to compare the suggested algorithms to other general purpose algorithms.

The second synthetic dataset group examined the ability of the proposed algorithms to converge to the optimal decomposition structure as presented in Lemma 6.2. All datasets in this group contained 40 binary input features and binary class. The synthetic data was generated in such a manner that all features were relevant for modeling the class and that the feature set could be divided into 10 conditionally independent groups of 4 features each. In order to obtain this synthetic dataset, the following procedure was performed for each class:

(1) All input features were randomly allocated into ten equally sized groups.
(2) For each value combination (i) of each group (j) and for each value of the target feature, a random value $0 \leq p_{i,j,k} \leq 1$ was selected such that $\sum_{i=1}^{16} p_{i,j,k} = 1 \, \forall j, k$ where $p_{i,j,k}$ denotes the probability of the attributes in group j to obtain this value combination i when the target feature obtains the value k.

Note that because in each group there are exactly four binary features, there are then 16 value combinations. In order to fabricate one instance, the value of the target feature was sampled first (assuming uniform distribution) then the values of all input features were sampled according to the appropriate distribution generated in step 2.

6.6.4 *Metrics Measured*

In this experiment the following metrics were measured:

- Generalized Accuracy: Represents the probability that an instance was classified correctly. In order to estimate the generalized accuracy, a 10-fold cross-validation procedure was used. Under this procedure, the training set was randomly partitioned into 10 disjoint subsets. Each subset was used once in a test set and nine times in a training set. Since the average accuracy on the validation instances is a random variable, the confidence interval was estimated by using the normal approximation of the binomial distribution. Furthermore, the one tailed paired t-test with a confidence level of 95% was used in order to verify whether the differences in accuracy between the DOG algorithm and other algorithms were statistically significant.

- Classifier Complexity: As this book focuses on decision trees, the classifier complexity was measured as the total number of nodes, including the leaves. It should be noted that for multiple decision trees classifiers, the complexity was measured as the total number of nodes in all trees.

The following additional metrics were measured in order to characterize the decomposition structures obtained by DOG and BCW algorithms:

- Number of Subsets
- Average Number of features in a single subset.
- Structure Similarity to the optimal complete equivalent — this measure can be measured only in synthetic cases where the complete equivalence decomposition structure is known based on Lemma 6.2 and Lemma 6.3.

6.6.5   *Comparison with Single Model Algorithms*

Tables 6.1, 6.2, 6.3 and 6.4 present the results obtained by using 10-fold-cross-validation. The superscript "+" indicates that the accuracy rate of DOG was significantly higher than the corresponding algorithm at a confidence level of 5%. The "-" superscript indicates the accuracy was significantly lower.

Tables 6.1 and 6.2 indicate that there is no significant case where Naïve Bayes or IFN were more accurate than DOG. On the other hand, DOG was significantly more accurate than Naïve Bayes and IFN in 24 databases and 22 databases respectively. Moreover, DOG was significantly more accurate than C4.5 in 19 databases, and less accurate in only 3 databases. DOG's model complexity (total number of nodes) was comparable to the complexity obtained by C4.5 algorithm in most of the cases.

The results of the experimental study are very encouraging. The superiority of DOG is particularly remarkable in the synthetic datasets. In the

$DNF(k,3)$ datasets, the DOG's superiority increased with the dimensionality.

The results of the experimental study are encouraging. On the datasets obtained from the UCI repository, the DOG outperformed Naïve Bayes mostly when the data was large in size or had a small number of features. For moderate dimensionality (from 50 features up to 500), the performance of Naïve Bayes was not necessarily inferior. More specifically, regarding the datasets: OPTIC, SONAR, SPI, AUDIOLOGY, LUNG-CANCER, only in three of the datasets (SPI, AUDIOLOGY, LUNG-CANCER), was the superiority of DOG over Naïve Bayes statistically significant. However, for high dimensionality datasets (having at least 500 features), DOG significantly outperforms Naïve Bayes in all cases.

Comparing the accuracy of DOG and BCW indicated that in most of the cases DOG and BCW obtained similar results. This observation is surprising, considering the facts that C4.5 outperforms IFN and that the computations of BCW are much more intensive than DOG computations. Note that BCW uses Multi-Search (and not Serial Search), it executes the C4.5 inducer in each iteration from scratch (instead of using simple oblivious decision tree constructed incrementally), and it uses the wrapper evaluation approach. These surprising results can be explained two-fold. First in small decision trees, despite its restricted structure, oblivious decision trees perform as well as regular decision trees. Second, the serial search in most of the cases is sufficient.

Analyzing the number of features in each subset shows that the DOG algorithm tends to build small subsets. Moreover, there are 6 cases in which the DOG algorithm used only one feature in each tree. In these cases the classifiers built are equivalent to Naïve Bayes, besides the fact that not all input features are necessarily used (non relevant features might be dropped). This suggests that in some cases DOG acts as a feature selection procedure for Naïve Bayes.

6.6.6 Comparing to Ensemble Algorithms

Since the accuracy and the model complexity is affected by the ensemble size (number of classifiers), we have examined various ensembles sizes. Following the empirical results for asymptotic convergence of ensembles [Opitz and Maclin (1999)], the ensemble size created using the bagging algorithm have been up to 15 classifiers. Similarly the ensemble size created using the AdaBoost have been up to 25 classifiers. The results indicate that there are datasets in which DOG algorithm obtained accuracy similar to the accuracies obtained by bagging and AdaBoost (like in the case of AUST dataset). There are cases in which bagging or AdaBoost have achieved much higher accuracies (like in the cases of AUDIOLOGY and HEPATITIS datasets). There are cases in which DOG achieved the best accuracies (like in the case of BCAN or MADELON).

Analyzing the results of the entire datasets collection indicates that in 7 datasets AdaBoost achieved significantly higher accuracies (note that the compared value is the best accuracy achieved by enumerating the ensemble size from 1 to 25). On the other hand, DOG was significantly more accurate than AdaBoost in only 4 datasets, including the high-dimensional datasets MADELON and DEXTER.

DOG was significantly more accurate than Bagging in 10 datasets. While bagging was significantly more accurate than DOG in only 4 datasets.

The above results disregard the model complexity. For instance AdaBoost obtained an accuracy of 87.76% for the LETTER dataset (in comparison with an accuracy of 73.46% obtained by DOG algorithm). However, the average complexity of AdaBoost model in this case was 240318.6 nodes (in comparison with only 272 nodes of DOG in this case).

Taking into consideration the model's complexity, we have compared the accuracy obtained by the AdaBoost algorithm to that of DOG algorithm using the same complexity of the DOG's model. Because it is challenging to tune the AdaBoost model's complexity to a certain value, we use interpolation of the two closest points in the AdaBoost's accuracy-complexity graph that bounds this value, on condition that these points are "dominant", namely there are no less complicated points in the AdaBoost's graph that has higher accuracy. Geometrically this examines on what datasets the DOG point is significantly above or below the AdaBoost's trend line. If no such pair of points could be found we used the highest accuracy that its complexity is less or equal to the DOG's model complexity. If no such point can be found, we used the first point (ensemble of size one).

The accuracy-complexity tradeoff analysis indicates that DOG has significantly outperformed AdaBoost in 10 datasets while AdaBoost has significantly outperformed DOG in 4 datasets, in which two, the complexity of AdaBoost was much higher than the DOG complexity (because the ensemble of size one is already more complicated), namely AdaBoost is not necessary better in these cases because DOG introduce new points in the complexity-accuracy tradeoff. Furthermore, in three of these four datasets, a single C4.5 has already significantly outperformed the DOG algorithm.

Furthermore, DOG has obtained better accuracy-complexity tradeoff than AdaBoost for all datasets with moderate dimensionality (number of features between 50 to 100) and with high dimensionality (number of features greater than 100).

6.6.7 *Discussion*

6.6.7.1 *The Relation of Feature Set Decomposition Performance and Node-Sample Ratio*

The results presented above indicate that feature set decomposition may be beneficial for improving the decision tree accuracy. However, there is still no clear understanding under what circumstances the feature set decomposition can improve the performance of a decision tree. This is important for deciding whether to perform a feature set decomposition for an unseen dataset.

It is well known that the number of nodes in a tree is bounded by the training set size. Hence, when there are not enough instances, a single decision tree may not be capable of representing a complicated classifier in a reliable way. In this case reliability can be obtained by having enough instances assigned to each leaf. In any other case the tree might be too short to present the classification function completely or its classifications in some of the leaves are based on a small number of instances resulting in a potentially unreliable classification.

A simple way to measure the shortage of instances is to use the node-sample ratio, which is computed as the ratio of the number of nodes in the decision tree to the training set size. A low value of the node-sample ratio indicates that there are abundant instances, while a high value may indicate a shortage of instances.

Using this ratio has a drawback because it assumes that the decision tree is balanced and that the instances are uniformly distributed. If the number of instances assigned to a certain leaf is much less than the other (because its distance from the root is longer or just because the distribution is not uniform) then the value of the nodes-sample ratio may be misleading. However the advantage of this measure is its simplicity.

The datasets from Tables 6.1 and 6.2 are divided into three groups: Datasets that DOG outperforms C4.5, Datasets that DOG and C4.5 had similar accuracies and datasets where C4.5 outperforms DOG. The node-sample ratio has been measured on each dataset and the average values for each group are presented in Table 6.5. The results indicate that feature set decomposition improves single decision tree performance when the node-sample ratio is high, and deteriorates when this ratio has low values. In an attempt to disable the potentially biased effect of the synthetic datasets, Table 6.5 presents also the values measured for the datasets obtained from the UCI repository only. In this case the differences between the groups are smaller but still noticeable.

In order to validate that the differences observed in Table 6.5 are statistically significant, the Kruskal–Wallis one-way analysis of variance by ranks was applied here. This nonparametric hypothesis test is extremely useful for deciding whether k independent samples are from a different population. The Kruskal–Wallis technique tests the null hypothesis that the k samples come from the same population or from identical populations with the same median. In the first case (all datasets), the null hypothesis was rejected with $\alpha = 1\%$ while in the second case (UCI Repository only) the null hypothesis was rejected with $\alpha = 2.5\%$.

Given that there are enough instances, a decision tree built on a dataset that contains more independent relevant features, tends to have more nodes, meaning a higher value of nodes-sample ratio. This is particularly noticeable on the $DNF(k,3)$ syntactic datasets where the number of nodes increased from 15 in $DNF(3,3)$ to 1710 in $DNF(6,3)$. This phenomenon occurs in most of the datasets which are not necessarily synthetic. Combining the results in Table 6.5 and the last observation indicates that feature set decomposition is potentially useful when there are many contributing features relative to the training set size.

6.6.7.2   *The Link Between Error Reduction and the Problem Complexity*

In order to understand when the suggested approach introduces considerable performance enhancement, the correlation between error reduction and the problem complexity has been examined.

There are two obvious alternatives for measuring the error reduction achieved by using the Feature Set Decomposition approach: measuring the error difference between IFN and DOT or measuring the error ratio (i.e. the error of DOT divided by the error of single IFN). Following [Ali and Pazzani (1996)], this book uses error ratio because it manifests the fact that it becomes gradually more difficult to achieve error reduction as the error of single IFN converges to zero.

The problem complexity has been estimated by the following ratio $\log(|H|)/m$ where m is the training set size and $|H|$ is the hypothesis space size of all possible labeling functions of the investigated problem after eliminating redundant and irrelevant attributes. The feature selection procedure used for discovering the relevant features was the wrapper approach using C4.5 as the induction algorithm.

Note that the problem complexity increases as the problem dimensionality grows. The estimated linear correlation coefficient (r) is 0.9. This result is quite encouraging as it evidently indicates when the Feature Set Decomposition may potentially contribute.

6.6.8 *The Suitability of the Naïve Bayes Combination*

In this section we investigate whether the Naïve Bayes combination is suitable to feature set decomposition. For this purpose we compare it to the Distribution Summation combination using the DOG algorithm with the C4.5 as the base classifier. The results obtained indicated that in most of the cases these combining methods have obtained similar results. There are two cases (AUDIOLOGY and SONAR) in which the superiority of distribution summation was statistically significant. On the other hand, there are two cases (SPI and ZOO) in which the results are opposite. Nevertheless,the grand averages of these methods are almost equal. We conclude that the Distribution Summation combination and the Naïve Bayes combination are equivalent methods.

6.6.9 *The Effect of Subset Size*

In this section we examine how the subset size affects the performance of the combined classifiers. For this purpose the DOG algorithm was executed several times, each time with a different setting of the C4.5's parameter: "minimum number of instances per leaf". In this experiment we have examined the following values: 2, 4, 8, 16, 32, 64, 128. A higher value will result with a smaller decision tree and consequently a smaller subset size. The number of iterations was set to 10 in all cases. The results obtained in this experiment indicated that the datasets can be divided into two groups: In the first group (AUDIOLOGY, HEPATITIS, IRIS, KR-VS-KP, LED17, LETTER, MONKS1, MUSHROOM, NURSE, SOYBEAN, TTT, VOTE) the accuracy is decreasing as a function of the minimum number of instances per leaf. In the remaining datasets (BCAN, LUNG-CANCER,

MONKS2, MONKS3, OPTIC, SONAR, SPI, WINE, ZOO) the graph is concave, meaning a maximum accuracy value is obtained for a certain value of the parameter that is greater than 2.

Table 6.1   Summary of Experimental Results of the Single Classifier Methods on UCI Repository.

Dataset	# Instances	# Features	Naïve Bayes		C4.5		IFN	
			Accuracy	# Nodes	Accuracy	# Nodes	Accuracy	# Nodes
AUST	690	15	84.93±2.7	80	85.36±5.1	30	84.49±5.1	27
AUDIOLOGY	200	70	+65.5±7.39	223	75±6.95	52	74±7.95	100
BCAN	699	10	97.4249±1.17	99	+92.99±2.87	61	+94.39±3.5	55
HEPATITIS	155	20	82.58±7.56	82	70.32±8.46	5	70.97±8.99	68
IRIS	150	5	95.33±5.05	40	96±3.33	11	96±3.33	90
KR-VS-KP	3197	37	+87.86±1.41	108	99.44±0.55	87	98.06±0.42	220
LABOR	57	16	98.24±4.52	67	+87.72±12.72	12	+84.63±8.14	32
LED17	220	24	+63.18±8.7	72	+59.09±6.9	69	+55.55±6.3	73
LETTER	15000	16	73.29±1	272	74.96±0.8	11169	+69.56±0.7	5321
LUNG CANCER	31	56	+41.94±19.96	228	+38.71±17.82	16	+38.71±17.82	16
MONKS1	124	6	+73.39±6.7	23	+75.81±8.2	18	+75.00±10.7	40
MONKS2	169	6	+56.21±6.1	23	61.54±8.6	31	62.72±10.4	194
MONKS3	122	6	93.44±3.7	23	93.44±3.7	12	92.38±3.3	12
MUSHROOM	8124	22	+95.48±0.9	137	100±0	28	100±0	30
NURSE	12960	8	+65.39±24	34	-97.45±0.4	527	92.47±0.5	135
OPTIC	5628	64	91.73±1.3	981	+62.42±2	4059	+48.90±2.5	1257
SONAR	208	60	75.48±7.3	660	+69.71±5.4	51	76.48±6.8	97
SOYBEAN	683	35	91.95±1.99	135	92.83±1.52	85	92.24±2.46	72
SPI	1000	60	+94.1±0.4	300	+91.2±1.9	117	+87.00±2.6	523
TTT	958	9	+69.27±3.2	36	-85.7±1.65	142	73.19±3.9	540
VOTE	290	16	90.34±3.44	48	-96.21±2.45	16	93.79±2.8	23
WINE	178	13	96.63±3.9	143	+85.96±6.9	41	+91.45±5	41
ZOO	101	8	+89.11±7	52	+93.07±5.8	21	+90.89±9.7	21

Table 6.2   Summary of Experimental Results of the Single Classifier Methods on Remaining Datasets.

Dataset	# Instances	# Features	Naïve Bayes		C4.5		IFN	
			Accuracy	# Nodes	Accuracy	# Nodes	Accuracy	# Nodes
ARCENE	100	10000	+70±12.3	1000	75 ±9.2	9	+54±8.3	46
DEXTER	300	20000	+86.33±3.9	3000	+78.33 ±3.6	53	+76.13 ±2.1	47
MADELON	2000	500	+58.3±1.5	20000	69.8±4.7	259	+62±3.4	127
DNF(2,2)	20	4	+69.75±7	12	+93.41±2.5	9	+93.41±2.5	9
DNF(3,3)	128	9	+80.47±2.1	27	87.5±1.9	15	85.15±1.3	9
DNF(4,3)	1024	12	+74.61±3.51	36	+93.75±2.6	124	+72.65±3.5	16.1
DNF(5,3)	8192	15	+73.88±2.9	45	+97.78±0.3	489.6	+64.16±4.62	103.4
DNF(6,3)	50000	18	+66.40±4.72	54	99.1±0.6	1710.4	+63.84±5.23	269
INDEP(10,4)	1000	40	+68.64±0.1	120	+72.71±0.4	1415	+71.86±0.2	4323
INDEP(10,4)	2000	40	+69.29±0.1	120	+75.33±0.8	1415	+76.28±0.9	5853
INDEP(10,4)	3000	40	+68.95±0.2	120	+76.12±0.3	1340	+76.74±0.3	5853
INDEP(10,4)	4000	40	+69.37±0.1	120	+76.94±0.3	1320	+77.12±0.5	5853
INDEP(10,4)	5000	40	+69.48	120	+77.46±0.2	1415	+79.86±0.4	5853

Table 6.3 Summary of Experimental Results of the Feature Set Decomposition Methods on UCI Repository.

Dataset	DOG				BCW			
	Accuracy	# Nodes	# Subsets	Mean Subset Size	Accuracy	# Nodes	# Subsets	Mean Subset Size
AUST	86.52±2.5	84	11	1.27	84.35±4.6	56	3	3.33
AUDIOLOGY	78.5±6.54	64	3	4.67	81.5±4.29	124	6	2.12
BCAN	97.42±1.17	99	9	1	96.13±4.2	76	6	1.12
HEPATITIS	80±6.89	8	2	6.5	79.35±5.71	12	3	4
IRIS	95.33±5.05	40	4	1	96±3.33	11	1	4
KR-VS-KP	98.47±0.63	330	2	7	99.44±0.35	140	2	7.5
LABOR	98.24±4.52	67	16	1	96.75±3.5	123	5	3
LED17	73.64±5.5	370	7	3.28	$^{+}$66.36±3.7	47	3	3.33
LETTER	73.46±0.64	272	16	1	75.02±1.7	313	9	1.67
LUNG CANCER	93.55±10.05	13	2	2	93.55±10.05	13	2	2
MONKS1	98.39± 2.3	28	5	1.2	$^{+}$89.51± 5.5	12	2	2
MONKS2	60.36 ±7.55	30	4	1.5	59.56±7.6	24	1	5
MONKS3	93.442±3.3	19	5	1.2	93.44±5.34	6	2	1
MUSHROOM	100±0	28	1.2	7.67	100±0	37	1	5
NURSE	91.65±0.6	38	6	1.33	$^{-}$96.82±1.159	339	2	4
OPTIC	91.73±1.4	981	64	1	91.73±1.4	981	64	1
SONAR	77.12±8.7	98	35	1.657	71.42±3.23	125	5	2.2
SOYBEAN	92.9±2.56	122	3	4	91.95±1.56	134	2	5
SPI	95.8±0.9	300	50	1.2	96.3±0.7	420	20	3
TTT	73.33±4	51	6	2.5	84.24±2.7	95	2	4.5
VOTE	90.52±1.23	18	6	1.333	93.79±2.8	23	1	7
WINE	96.63±3.9	143	13	1	84.27±4.41	65	5	1.8
ZOO	98.02±3.02	50	4	4	$^{+}$93.01±3.42	18	2	2.5

Table 6.4 Summary of Experimental Results of the Feature Set Decomposition Methods on Remaining Datasets.

Dataset	DOG				BCW			
	Accuracy	# Nodes	# Subsets	Mean Subset Size	Accuracy	# Nodes	# Subsets	Mean Subset Size
ARCENE	76±8.1	97	12	3.2	77±7.2	119	7	4.8
DEXTER	89.33±2.7	562	11	52.72	90.28±1.9	789	16	47.33
MADELON	71.4±2.6	660	2	117.8	71.2±2.9	990	3	95.42
DNF(2,2)	100±0	10	2	2	100±0	10	2	2
DNF(3,3)	87.5±1.2	21	1.67	5.33	-90.2±1.2	25	2.7	4.33
DNF(4,3)	98.7±0	29	3.85	2.65	91.41±1.4	37	3	3.67
DNF(5,3)	100±0	35	5	3	100±0	35	5	3
DNF(6,3)	100±0	42	6	3	100±0	42	6	3
INDEP(10,4)	93.81±0.5	180	9	3.7	94.70±0.5	180	10	3.6
INDEP(10,4)	94.12±0.4	205	10	3.3	94.1±0.4	205	10	3.3
INDEP(10,4)	94.78±0.4	225	10	3.5	94.8±0.4	225	10	3.5
INDEP(10,4)	95.67±0.2	275	10	3.5	95.7±0.2	275	10	3.5
INDEP(10,4)	97.92±0.1	300	10	4	97.9±0.1	300	10	4

Table 6.5   Node-Sample Ratio

Group	Node-Sample Ratio for datasets in Tables 6.1 and 6.2	Node-Sample Ratio for datasets in Table 6.1 only
DOG outperforms C4.5	36.71%	27.94%
DOG and C4.5 had similar accuracies	15.55%	17.31%
C4.5 outperforms DOG	8.13%	8.13%

Chapter 7

Space Decomposition

7.0.10 *Overview*

Data mining algorithms aim at searching interesting patterns in a large
amount of data in manageable computational complexity and high classification performance. Decomposition methods are used to improve both
criteria. This chapter presents a decomposition method that partitions the
instance space using the K-means algorithm and then employs an induction
algorithm on each cluster. Because space decomposition is not necessarily
suitable to any given dataset, and in some cases it might reduce the classification accuracy, we suggest a homogeneity index that measures the initial
reduction in a sum of square errors resulting from the clustering procedure.
Consequently, the decomposition method is executed only if the homogeneity index obtained a certain threshold value. Additionally, the proposed
procedure ensures that there is a suffice number of instances in each cluster
for inducing a classifier. An empirical study conducted shows that the proposed method can lead to a significant increase of classification accuracy,
especially in numeric datasets.

7.0.11 *Motivation*

Clustering and classification are both considered fundamental tasks in data
mining. In essence, the difference between clustering and classification lies
in the manner that knowledge is extracted from data: whereas in classification, the knowledge is extracted in a supervised manner based on
pre-defined classes, in clustering the knowledge it is extracted in an unsupervised way without any guidance from the user.

    Decomposition may divide the database horizontally (subsets of rows
or tuples) or vertically (subsets of attributes). This chapter deals with the

former, namely tuple decomposition.

Many methods have been developed for partitioning the tuples into subsets. Some of them are aimed at minimizing space and time needed for the classification of a dataset; whereas others attempt to improve accuracy. These methods may be roughly divided according to the manner in which tuples are divided into subsets:

Sample-based tuple decomposition tuples are divided into subsets via sampling. This category includes sampling, a degenerate form of decomposition that decreases complexity but also accuracy [Catlett (1991)], as well as multiple model methods. The latter may be sequential in an attempt to take advantage of knowledge gained in one iteration, and uses it in the successive one. Such methods include algorithms as windowing [Quinlan (1983)], in an attempt to improve the sample they produce from one iteration to another, and also the boosting algorithm [Schapire (1990)], increasing the probability of selecting instances that are misclassified by the current classifier for constructing the next one, in order to improve accuracy. Sample-based decomposition may also be concurrent, thus enabling parallel learning. Classifiers produced by concurrent methods may be combined using a number of methods, varying from simple voting (e.g. bagging) to more sophisticated meta-classifying methods, such as stacking [Wolpert (1992)], grading [Seewald and Furnkranz (2001)] and arbiter tree [Chan and Stolfo (1993)]. Many multiple model methods were showed to improve accuracy. This accuracy gain may stem from the variation in classifiers, built by the same algorithm, or from the advantages of the sequential process.

Space-based decomposition Tuples are divided into subsets according to their belonging to some part of space. [Kusiak (2000)] describes the notion of "feature value decomposition" in which objects or instances are partitioned into subsets according to the values of selected input attributes. Kusiak also suggests the notion of "decision value decomposition" in which objects are partitioned according to the value of the decision (or more generally, the target attribute). Kusiak does not describe a method for selecting the set of attributes according to which the partition is performed. In fact his work deals only with the decision-making process, and does not offer an automated procedure for space-based decomposition.

A Model Class Selection (MCS) — a system that searches for different classification algorithms for different regions in the instance-space is proposed by [Brodley (1995)]. The MCS system, which can be regarded as implementing an instance-space decomposition strategy, uses dataset characteristics and expert-rules to select one of three possible classification methods (a decision tree, a discriminant function or an instance-based method) for each region in the instance-space. The expert-rules are based on past empirical comparisons of classifier performance, which can be considered as prior knowledge.

In the neural network community, several researchers have examined the decomposition methodology. [Nowlan and Hinton (1991)] examined the Mixture-of-Experts (ME) methodology that decomposes the input space, such that each expert examines a different part of the space. However, the subspaces have soft "boundaries", namely subspaces are allowed to overlap. A gating network is responsible for combining the various experts. [Jordan and Jacobs (1994)] have proposed an extension to the basic mixture of experts, known as Hierarchical Mixtures of Experts (HME). This extension decomposes the space into subspaces and then recursively decomposes each subspace into subspaces.

Variations of the basic mixture-of-experts method have been developed to accommodate specific domain problems. [Hampshire and Waibel (1992)] and [Peng *et al.* (1995)] have used a specialized modular network called the Meta-p_i network to solve the vowel-speaker problem. [Weigend *et al.* (1995)] proposed nonlinear gated experts for time-series while [Ohno-Machado and Musen (1997)] used a revised modular network for predicting the survival of AIDS patients. [Rahman and Fairhurst (1997)] proposed a new approach for combining multiple experts for improving recognition of handwritten numerals.

NBTree [Kohavi (1996)] is an instance space decomposition method that induces a decision tree and a Naïve Bayes hybrid classifier. Naïve Bayes, which is a classification algorithm based on Bayes' theorem and a Naïve independence assumption, is very efficient in terms of its processing time. To induce an NBTree, the instance space is recursively partitioned according to attributes values. The result of the recursive partitioning is a decision tree whose terminal nodes are Naïve Bayes classifiers. Since subjecting a terminal node to a Naïve Bayes classifier means that the hybrid classifier may classify two instances from a single hyper-rectangle region into distinct classes, the NBTree is more flexible than a pure decision tree. In order to decide when to stop the growth of the tree, NBTree compares two alternatives in terms of error estimation - partitioning into a hyper-rectangle region and inducing a single Naïve Bayes classifier. The error estimation is calculated by cross-validation, which significantly increases the overall processing time. Although NBTree applies a Naïve Bayes classifier to decision tree terminal nodes, classification algorithms other than Naïve Bayes are also applicable. However, the cross-validation estimations make the NBTree hybrid computationally expensive for more time-consuming algorithms such as neural networks.

NBTree uses a simple stopping criterion according to which a split is not considered when the dataset consists of 30 instances or less. Splitting too few instances will not affect the final accuracy, in fact will lead, on the other hand, to a complex composite classifier. Moreover, since each sub classifier is required to generalize instances in its region, it must be trained on samples of sufficient size. [Kohavi (1996)] suggested a new splitting criterion which is to select the attribute with the highest utility. Kohavi defined utility as the 5-fold cross-validation accuracy estimate of using a Naïve Bayes algorithm for classifying regions generated by a split. The regions are partitions of the initial subspace according to a particular attribute value.

Although different researchers have addressed the issue of instance space decomposition, there is no research that suggests an automatic procedure for mutually exclusive instance space decompositions, which can be employed for any given classification algorithm and in a computationally efficient way. This chapter presents an algorithm for space decomposition, which exploits the K-means clustering algorithm. It is aimed at reducing the error rate compared to the simple classifier embedded in it, while keeping the comprehensibility level.

7.1   Problem Formulation

The problem of decomposing the data space presented in this chapter is accuracy oriented. Our aim is to achieve a decomposition of the data space, such that if a learning algorithm is built on each data subset, it will achieve a lower generalization error compared to a classifier built on the entire data set using the same algorithm.

Recall from Chapter 5, the formal definition of Space Decomposition problem:

Given a learning method I, and a training set S with input attribute set

$A = \{a_1, a_2, \ldots, a_n\}$ *and target attribute* y *from a distribution* D *over the labeled instance space, the goal is to find an optimal decomposition* W_{opt} *of the instance space* X *into* ψ *subspaces* $B_k \subseteq X$; $k = 1, \ldots, \psi$ *fulfilling* $(\bigcup_{k=1}^{\psi} B_k) = X$ *and* $B_i \cap B_j = \emptyset$; $i, j = 1, \ldots, \psi$; $i \neq j$ *such that the generalization error of the induced classifiers* $M_k = I(\sigma_{x \in B_k} S)$; $k = 1, \ldots, \psi$ *will be minimized over the distribution* D.

The generalization error in this case is defined as:

$$\varepsilon(B_1, \ldots, B_\psi, M_1, \ldots, M_\psi) = \sum_{k=1}^{\psi} \sum_{x \in B_k} \sum_{c_j \in dom(y)} L(x, c_j, M_k) \cdot D(x, c_j)$$

(7.1)

where the loss function is defined as:

$$L(x, c_j, M_k) = \begin{cases} 0 c_j = \underset{c_j^* \in dom(y)}{\operatorname{argmax}} \hat{P}_{M_k}(y = c_j^* | x) \\ 1 c_j \neq \underset{c_j^* \in dom(y)}{\operatorname{argmax}} \hat{P}_{M_k}(y = c_j^* | x) \end{cases}$$

(7.2)

where M_k is the corresponded classifier of subspace B_k.

7.1.1 *Manners for Dividing the Instance Space*

One of the main issues arising when trying to address the problem formulated in the last section concerns the question of what sort of instance space division should be taken in order to achieve as high accuracy as possible. One may come up with quite a few ways for dividing the instance space, varying from using one attribute at a time (similarly to decision tree construction) to the use of different combinations of attribute values.

Inspired by the idea that similar instances should be assigned to the same subspace, it lead us towards using clustering methods. We choose to define the similarity of unlabeled data via the distance metric. In particular, the metric used will be the Euclidean metric for continuous attributes, involving simple matching for nominal ones (very similar to the similarity measure used by [Haung (1998)] in the K-prototypes algorithm, except for the fact that there is no special cluster-dependent weight for the categorical attributes). The reason for this particular metric chosen lies in the clustering method we preferred to use for this work, namely the K-means algorithm.

7.1.2   The K-Means Algorithm as a Decomposition Tool

The K-means algorithm presented in Chapter 3 is one of the simplest and most commonly used clustering algorithms. Recall that this algorithm heuristically attempt to minimize the sum of squared errors:

$$SSE = \sum_{k=1}^{K} \sum_{i=1}^{N_k} \|x_i - \mu_k\|^2 \qquad (7.3)$$

where N_k is the number of instances belonging to cluster k and μ_k is the mean of k'th cluster, calculated as the mean of all the instances belonging to that cluster:

$$\mu_{k,i} = \frac{1}{N_k} \sum_{q=1}^{N_k} x_{q,i} \forall i \qquad (7.4)$$

The algorithm starts with an initial set of cluster centers, chosen at random or according to some heuristic procedure. In each iteration, each instance is assigned to its nearest cluster center according to the Euclidean distance between the two. Then the cluster centers are re-calculated.

A number of convergence conditions are possible, including no reduction in error as a result of the relocation of centers, no (or minimal) reassignment of instances to new cluster centers, or exceeding a pre-defined number of iterations.

For T iterations of the K-means algorithm performed on a dataset containing m instances, each has n attributes, its complexity may be calculated as: $O(T \cdot K \cdot m \cdot n)$. This linear complexity with respect to m is one of the reasons for the popularity of K-means: Even if the number of instances is substantially large (which often is the case nowadays) — this algorithm is computationally attractive. Thus, K-means has an advantage in comparison to other clustering methods (e.g. hierarchical clustering methods), which have non-linear complexity with respect to the number of instances.

Other reasons for the algorithm's popularity are its ease of interpretation, simplicity of implementation, speed of convergence and adaptability to sparse data [Dhillon and Modha (2001)].

Having intended to use a clustering algorithm as a means for partitioning the dataset, and taking into account the availability, linear complexity and high understandability of the K-means algorithm, we choose to integrate this specific clustering method in our algorithm.

The K-means algorithm may be considered as a simplification of the expectation maximization algorithm [Dempster *et al.* (1977)]. This is a density based clustering algorithm used for identifying the parameters of different distributions from which the data objects are assumed to be drawn. In the case of K-means, the objects are assumed to be drawn from a mixture of K multivariate normal distributions, sharing the same known variance, whereas the mean vectors of the K distributions are unknown [Estivill-Castro (2000)]. When employing the K-means on the unlabeled data, this underlying assumption of the algorithm may be written as:

$$x \sim N(\mu_k, \sigma^2) \forall k = 1, 2, \ldots, K, x \in C_k \qquad (7.5)$$

According to Bayes' theorem:

$$p(y = c_j^* \,|x) = \frac{p(y = c_j^*, x)}{p(x)} \qquad (7.6)$$

Since $p(x)$ depends on the distribution from which the unlabeled instances are drawn and since it is plausible to assume that different clusters have different distributions, it implies that $p(y = c_j^* \,|x)$ is distributed differently on various clusters. The latter distribution has a direct influence on the predicted value of the target attribute, since:

$$\widehat{y}(x) = \underset{c_j^* \in dom(y)}{\arg\max} \; p(y = c_j^* \,|x) \qquad (7.7)$$

This supports the idea of using the clustering algorithm.

7.1.3 *Determining the Number of Subsets*

In order to proceed with the decomposition of unlabeled data, a significant parameter should be at hand — the number of subsets, or in our case, clusters, existing in the data.

The K-means algorithm requires this parameter as input, and is affected by its value. Various heuristics attempt to find an optimal number of clusters, most of them referred to as inter-cluster distance or intra-cluster similarity. Nevertheless, in this case as we know the actual class of each instance, we suggest using the mutual information criterion for clustering [Strehl *et al.* (2000)]). The criterion value for m instances clustered using

$C = \{C_1,...,C_g\}$ and referring to the target attribute y whose domain is $dom(y) = \{c_1,...,c_k\}$ is defined as follows:

$$C = \frac{2}{m}\sum_{l=1}^{g}\sum_{h=1}^{k} m_{l,h} \log_{g \cdot k}\left(\frac{m_{l,h} \cdot m}{m_{.,l} \cdot m_{l,.}}\right) \qquad (7.8)$$

where $m_{l,h}$ indicate the number of instances that are in cluster C_l and also in class c_h. $m_{.,h}$ denotes the total number of instances in the class c_h. Similarly $m_{l,.}$ indicates the number of instances in cluster C_l.

7.1.4   The Basic K-Classifier Algorithm

The basic K-classifier algorithm employs the K-means algorithm for the purpose of space decomposition and uses mutual information criterion for clustering for determining the number of clusters. The algorithm follows the following steps:

Step 1 Apply the K-means algorithm to the training set S using $K = 2, 3, \ldots K_{max}$

Step 2 Compute the mutual information criterion for clustering for $K = 2, 3, \ldots, K_{max}$ and choose the optimal number of clusters K^*.

Step 3 Produce K classifiers of the induction algorithm I, each produced on the training data belonging to a subset k of the instance space. A decomposition of the space is defined as follows: $B_k = \{x \in X : k = \arg\min \|x - \mu_k\|\}$ $k = 1, 2, \ldots, K^*$ and therefore the classifier constructed will be: $I(x \in S \cap B_k)$ $k = 1, 2, \ldots, K^*$

New instances are classified by the K-classifier as follows:

- The instance is assigned to the cluster closest to it: B_k : $k = \arg\min \|x - \mu_k\|$.
- The classifier induced using B_k is employed for assigning a class to the instance.

We analyze the extent to which the conditions surrounding the basic K-classifier may lead to its success or failure. This is done using three representative classification algorithms: C4.5, Neural network and Naïve Bayes. These algorithms, denoted by "DT", "ANN" and "NB" respectively, are employed on eight databases from the UCI repository, once in their basic form and once combined with the K-classifier. The classification error rate, resulting from the decomposition, is measured and compared to that achieved by the basic algorithm using McNemar's test [Dietterich (1998)]. The maximum number of clusters is set to a sufficiently large number (25). These experiments are executed 5 times for each database and each classifying algorithm, in order to reduce the variability resulting from the random choice of training set in McNemar's test.

In order to analyze the causes for the K-classifier's success/failure, a Meta dataset has been constructed. This dataset contains a tuple for each experiment on each database with each classifying algorithm. Its attributes correspond to the characteristics of the experiment:

Record-attribute ratio Calculated as the training set size divided by the attribute set size.

Initial PRE the reduction in the SSE, resulting from partitioning the dataset from one cluster (the non partitioned form) to two. This characteristic was chosen since we suspect it indicates whether the data set should be partitioned at all.

Induction method the induction algorithm employed on the database.

In order to analyze the reduction in error rate as a function of the method and dataset characteristics, a meta-classifier is constructed. The inducer employed for this purpose is the C4.5 algorithm.

As for the target attribute, it represents the accuracy performance of the basic K-classifier algorithm relatively to the appropriate accuracy performance of the inducer employed in the base form. The target attribute can have one of the following values: non-significant decrease/increase of up to ten percent ("small ns dec/inc"), non-significant decrease/increase of ten percent or more ("large ns dec/inc"), significant decrease/increase of up to ten percent ("small s dec/inc"), significant decrease/increase of ten percent or more ("large s dec/inc"), and a decrease rate of 0 percent ("no change"). The resultant decision tree is presented in Figure 7.1.

As may be learned from the tree, the two attributes that determine whether or not the K-classifier would achieve a significant decrease in error rate are the record-attribute ratio and the initial PRE. A significant decrease in error rate may occur when the former characteristic exceeds 20.67 and the latter exceeds 0.2. This result also answers the question: should there always be a recommended partition? This question may be viewed as a preliminary check of the dataset, aiming at discovering whether or not it requires space decomposition.

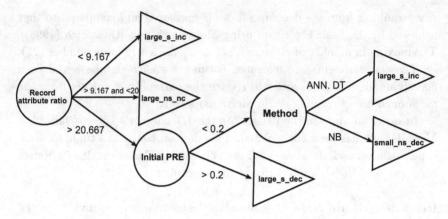

Fig. 7.1   A Decision Tree Describing the Change in Error Achieved by the K-Classifier.

When the record-attribute ratio is smaller than 20.67 or is equal to, the result will be a significant increase in the error rate, or at the very least — a non-significant increase. Therefore, it may be concluded that datasets containing a small number of records compared to their number of attributes should not be partitioned using the K-classifier algorithm.

Another conclusion that may be drawn from this stage is that the K-classifier algorithm works better on integer or continuous-valued attributes. Though the algorithm did not significantly decrease the error on all databases of such values, the ones on which the error decreased significantly contained integer attributes, continuous-valued attributes or some combination of these two kinds.

7.2   The Heterogeneity Detecting K-Classifier (HDK-Classifier)

7.2.1   *Overview*

The analysis of error reduction rate provides the basic K-classifier with the missing link concerning when clustering should be used. As we suspected, decomposition does not always yield an accuracy gain, and may deteriorate on many occasions. Such results may derive from the homogeneity, or lack of heterogeneity of the dataset: there are no distinct clusters or populations in the dataset, and therefore it should not be partitioned.

The mutual information criterion, used in the basic K-classifier, does not examine whether heterogeneity exists. It simply assumes it exits and aims at finding the number of populations in the data, given that the dataset is indeed composed of different populations.

Should we detect non-heterogeneous datasets, there is no need to decompose them, since their error will not decrease. The current K-classifier, increasing the running time complexity compared to the basic learning algorithm, only yields worse results on such datasets. We refine the basic K-classifier, and add another step, to be taken first. In this step the K-means is employed for $K = 1$ and $K = 2$, and it is checked whether the resultant PRE is larger than 0.2. If so, the rest of the K-classifier stages follow. If this is not so, it is assumed that there is no use in decomposition, therefore instead of so the inducer in its base form is employed on the entire dataset. Thus, the algorithm maintains the accuracy of non-heterogeneous datasets at the expense of an additional complexity that is much smaller compared to the basic K-classifier.

7.2.2 Running-Time Complexity

The offered training algorithm requires the following computations:

- During the stages of determining the best number of clusters, the K-means algorithm is run $K_{max} - 1$ times, leading to a complexity of $O(T \cdot K_{max}^2 \cdot n \cdot m)$.
- Computation of the PRE's value for $K = 1$ and $K = 2$ is of $O(n \cdot m)$ complexity and is therefore negligible.
- Constructing a classifier on each of the K^* partitions requires at most $O(K_{max} \cdot G_I(m, n))$, where G_I is the classifier's training complexity time. For instance, when employing the decision tree algorithm, the time complexity of this stage will be at most $O(K_{max} \cdot m\sqrt{l})$, where the number of leaves of the decision tree is l.

In light of the above analysis the total running-time complexity of the training algorithm is $O(T \cdot K_{max}^2 \cdot n \cdot m + K_{max} \cdot G_I(m, n))$. In the case of decision trees classifiers, for instance, the time-complexity would be: $O(T \cdot K_{max}^2 \cdot n \cdot m + K_{max} \cdot m\sqrt{l})$.

7.3 Experimental Study

We evaluate the performance of the HDK-classifier on a set of 9 UCI datasets, using the same learning methods combined with the K-classifier and McNemar's test for algorithm comparison. Note that the datasets used in this experiment have not been used in the preliminary experimental study. This fact is important as the HDK-classifier has been built based upon the results of the preliminary experimental study. Using a different set of datasets can be useful to validate that the HDK-Classifier has generalized beyond the first set of datasets.

The results obtained in this experiment indicate that employing the HDK-classifier algorithm has increased the misclassification rate on some occasions. An examination of these datasets indicates that this undesired outcome occurs when the training set has been relatively small. It is very likely that partitioning small databases into many subsets damaged the accuracy since each subset consisted of only a few records, thus containing very little information and was not well generalized. In order to prevent such phenomenon, it is required that each cluster will have at least 80 records. Such requirement is simply translated into a limitation of the number of clusters, since the K-means produces approximately equal-sized clusters.

The results of employing the HDK-classifier algorithm with the above limitation indicates that the new limitation seemed to have prevented the increase in error in most cases: Former non-significant increase in error rate turned into a non-significant decrease or even into a significant decrease, and significant increase in error rate turned into a non-significant increase.

7.4   Conclusions

In this chapter we presented a space decomposition approach to data mining. We implemented such a decomposition using the K-means clustering algorithm.

An important conclusion derived from our experiments regarding the heterogeneity of the data set: If it exists, it is very likely that space-based decomposition would improve accuracy. Specifically, we derived a PRE threshold for determining heterogeneity and combined it in our algorithm.

Other parameters that affect the effectiveness of the decomposition are also related to the degree to which the instance space and dataset are likely to be separable: record-attribute ratio as well as input data type.

Our heterogeneity detecting decomposition algorithm decreased error rate on what appeared to be heterogeneous datasets and did not increase it on almost all of the others. This was done at in the expense of some additional complexity. In contrary to popular sample-based decomposition methods, such as bagging, this method is also relatively understandable: it may be translated into a decision-tree-like scheme, describing the model to be used in case an instance is close to any of the cluster means (which are also easy to understand).

In this chapter we have presented a methodology for partitioning the instance space so as to decrease the generalization error. This methodology may be further examined and extended in several directions:

- Developing a combination method, taking into consideration all classifiers, built on the different subsets (for instance, using an EM clustering algorithm, and making some probabilistic combination)
- Adjusting the HDK-classifier algorithm to datasets with a continuous target attribute
- Suggesting alternative criteria for determining whether the dataset should be divided at all
- Examining whether different clustering algorithms yield various results
- Using clustering as a means for partitioning the attribute space, thus attempting to improve accuracy by attribute decomposition, rather than tuple decomposition

Chapter 8

Sample Decomposition

8.1 Overview

This chapter introduces a concurrent sample decomposition technique, known as Cluster Based Concurrent Decomposition (CBCD) that decomposes the training set into mutually exclusive equal-size sub-samples. This algorithm first clusters the instance space by using the K-means clustering algorithm. Afterwards it produces the disjoint sub-samples using the clusters such that each sub-sample is comprised from tuples of all clusters and hence represents the entire dataset. An induction algorithm is applied to each subset in turn, followed by a voting mechanism that combines the classifiers predictions. The CBCD algorithm has two tuning parameters: the number of clusters and the number of subsets to create. Using a suitable meta-learning it is possible to tune these parameters properly. In the experimental study conducted the CBCD algorithm using the embedded C4.5 algorithm has outperformed the bagging algorithm with the same computational complexity.

8.2 Tuple Sampling

Tuple sampling is an approach for coping with very large databases. It involves the selecting of a single small sample (subset) from the entire dataset for the learning task. [Blum and Langley (1997)] mention three main reasons for sampling examples during the learning phase:

(1) If sufficient training data is available, it makes sense to learn only from some examples for purposes of computational efficiency.
(2) If cost of labeling is high, one can use unlabeled examples, which are

available or are easy to generate.

(3) It increases the rate of learning by focusing attention on informative examples.

The differences between the sampling techniques involve the selection procedure used. [Catlett (1991)] studied the following three methods for sampling:

- Random sampling — samples are selected randomly.
- Duplicate compaction — duplicated instances are removed from the database. This technique assumes that repeated tuples are redundant. However, this technique distorts the original distribution of the database.
- Stratified sampling — a technique that is applicable when the class values are not uniformly distributed in the training sets. Instances of the minority classes are selected with a greater frequency in order to even out the distribution. The main claim of the technique is that increasing the proportion of rare classes may lead to better accuracy on data instances labeled with those rare classes.

In general Catlett showed that learning through sampling decreases accuracy in comparison to using the entire dataset. However, using smaller samples may be necessary and essential when the databases are very large and could reduce complexity and the run time of learning algorithms.

8.3   Problem Formulation

Recall from Chapter 5 the basic problem discussed in this chapter can be phrased as follows:

Given a learning method I, a combination method C, and a training set S with input attribute set $A = \{a_1, a_2, \ldots, a_n\}$ and target attribute y from a distribution D over the labeled instance space, the goal is to find an optimal decomposition T_{opt} of the training set S into ξ subsets $E_k \subseteq S$; $k = 1, \ldots, \xi$ fulfilling ($\bigcup_{k=1}^{\xi} E_k$) $\subseteq S$ and $E_i \cap E_j = \emptyset$; $i, j = 1, \ldots, \xi$; $i \neq j$ such that the generalization error of the C-combination of the induced classifiers of the induced classifiers $I(E_k), k = 1, \ldots, \xi$ will be minimized over the distribution D.

It should be noted that the sample selection problem could be considered as a specific case of the sample decomposition problem defined here. The aim is to find the smallest sufficient subset of the dataset and by using a superset of it will not improve accuracy. The rational of using the sampling idea is that having massive amounts of data does not necessary imply that induction algorithms must use the entire dataset. Samples often provide the same accuracy with far less computational cost. Sampling techniques, which give only an approximate quality guarantee, but can make runtimes almost independent of the size of the dataset, are presented in [Provost *et al.* (1999)].

This chapter focusses on exhaustive sample decomposition (namely $\bigcup_{k=1}^{\xi} E_k = S$) designed for decision trees ($I = C4.5$ Algorithm) which are combined using the simple voting combination ($C=Voting$).

8.4 The CBCD Algorithm

The suggested algorithm denoted as CBCD (**C**luster **B**ased **C**oncurrent **D**ecomposition) creates mutually exclusive equal-sized subsets of training data by using the K-means clustering method. Each of these disjoint subsets is comprised of tuples from each cluster and hence represents the entire dataset. The C4.5 decision tree is then applied to each subset in turn, followed by a voting method that combines the classifiers predictions.

The main stages of CBCD algorithm are:

- Dividing the instance space into K clusters.
- Creating ψ subsets, based on the clusters.
- Constructing a classifier for each subset.

When a new instance is required to be classified the following steps are performed:

- Classify the new instance according to the classifiers constructed from each subset.
- Applying a combination procedure that combines the classifiers predictions.

The input of the algorithm is the training set, the number of subsets to be examined (ψ) and the number of clusters (K).

8.4.1 *Stages of the Algorithm*

The following subsections present the three stages of the proposed algorithm.

8.4.1.1 *Stage 1 — Apply the K-Means Algorithm on the Entire DataSet S.*

A given training set is clustered into K mutually exclusive clusters (namely, each instance belongs to only one group): $C_k \subseteq S$ $k = 1, \ldots, K$, resulting from the K-means clustering algorithm, fulfilling ($\bigcup_{k=1}^{K} C_k$) = S and $C_i \cap C_j = \emptyset; i, j = 1, \ldots, K; i \neq j$.

Clustering methods group the data instances in such a manner that instances that bear a strong resemblance to one another are grouped together within the same cluster, while those that are dissimilar are grouped into other clusters. The aim of the clustering method is to form high intraclass similarity and low interclass similarity.

The clustering method chosen for this task is the K-means algorithm, extended to allow mixed-type attributes. This extension uses a similarity measure that is suited for mixed-type attributes and calculates the cluster centers of non-numeric attributes using their modes instead of means. The K-means was chosen for several reasons:

- The K-means algorithm is suited to data mining and very efficient in processing large databases due to its linear complexity. It is much faster than the hierarchical methods whose general computational complexity is non-linear.
- The K-means algorithm is simple, easy to interpret and understandable to the user.
- It is the most common clustering algorithm and therefore highly accessible and relatively available.

8.4.1.2 *Stage 2 — Produce the ψ Subsets Based on the K Clusters Created Sn Stage 1.*

The given clustered training set is partitioned into ψ mutually exclusive subsets $B_k k = 1, \ldots, \psi$. After grouping the data into clusters (in Stage 1), we then randomly select some records from each cluster in order to form each of the ψ subsets. The distribution of instances from each cluster in the subsets is proportional to the size of the cluster (i.e. the ratio of instances from each cluster in the whole dataset is preserved). That process yields mutually exclusive subsets that represent the whole database. For example, in the case of building 4 subsets based on 3 clusters, randomly different quarters of the instances from each cluster are used to form each of the four subsets.

8.4.1.3 *Stage 3 — Produce ψ Classifiers by Applying the C4.5 Learning Algorithm on the ψ Cluster-Based Subsets.*

Induction algorithms are applied on each of the K subsets. A classifier (model) is produced from each one. A beneficial side effect of using smaller datasets for classifiers such as decision trees is that the classifiers obtained are smaller in size [Oates and Jensen (1998)]. The induction algorithm chosen for this task is the C4.5 algorithm for the following reasons:

- The algorithm deals both with numerical and nominal attributes.
- Research results have demonstrated that this algorithm achieves quite good results [Brazdil *et al.* (1994)].
- The decision tree generated by C4.5 can be inspected and analyzed quite easily by the user.

Figure 8.1 illustrates the various stages of the CBCD algorithm.

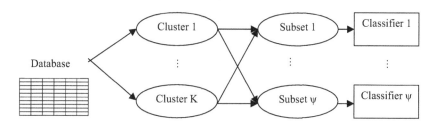

Fig. 8.1 The CBCD Stages.

8.4.2 *Running-Time Complexity Analysis*

The offered training algorithm requires the following computations:

- The first step of the CBCD algorithm is the running of the K-means algorithm, it leads to complexity of: K-means $(m, K) \rightarrow O(TKnm)$, where n is the number of attributes, m is the number of instances, K is the number of clusters and T is the number of the algorithm's iterations.

- Creating the subsets from the clustered instances is negligible due to the fact that the complexity of this process is: $O(m)$.
- Building the ψ classifiers from the subsets (each contains m/ψinstances) leads to the following complexity: $\psi \cdot InducerComplexity(m/\psi)$. The complexity of the C4.5 algorithm used here strongly depends on whether there are numeric attributes in the dataset.

8.4.3   *Classifying New Instances*

Figure 8.2 describes the procedure for classifying new instances. New instance would be classified as follows:

- The ψ classifiers induced will be employed on the new instance
- Voting method will be applied in order to coalesce the ψ predictions and to yield a final prediction.

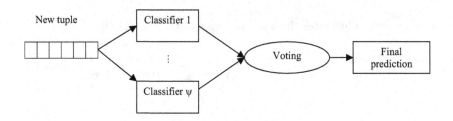

Fig. 8.2   Classifying New Instance.

8.5   An Illustrative Example

For demonstrating the suggested algorithm we use the weather dataset [Mitchell (1997)]. This tiny dataset describes the days on which a certain person is willing to play tennis. Each day is characterized using four input attributes that measure different weather conditions. The target attribute indicates whether that person decided to play on these days.

As shown in Table 8.1, two of the four attributes are categorical and the other two are numeric. The outlook can be *sunny, overcast* or *rainy*;

temperature and humidity have numeric values; and windy can be *true* or *false*. Fourteen different combinations are present in the set of input examples. The following sections demonstrate our suggested technique, and include error estimation by using training and test sets.

Table 8.1 The Weather Dataset.

Outlook	Temperature	Humidity	Windy	Play
sunny	75	70	TRUE	yes
rainy	71	91	TRUE	no
sunny	69	70	FALSE	yes
rainy	65	70	TRUE	no
rainy	70	96	FALSE	yes
rainy	75	80	FALSE	yes
sunny	72	95	FALSE	no
overcast	72	90	TRUE	yes
overcast	83	86	FALSE	yes
rainy	68	80	FALSE	yes
overcast	64	65	TRUE	yes
sunny	80	90	TRUE	no
sunny	85	85	FALSE	no
overcast	81	75	FALSE	yes

8.5.1 Step 1 – Creating a Training Set

The available training set S is randomly divided into a training set of specified size (two thirds of the data, namely nine instances) and a test set, which contains the remaining instances.

Table 8.2 Train Set.

Outlook	Temperature	Humidity	Windy	Play
sunny	75	70	TRUE	yes
rainy	71	91	TRUE	no
sunny	72	95	FALSE	no
overcast	83	86	FALSE	yes
rainy	68	80	FALSE	yes
sunny	80	90	TRUE	no
overcast	72	90	TRUE	yes
overcast	81	75	FALSE	yes
rainy	70	96	FALSE	yes

Table 8.3   Test Set.

Outlook	Temperature	Humidity	Windy	Play
rainy	75	80	FALSE	yes
sunny	69	70	FALSE	yes
rainy	65	70	TRUE	no
sunny	85	85	FALSE	no
overcast	64	65	TRUE	yes

8.5.2   Step 2 – Performing Clustering

The training set contains nine instances and is divided into clusters by applying the K-means clustering algorithm on the dataset. For the purpose of this example, we decided to divide the instances into two clusters, from which two subsets are created.

Table 8.4   First Cluster.

Outlook	Temperature	Humidity	Windy	Play
rainy	71	91	TRUE	no
sunny	72	95	FALSE	no
rainy	68	80	FALSE	yes
rainy	70	96	FALSE	yes

Table 8.5   Second Cluster.

Outlook	Temperature	Humidity	Windy	Play
sunny	75	70	TRUE	yes
overcast	83	86	FALSE	yes
sunny	80	90	TRUE	no
overcast	72	90	TRUE	yes
overcast	81	75	FALSE	yes

8.5.3   Step 3 – Creating the Subsets

In order to create the two subsets, we then unify half of the instances of each cluster ($1/_{\psi=2}$) into one final subset that represents the whole database. A total of two such subsets are created.

8.5.4   Step 4 – Performing Induction

After creating the subsets, induction algorithms (learning algorithms) are trained on each subset. From each one a classifier (model) is produced. The

Table 8.6   First Subset.

Outlook	Temperature	Humidity	Windy	Play	Origin Cluster
rainy	71	91	TRUE	no	cluster 1
sunny	72	95	FALSE	no	cluster 1
sunny	75	70	TRUE	yes	cluster 2
overcast	83	86	FALSE	yes	cluster 2

Table 8.7   Second Subset.

Outlook	Temperature	Humidity	Windy	Play	Origin Cluster
rainy	68	80	FALSE	yes	cluster 1
rainy	70	96	FALSE	yes	cluster 1
sunny	80	90	TRUE	no	cluster 2
overcast	72	90	TRUE	yes	cluster 2
overcast	81	75	FALSE	yes	cluster 2

following figure presents the results obtained by running the J4.5 algorithm in the Weka package. Note that the decision tree of subset 2 is degenerate, as it classifies all instances as "yes", ignoring the input attributes values.

8.5.5   *Step 5 – Testing the Classifiers*

The resulting classifiers are tested on the test set and the voting method is applied in order to combine the two classifications for a given instance. The C4.5 decision tree provides at the leaf nodes the classification, namely in the voting method the class with the highest classification frequency is chosen to be the final decision. Using the voting method on labeled test data enable us to estimate the accuracy level. In this example an accuracy level of 80% is achieved (see Table 8.8). In the case of only one classifier trained from the entire training set, only 60% accuracy is obtained.

Table 8.8   The Classifier Prediction Table.

Test Set Instance	Class value	Classifiers prediction
rainy,75,80,FALSE,yes	yes	yes
sunny,69,70,FALSE,yes	yes	yes
rainy,65,70,TRUE,no	no	no
sunny,85,85,FALSE,no	no	yes
overcast,64,65,TRUE,yes	yes	yes

```
Decision tree (subset 1)


Temperature <= 72:  no (2.0)
Temperature > 72:  yes (2.0)


Number of Leaves:  2
Size of the tree:  3




Decision tree (subset 2)


yes (5.0/1.0)


Number of Leaves:  1
Size of the tree:  1
```

Fig. 8.3   The J4.5 Output.

8.6   Experimental Study

In order to evaluate the efficiency of the technique, we compare the results achieved using two different methods:

- The C4.5 algorithm applied to the entire dataset.
- The CBCD algorithm, which uses the same basic learning algorithm, C4.5, on each of the data subsets.

The experimental study has multiple aims:

- To find the circumstances under which the CBCD algorithm performs better than the implementation of C4.5 on the entire dataset.
- Using the results to determine what number of clusters and subsets is needed, for a given database, in order to yield a significant accuracy

improvement using the CBCD algorithm.

8.6.1 *Data Sets Used*

Most of the databases in this experiment were taken from the UCI-Machine Learning Repository. As most of the datasets are real-world data, they tend to be incomplete, noisy and inconsistent. One of the KDD stages that attempt to handle such problems is the data cleaning process. This stage includes the filling of missing values. Several solutions are offered in such cases [Han and Kamber (2001)]:

- Ignore the instance.
- Fill in the missing value manually.
- Use the attribute mean or mode to fill in the missing value.
- Use the attribute mean or mode for all samples belonging to the same class as the given instance.
- Use the most probable value to fill in the missing value.

In this experiment missing data have been replaced with the attribute mean or mode. We avoided ignoring instances due to the fact that some of the databases are not large enough and instances containing missing values may enclose relevant information.

8.6.2 *Experimental Stages*

As stated above the number of subsets generated may affect the accuracy obtained. During the experimental stages, we examined the accuracy level obtained by using different combinations of clusters and subsets.

8.6.2.1 *Stage 1 — Partitioning the Dataset*

Using the same instances to train the classifiers and then to estimate their accuracy may result in misleading estimates due to overfitting. Therefore, as a preliminary step, before employing any induction algorithm on the data, we randomly partitioned the datasets into two independent sets. Two thirds of the original dataset is allocated to the training set from which the classifiers were derived. The remaining instances were allocated to the test set, from which the accuracy of the classifiers is estimated.

8.6.2.2 *Stage 2 — Applying the CBCD Algorithm on the Datasets*

In order to examine in which cases the CBCD algorithm performs well, we varied the number of clusters and number of subsets from 1 to 10. Namely, we applied the CBCD for all of the possible combinations of the two parameters: the number of clusters and the number of subsets (totally 100 combinations).

Following the completion of the test instances' classification, it was possible to achieve the accuracy result. Table 8.9 presents the accuracy results achieved while applying the CBCD algorithm on the Aust database, using the different combinations of the two parameters.

Table 8.9   Accuracy of Different Clusters and Subsets Combinations (AUST).

	Subset									
Cluster	1	2	3	4	5	6	7	8	9	10
1	0.830	0.8	0.821	0.847	0.830	0.843	0.847	0.847	0.856	0.847
2	0.830	0.778	0.821	0.817	0.839	0.843	0.847	0.847	0.852	0.847
3	0.830	0.786	0.813	0.847	0.839	0.821	0.847	0.826	0.847	0.847
4	0.830	0.795	0.821	0.834	0.839	0.856	0.852	0.847	0.852	0.847
5	0.830	0.782	0.821	0.847	0.847	0.847	0.852	0.847	0.847	0.852
6	0.830	0.795	0.821	0.817	0.821	0.852	0.852	0.843	0.826	0.847
7	0.830	0.795	0.830	0.839	0.834	0.843	0.847	0.847	0.852	0.852
8	0.830	0.795	0.830	0.782	0.8	0.847	0.839	0.843	0.847	0.856
9	0.830	0.826	0.8087	0.834	0.847	0.817	0.847	0.847	0.847	0.839
10	0.830	0.804	0.813	0.821	0.839	0.830	0.852	0.847	0.839	0.847

Note that the values in the first column (for the one subset case) are identical over the different cluster numbers due to the fact that one subset yields one decision tree, thus the division to clusters is superfluous. The first row's values are, in fact, the results obtained from using random subsets due to the fact that they based on a single cluster only, thus the subsets are not comprised of instances from different clusters.

In order to examine the significance of the results, the test has been repeated ten times. In each of the runs, the database is randomly split into a training set (two thirds of the data) and a test set (one third of the data). At the end of this running process, ten accuracy levels are achieved for each combination.

8.6.2.3 *Stage 3 — Employing the Paired T Test*

After completing the ten runs, a paired T test is employed in order to compare the performance of the CBCD algorithm (using different combinations of cluster and subset numbers) to that of the basic C4.5 learning algorithm applied to the entire data.

Table 8.10 shows the accuracy levels achieved in ten trials for both methods: the basic algorithm, applied on the entire dataset, and the CBCD approach for the specific combination of two clusters from which two subsets were created. Table 8.11 shows the results of the paired T test applied on the data from Table 8.10.

Table 8.10 Comparing the Accuracy of the Two Different Methods.

Trial ♯	The C4.5 applied on the entire dataset.	2 subsets 2 clusters
Trial 1	0.830435	0.778261
Trial 2	0.817391	0.83913
Trial 3	0.813043	0.843478
Trial 4	0.795652	0.83913
Trial 5	0.826087	0.847826
Trial 6	0.852174	0.86087
Trial 7	0.83913	0.852174
Trial 8	0.821739	0.830435
Trial 9	0.830435	0.817391
Trial 10	0.782609	0.817391

Table 8.11 Example of the Results of T Rest: Paired Two Samples for Means.

	2 subset	C4.5 Applied on the entire dataset
Mean	0.832609	0.82087
Variance	0.00056	0.000411
Observations	10	10
Pearson Correlation	0.223378	
Hypothesized Mean Difference	0	
df	9	
t Stat	1.34981	
$P(T <= t)$ one-tail	0.105022	
t Critical one-tail	1.833114	
$P(T <= t)$ two-tail	0.210045	
t Critical two-tail	2.262159	

The results of the T test are represented in the form of P values. Once the P value is known, it is easer to determine how significant the results are without formally imposing pre-selected levels of significance.

Table 8.12 shows the P values achieved by implementing the CBCD algorithm using different combinations of the two parameters, ten times, and comparing the results to the C4.5 applied on the entire dataset (one subset).

Table 8.12   P-values of AUST Dataset.

Cluster	Subset 2	3	4	5	6	7	8	9	10
1	.02695	.00979	.0003	.00026	7E-5	8E-5	3E-5	3E-5	.00011
2	.10502	.01109	.011	.00026	9E-5	5E-5	8E-5	5E-5	.00015
3	.05061	.00348	.00072	.00024	.00124	5E-5	.00054	9E-5	.0001
4	.03629	.03178	.00577	.00039	9E-5	.00016	7E-5	.00022	6E-5
5	.13173	.00382	.00151	3E-5	.00012	8E-5	7E-5	4E-5	3E-5
6	.09264	.00757	.00262	.00096	6E-5	.00018	6E-5	.00048	.00012
7	.02228	.00695	.00399	.00017	.00021	8E-5	7E-5	2E-5	6E-5
8	.01809	.00461	.03218	.01535	7E-5	.00029	.00021	5E-5	2E-5
9	.00714	.00905	.00936	4E-5	.00464	.00016	6E-5	.00013	.00012
10	.01723	.00737	.00766	.00095	.00095	5E-5	9E-5	.00057	6E-5

It is useful to categorize the results into different classes according to the P values:

A significant improvement $P_{value} < 0.05$ and the accuracy level mean (obtained by ten runs) achieved by implementing the proposed method is greater than the serial case mean.

An insignificant improvement $P_{value} > 0.05$ and the accuracy level mean achieved by implementing the proposed method is greater than the serial case mean.

No change $P_{value} = 0.5$, namely the two means are equal.

An insignificant decrease $P_{value} > 0.05$ and the accuracy level mean achieved by implementing the proposed method is lower than the serial case mean.

A significant decrease $P_{value} < 0.05$ and the accuracy level mean achieved by implementing the proposed method is lower than the serial case mean.

In the cases of insignificant improvement or a decrease in accuracy, it is possible to divide the category into two subcategories. For example: An insignificant improvement in which $0.05 < P_{value} < 0.1$ and an insignificant improvement in which $P_{value} > 0.1$.

The categorization process of the test results, as described above, can be seen as a preparatory step for the meta-level learning task that will be detailed later.

The results indicates that there are databases (such as AUST, PAGE-BLOCK and VOTE) in which the CBCD algorithm outperforms the C4.5 run upon the entire dataset for all subsets and clusters combinations. Namely, the P values obtained for the T test results indicate a significant or non-significant improvement in all combinations examined. This result is encouraging considering the fact that in the worst case the computational complexity of C4.5 is greater than linear in the number of tuples. This means that the CBCD has obtained in these cases a higher accuracy in a less computational effort. However, in some other databases (such as TTT, DERMATOLOGY and NURSE), the proposed algorithm performed less than the opponent algorithm in all the combinations examined. In other databases (such as: GLASS and LED17) certain combinations performed better than the serial case and others performed worse. These combinations were mostly grouped into "areas" (clusters of combinations) that were characterized with similar behavior of accuracy.

It is possible to conclude that the behavior of the average accuracy obtained is strongly affected by the number of subsets, i.e. areas are formed where accuracy levels are similar and defined mainly by the number of subsets.

8.7 Conclusions

This chapter presented the sample decomposition problem and suggested the CBCD algorithm to address it. The experimental study conducted shows that the CBCD algorithm outperforms bagging with the same complexity. In some cases the CBCD algorithm even outperforms C4.5 run upon the entire dataset.

There are several issues that may be further investigated such as

- Extending the scope of the experimental stages, i.e. examining a larger amount of combinations of the two algorithm's parameters and examining more databases.
- Suggesting a method for predicting a useful combination of the numbers of subsets and clusters.

- Examining whether different clustering algorithms yield better accuracy results.

Chapter 9

Function Decomposition

9.1 Data Preprocessing

Many real-world databases contain noisy, incomplete and inconsistent data, i.e., data with errors, missing attribute values and inconsistency. This can occur for many reasons, such as faulty data collection instruments, human or computer errors during data entry, errors in data transmission, technology limitations, unavailable data, misunderstandings regarding the data recordings, inconsistencies in naming conventions or data codes and many more. In order to overcome these limitations and effectively use data mining tools, data should be preprocessed before it is presented to any learning, discovering or visualizing algorithms [Liu and Motoda (1998); Han and Kamber (2001)]. There are many data preprocessing techniques, divided by Han and Kamber into four categories: data cleaning techniques, data integration techniques, data transformation techniques and data reduction techniques. Some of the suggested methods may fall into more than one category.

Data cleaning techniques fill in missing values, smooth noisy data, identify outliers and correct inconsistencies in the data. Methods used for dealing with missing values include ignoring the tuple, filling in the missing value manually, using a global constant to fill in the missing value, using the attribute mean to fill in the missing value, using the attribute mean for all samples belonging to the same class as the given tuple, or using the most probable value to fill in the missing value. In order to deal with noisy data one can use mining methods, clustering methods, a combination of human and computer inspection techniques or regression techniques. Inconsistencies in the data can be detected and corrected manually using external references or by knowledge engineering tools.

Data integration techniques combine data from multiple sources into a coherent data store. These techniques deal with issues such as combining equivalent entities from multiple data sources, in which the entities appear differently. Metadata techniques are used in order to avoid this kind of problem. Another problem which data integration techniques deal with is redundancies. Redundancies may be caused by deriving the same attribute from different tables due to inconsistencies in attribute naming. Redundancies may be detected by correlation analysis. Detection and resolution of data value conflicts is also an issue in data integration.

Data transformation techniques transform the data into forms appropriate for mining. Data transformation methods include smoothing, aggregation, discretization, normalization, feature content modification (generalization, specialization) and feature bundling.

Data reduction techniques create a new representation for the data which is smaller in volume and has the same analytical results as the original representation. There are various strategies for data reduction: aggregation, dimension reduction, data compression, discretization and concept hierarchy.

9.2 Feature Transformation

Frequently, original data should be transformed into new forms in order to perform the mining task. Feature transformation techniques transform data into such mining appropriate forms. After removing noise from data, different transformation operations may be applied. Aggregation techniques are thoroughly discussed in the next section. Here, we present some other transformation methods.

Normalization is a kind of data transformation in which attribute values are scaled to fall within a specified range, such as 0 to 1. Normalization is usually carried out when neural networks or distance measurements are involved in the classification process. When using distance measurements normalization is very important, since it prevents attributes with large ranges from outweighing attributes with smaller ranges. Two examples of normalization methods are the *min-max normalization* and the *z-score normalization*.

In min-max normalization, a linear transformation is performed on the original data. The original values of the attribute a are mapped to new values such that:

$$v' = \frac{v - \min_a}{\max_a - \min_a}(new\_\max_a - new\_\min_a) + new\_\min_a \qquad (9.1)$$

where v is the original attribute value, v' is the new attribute value, $\min_a$ ($\max_a$) is the original minimum (maximum) value of attribute a and $new\_\min_a$ ($new\_\max_a$) is the new minimum (maximum) value of attribute a.

In z-score normalization, the normalization of an attribute value is based on its mean and standard deviation:

$$v' = \frac{v - \overline{a}}{\sigma_a} \qquad (9.2)$$

Discretization is another type of transformation applied on continuous data. In discretization the continuous attribute range is divided into intervals and a single label is assigned to the data values in each interval. The attribute is therefore represented by a reduced number of discrete values. Numerous methods exist for discretization, based on different theoretical origins such as, statistics, Boolean reasoning, clustering techniques and error and entropy calculations. These approaches can be roughly divided into unsupervised methods and supervised methods. Unsupervised methods rely on assumptions of the distributions of the attribute values, since there is no classification information available for the object being considered. In supervised methods classification information is available and taken into consideration in the discretization process. The ChiMerge algorithm [Kerber (1992)] and Entropy-Based Discretization [Han and Kamber (2001)] are examples for supervised discretization techniques. We present here one simple unsupervised discretization method which we use in our work.

The *Equal width discretization* is the simplest approach for discretization, in which the attribute values are partitioned into k equal-sized ranges. For each numerical attribute, a_i, with minimum value, $\min(v_{a_i})$, and maximum value, $\max(v_{a_i})$ the size of the interval, d, is calculated according to k:

$$d = \frac{\max(v_{a_i}) - \min(v_{a_i})}{k} \qquad (9.3)$$

This yields the following cuts in the intervals:

$$\min(v_{a_i}) + d, \min(v_{a_i}) + 2d, \ldots, \min(v_{a_i}) + (k-1)d \qquad (9.4)$$

Generalization is data transformation in which low-level data are replaced by higher-level concepts, using a concept hierarchy. The generalized data may be more meaningful and easier to interpret, and will require less space than the original data. Concept hierarchies for numeric attributes can be constructed based on data distribution analysis. There are various methods for numeric concept hierarchy generation. Binning, histogram analysis and entropy-based discretization can be applied recursively on the resulting partitions in order to generate concept hierarchies. Cluster analysis, in which clusters may be further decomposed into sub clusters to form a lower level of the hierarchy, or be grouped together in order to form a higher conceptual hierarchy level. Concept hierarchy may also be generated for categorical attributes, i.e., attributes which have a finite number of distinct values, with no ordering among the values. This is usually done manually by users or experts.

Another kind of feature transformation is Feature Bundling [Kusiak (2001B)], primarily intended for integer, normative and categorical features. A feature bundle is a collection of features in its pure or transformed form. In feature bundling, relationships are formed among features using logical operators, arithmetic operators or a regression function defined on a subset of features. Once the feature sequences are defined, the original dataset is transformed according to the newly created features and it is used for mining. In the new dataset feature values corresponding to feature sequences are merged.

9.2.1 *Feature Aggregation*

Feature aggregation is a feature transformation process through which a set of new features is created. The purpose of this process is to improve the estimated accuracy, visualization and comprehensibility of the learned knowledge. The two main feature aggregation approaches are feature construction and feature extraction.

Feature extraction is a process that extracts a set of new features from the original features through some functional mapping [Wyse *et al.* (1980)]. If we originally have n features, $a_1, a_2, \ldots, a_n$, after feature extraction we have a new set of m features, $b_1, b_2, \ldots, b_m$ $(m < n)$, where $b_i = F_i(a_1, a_2, \ldots, a_n)$ and F_i is a mapping function. The goal is to find a good functional mapping which discovers a minimum set of new features. Usually, the dimensionality of the new set is smaller than the one of the original set and the representation of the data is changed such that many mining techniques can be used more efficiently.

Dimensionality reduction for further processing and visualization [Fayyad *et al.* (2001)] are the most common uses of feature extraction. The main limitations of this approach are the time it consumes in searching for new good features and the fact that the original features should be kept.

One example of a feature extraction algorithm is the *Principal component analysis* (PCA), in which new features are formed from linear combination of the original data. This algorithm does not require class information. Another example for a feature extraction algorithm is through the use of *Feedforward neural networks*, in which the hidden units are used as newly extracted features. This process employs class information of the data and generates a nonlinear mapping between original data and new data.

Feature construction is a process that discovers missing information about the relationships between features and augments the space of features by inferring or creating additional features. If we originally have n features, $a_1, a_2, \ldots, a_n$, after feature construction we have $n + m$ features, $a_1, a_2, \ldots, a_n, a_{n+1}, \ldots, a_{n+m}$, where $a_{n+1}, a_{n+2}, \ldots, a_{n+m}$ are newly constructed features. The dimensionality of the new set is usually bigger than the original dimensionality. The newly constructed features are defined in terms of the original features, but the new representation achieves the mining objectives more efficiently. Since the dimensionality of the new set is increased by adding additional newly constructed features, not all features are kept. Potentially useful new features are kept, while others are removed according to some goodness measure.

Feature construction approaches are categorized into four groups: data driven approaches, which use available data in constructing new features, hypothesis driven approaches, which use previously generated hypotheses, knowledge based approaches, which use existing knowledge and domain knowledge and hybrid approaches. Many operators can be used in constructing new features. Common constructive operators are conjunction, disjunction, negation and Cartesian product for nominal features, and algebraic operators for numerical features. Domain knowledge is very important in determining the set of operators and search strategies.

9.3   Supervised and Unsupervised Discretization

In the case of numerical target attributes, the problem of aggregating the target attribute may be perceived as feature discretization, i.e. can be accomplished by applying methods for discretization of continuous features. It is useful to distinguish between supervised and unsupervised discretization methods.

Supervised discretization methods are methods that utilize the class labels. The 1R algorithm attempts to divide the domain of every continuous variable into pure bins, each containing a strong majority of one particular class [Holte (1993)]. The ChiMerge system [Kerber (1992)] uses the χ^2 test to determine when adjacent intervals should be merged, testing the hypothesis that the two adjacent intervals are statistically independent by making an empirical measure of the expected frequency of the classes. [Fayyad and Irani (1992)] present an entropy minimization based discretization method offering further motivation for deciding on the number of intervals.

Unsupervised discretization methods are ones which do not utilize instance labels. They include methods such as Equal Interval Width and Equal Frequency Intervals. If such methods were applied on a numerical target attribute, it is likely that classification information will be lost.

Applying these methods for our purposes may even result in a decrease in accuracy rate, since values which naturally differ from each other, and should be seen as different concepts, may be aggregated.

9.4   Function Decomposition

9.4.1   *Boolean Function Decomposition in Switching Circuits*

Function decomposition has been extensively studied in switching circuits. [Ashenhurst (1952)] and [Curtis (1962)] were the first researchers to address this issue. They suggested a method to iteratively decompose a Boolean function represented by a truth-table. This was done in order to derive a hierarchical structure of smaller functions that are realizable with simple logic gates. This method was fully automated, but it requires that a dataset which completely covers the the input space will be provided. Moreover, it can handle only noise-free Boolean functions. These requirements are not realistic to data mining applications.

An extension to the Ashenhurst–Curtis approach was suggested by

[Biermann *et al.* (1982)]. This extension included a decomposition of nominal-valued attributes and classes, but the method still requires a complete set of examples. [Wan and Perkowski (1992)] presented an approach for decomposing incompletely specified Boolean functions. Their approach used a new graph coloring method for the "don't care" assignment, and therefore could accept an incompletely specified function and perform a quasi-optimum assignment to the unspecified part of the function.

A method for the decomposition of switching functions, which can be also applied to incompletely specified, multiple-valued functions was proposed by [Luba (1995)]. Each multi-valued variable is encoded by a set of Boolean variables. [Perkowski *et al.* (1995)] proposed a generalized decomposition approach for switching circuits. This approach can be applied to binary and multiple-valued functions, which are completely specified, incompletely specified, and with generalized "don't cares". Although the authors identified the potential usefulness of function decomposition for machine learning, they presented this approach for switching circuits only.

9.4.2   *Feature Discovery by Constructive Induction*

Feature discovery has been investigated by the constructive induction field. Constructive induction, as defined by [Michalski (1986)], is a knowledge-intensive, domain-specific learning process, in which the system is able to derive new concepts during the learning process. The system contains numerous predefined concepts, knowledge structures, domain constraints, heuristic rules, and built in transformations relevant to the specific domain for which the system is built. Not all the relevant attributes or concepts are proved initially: the system is expected to derive new ones in the process of learning. Michalski claims that "pure" induction, which is direct inference from facts to theories without any interpretive concepts, is impossible. These concepts are needed to describe the observations and are part of the learner's background knowledge. According to Michalski, this background knowledge is a necessary component of any induction process and it also includes goals of learning, domain-specific constraints, causal relationships, heuristics and biases that guide the generalization process, and the criteria for evaluating competing hypotheses. Some examples of constructive induction systems, which use a set of constructive operators to derive new attributes, are described in [Michalski (1983); Ragavan and Rendell (1993); Pfahringer (1994)]. The limitation of these systems is that the set of constructive operators should be defined in advance. In addition, the main goal of constructive induction approaches is accuracy improvement while function decomposition approaches aim at complexity reduction.

9.4.3 *Function Decomposition in Data Mining*

The machine learning community realized long ago the importance of problem decomposition. The possible benefits derived from this process are more tractable, less complicated sub-problems and meaningful intermediate concepts.

The first decomposition approach to machine learning was suggested by [Samuel (1967)]. He proposed a method based on a signature table system and used it as an evaluation mechanism for a checkers playing program. An improvement to this method was suggested by [Biermann *et al.* (1982)], but in both approaches the concept structures which were used had to be given in advance.

An approach for problem decomposition by human expert is proposed by [Shapiro and Niblett (1982)]. The expert selects the relevant set of examples for each of the concepts from the training set and a decision tree is then built for each of these subsets. As a result, the structured classifier is checked against all the examples in the training set and improved by changing the concept representations, until all the training set is classified correctly. [Shapiro (1987)] implemented this approach for the classification of chess endgame. He showed that the complexity and comprehensibility of the obtained solution were superior to the unstructured one. The major drawback of this method is the manual selection of the hierarchy by the human expert which is a tedious process. Another drawback of this method is the impossibility to handle noisy data, missing attribute values and continuously-valued data. This approach is an example of structured induction, which in comparison with standard decision tree induction techniques, creates classifiers with the same accuracy, higher comprehensibility and lower complexity.

A method for decomposition of Boolean functions given a predefined concept structure is suggested by [Tadepalli and Russell (1998)]. These algorithms differ from the function decomposition approaches in that they use both examples and membership queries. This means that the learner supplies an instance to an oracle (perhaps a human expert) and is told its classification label. It is used for checking decomposability of some subset of attributes. The need of the oracle is the main drawback of these algorithms.

Moreover [Kohavi (1994)] suggested the use of oblivious, read-once decision graphs (OODGs) as structures for representing concepts over discrete domains. OODGs are rooted, directed acyclic graphs that can be divided into levels. All nodes at a level test the same attribute, and all the edges that originate from one level terminate at the next level. The class assigned by a decision graph to a given variable assignment (an instance), is determined by tracing the unique path from the root to the class node. Kohavi also suggested a bottom-up, hill-climbing algorithm for OODG construction. OODGs can be regarded as a special case of decomposition, where decomposition structures intermediate concepts and examples that completely cover the attribute space are needed.

More recently [Zupan *et al.* (1998)] presented a new suboptimal heuristic machine learning algorithm based on function decomposition, which given a consistent set of training examples, automatically induces a definition of the target concept in terms of a hierarchy of intermediate concepts and their definitions. For each concept in the resulting hierarchy there is a corresponding function, which determines the dependency of the concept on its immediate descendants in the hierarchy. The basic decomposition step is the core of this algorithm.

The basic decomposition step is a process which, given a set of consistent examples that partially specify a function and a partition of the attributes to two subsets, constructs a hierarchy of two functions: the first function defines a new intermediate concept based on the first subset of attributes (referred to as the bound set) and the other one defines the target concept based on the new defined concept and the second subset of attributes (referred to as the free set). For each of these functions a new equivalent dataset is built, which is consistent with the original training set.

At the beginning of this step, the partition matrix is built. The partition matrix is a tabular representation of the training set with each row corresponding to a distinct combination of values of attributes in the free set, and each column corresponding to a distinct combination of values of attributes in the bound set. Each example in the training set has its corresponding entry in the partition matrix. The elements of the partition matrix with no corresponding examples in the dataset are treated as "don't care". Columns that exhibit non-contradicting behavior are called compatible. In order to label the non-empty columns, the column incompatibility graph is then derived and colored according to the rule that only compatible columns can be assigned the same label. The column incompatibility graph is then derived and colored. It is a graph where each non-empty column of the partition matrix is represented by a vertex and two vertices are connected if and only if the corresponding columns are incompatible. The preferred labeling is the one which introduces the fewest number of distinct labels and is done by coloring the incompatibility graph.

Selecting the best partition of the attributes in the original training set to bound set and free set is done according to a partition selection measure, based on the complexity of the original and new functions. A few partition selection measures are suggested by Zupan (1998).

The overall decomposition algorithm, as suggested by Zupan, is a suboptimal greedy algorithm, which aims at discovering a hierarchy of concepts. This algorithm applies the basic decomposition step over the evolving datasets in a concept hierarchy, starting with the original dataset. The main limitation of this algorithm is that it cannot handle databases with noise. A consistency over the dataset is required by this algorithm, and mostly this is not the case with real world databases. [Perkowski *et al.* (1998)] presented a constructive induction system based on function decomposition, where their goal was to extend the decomposition approach to realistic data that has continuous attribute values, missing attribute values and noise. Although they suggest the method for multivalued, multi-output relations, their presented program is limited to binary attributes and classes. In addition, the influence of their methods in terms of classification accuracy is not clear.

In order to overcome the limitation of noisy data, [Zupan *et al.* (2000)] presented an approach, which extends his previous function decomposition approach and is able to handle noise. The decomposition, in this approach, aims at minimizing the expected classification error.

The basic decomposition step, in this case, not only finds the corresponding new functions for a given attribute partition, but also estimates their classification error. The inconsistent dataset is first converted to the one that uses class distributions, that is, a class distribution vector is assigned to every distinct combination of attribute values in the training set. The accuracy of this dataset is estimated: each example in this dataset is classified to the class that minimizes the estimated error according to the m-error estimate. The sum of weighted errors (of all instances) is the estimated overall error if the classification is performed according to this set of examples. The algorithm then tries to derive an intermediate concept. The original dataset is represented by a partition matrix, where the entries of the matrix contain the distribution vectors of the corresponding value combinations. The algorithm tries to merge every two columns by summing-up the distribution vectors, resulting in a new partition matrix.

The estimated classification error of the new dataset is computed using the same method described above. The preferred merging is the one that gives the lowest estimated error and also a lower accuracy than the original one. The merging is continued until there is no improvement in the estimated accuracy. The new data sets, which represent the decomposed functions, are then constructed, according to the final partition matrix.

The overall decomposition uses its basic step to search for the attribute partition that minimizes the estimated error. The selected attribute partition is the one for which the column merging results in a dataset with the lowest estimated error. By applying the basic step recursively on the resulting two datasets, a concept hierarchy is discovered. Decomposition is not performed on a dataset if no attribute partition is found that would reduce the estimated error.

9.4.4 *Problem Formulation*

This chapter extends the single-step function decomposition defined in [Zupan *et al.* (1998)]. Recall from Chapter 5:

- $H = \{a_{\alpha(j)} \mid j = 1, \ldots, l\}$ —indicates a subset of A that contains l input attributes where i is the original attribute index in the set A.
- Intermediate concept F maps the space defined by the Cartesian product of the attributes in H into a single discrete attribute with ψ different values.
- We denote in x^1 the corresponding values of the attributes in H and in x^2 the values of the other attributes in A.

Consequently the function decomposition problem can be formally phrased as:

Given a learning method I and a training set S with input attribute set $A = \{a_1, a_2, \ldots, a_n\}$ and target attribute y from a distribution D over the labeled instance space, the goal is to find an optimal intermediate concept F over A such that the generalization error of the classifier $I(\{\langle F(x_i^1), x_i^2, y_i \rangle \mid i = 1, \ldots, m\})$ will be minimized over the distribution D.

9.5 The IBAC Algorithm

Currently available function decomposition methods can be either used as preprocessing algorithms or as inducers, but none of them use an induction algorithm as a part of the process. This section suggests a method based on function decomposition, which incorporates an induction method as a part of the process.

This section presents the IBAC (Inducer Based Attribute Combiner), a new algorithm for data preprocessing, which reduces the attribute dimension of a problem by combining attributes. The aim of this preprocessing algorithm is to improve the classification accuracy of the dataset. The new dataset, which contains the combined attributes instead of the original ones, may be more appropriate for the mining process and may produce better results than the original one. The algorithm combines classification methods and function decomposition, as it uses an internal inducer during the decomposition process.

The IBAC algorithm is an iterative preprocessing algorithm, which given an initial dataset, an inducer, and the maximum number of attributes to combine in a single iteration, produces a new dataset such that some of the attributes (denoted as H) is represented by a single attribute. The creation of this new attribute is performed as follows: First the original sample is partitioned into several sub-samples each of which refers to a certain value combination of the attributes in H. An inducer is activated on each sub sample. Then the obtained classifiers are compared. If two classifiers resemble each other it indicates that the two corresponding values should be represented in the new attribute as a single value. This process is repeated for all possible partitions of the attribute set A, and the best partition is selected. The output dataset from a certain iteration is the input dataset for the next iteration. The algorithm is performed iteratively until there is no improvement according to the stopping criterion.

In this algorithm, both input attributes and class are required to be nominal-valued with a finite cardinality of their set of values. In addition, the time complexity of the algorithm is reduced by bounding the number of attributes in H. In this work the size of H was limited to two.

Any induction algorithm can be chosen to be an internal inducer in this algorithm. This work employs the C4.5 and Naïve Bayes classification methods as internal inducers. Figure 9.1 outlines the flow of the IBAC Algorithm.

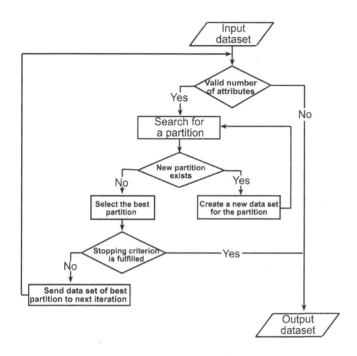

Fig. 9.1   The IBAC Algorithm.

9.5.1   *The Basic Stage*

9.5.1.1   *Initialization*

Given a partition of the attribute set, A, into two subsets, H and $A - H$, an inducer, I, and a division of the dataset into internal training set and internal test set, S_L and S_T, the basic stage of the algorithm creates a new dataset, which leaves the attributes in $A - H$ as-is and replaces the attributes in H with a single attribute.

The stage begins by finding all possible value combinations of the attributes in H. The cardinality of this Cartesian product is denoted as k. The instances in S_L and S_T are then divided into groups according to these value combinations. These sub-samples are denoted by $S_L = \{S_{L_1}, \ldots, S_{L_k}\}$ and $S_T = \{S_{T_1}, \ldots, S_{T_k}\}$ respectively. It is possible that $S_{L_i} = \emptyset$ or $S_{T_j} = \emptyset$ for some i, if there are no instances having the corresponding attribute value.

9.5.1.2   *Classifier Comparison*

The induction algorithm, I, is then activated on each of the nonempty subgroups of the internal training set, resulting in p classifiers, where p is the number of nonempty subgroups of the internal training set, $p \leq k$. The classifiers are represented as follows: $\{I(S_{L_i})|i = 1, \ldots, k; S_{L_i} \neq \emptyset\}$.

Each pair of classifiers is compared in order to determine if these classifiers are similar or not. Any two value combinations are considered similar if their corresponding classifiers $I(S_{L_i})$ and $I(S_{L_j})$ are similar. Any value combination that has no corresponding classifier ($S_{L_i} = \emptyset$), is determined to be similar to all other combinations.

For comparing classifiers the Cross Inspection procedure suggested by [Maimon, Rokach and Cohen (2002)] is used. This procedure gets two samples and two inducers as input parameters. It starts by randomly partitioning each sample into a training set and a test set. Then two classifiers are induced one from each training set. If the error of the first classifier over the first test set is significantly different from the error of the first classifier over the second test set, or vice versa, then the two classifiers are considered different. The hypothesis in cross inspection is tested by statistically estimating the difference in proportions of two binomial random variables.

The *dissimilarity matrix* is then built. The dissimilarity matrix is a squared matrix consisting of k rows and columns. Each row or column represents one value combination of the attributes in H. The entries of the matrix represents the dissimilarity between corresponded classifiers where a value of "0" represents "similar" while value of "1" represents "dissimilar". Note that the dissimilarity matrix is symmetric.

9.5.2   *Assigning Values to the New Attribute*

The dissimilarity matrix is converted into *dissimilarity graph*. The dissimilarity graph is a graph where each combination of values of attributes in H is represented by a vertex, v_i, and an edge (v_i, v_j) connects two vertices if the corresponding combinations are dissimilar. The number of values for the new attribute which replaces the attributes in H in the new resulting dataset is the lowest number of groups of mutually similar combinations. This number is derived by the coloring of the dissimilarity graph.

Graph coloring is an approach in which every two vertices linked by an edge are assigned different colors. In our case, the minimal number of colors needed to color the dissimilarity graph corresponds to the lowest number of groups of mutually similar combinations. Graph coloring is an NP-hard problem, so a heuristic approach should be employed here. In this case the Color Influence Method suggested by [Perkowski (1995)] has been chosen as it has polynomial complexity and good performance compared to the optimal algorithm.

The vertices (combinations) are first sorted in a decreasing order by their connectivity level (the number of vertices it is linked to). A color is assigned to each vertex in turn (according to the above sort order). The vertex can have a new color or a color that has already been used for other vertices. The decision depends on the following procedure. For every previously used color, the *degree of similarity* between the current vertex and each of the vertices assigned to that color is evaluated. The degree of similarity between two vertices is the number of vertices they are both either similar or dissimilar. The current vertex is assigned to the color that has obtained the highest degree of similarity on condition that the degree of similarity has passed a certain threshold. If no appropriate color has been found, then a new color is assigned to this vertex.

The colors correspond to values of the new combined attribute. The assigned values are *1,2,...,w*, where w is the number of different colors needed in order to color the graph. Each combination of values of the attributes in H is replaced by its corresponding value in the new dataset.

9.5.3   Creating the New Dataset

After assigning the values to the new attribute, the new dataset, S_{NEW} can be built. For each row $i = 1, \ldots, m$ in the original dataset, a corresponding row $i_{NEW} = 1, \ldots, m$ is built in the new dataset. First, the new row contains the values of the attributes in $A - H$ of the original row, j. Then, the new row contains the value of the new attribute which corresponds to the combination of values of the attributes in H in the original row, j. Finally, the new row contains the value of the target attribute, y, which appears in the original row.

9.5.4   Selection Criterion and Stopping Criterion

The basic stage is performed for every possible partition of the attribute set, A, into two subsets H and $A - H$, which fulfills the restriction on the size of H. For each partition, the basic stage builds a new dataset. After building all the new datasets for all possible partitions, the best partition is chosen, according to a selection criterion, and its new dataset is the new output dataset for the iteration.

For each partition i, the new dataset, S_{NEW}, is divided to internal training and test sets, S_{NL} and S_{NT}. The records of the new internal train set, S_{NL}, correspond to records in the original internal train set, S_L, and the records of the new internal test set, S_{NT}, correspond to the records of the original internal test set, S_T. A classifier is then built by activating the induction algorithm, I, on the new training set, S_{NL}, and the accuracy of this classifier over the records in the new internal test set, S_{NT}, is found.

According to the selection criterion, the best partition is the one which produces the dataset with minimal accuracy and its new attribute domain size, i.e. the number of values of the new attribute, does not exceed $\overline{D}$ which is a predefined limitation on the domain size of any new attribute. If more than one partition can be selected, the one with the minimal number of values of the new attribute will be preferred.

The new dataset contains m rows as the original number of rows, and a smaller number of attributes. Since we also limit the domain size of the new attribute, the attribute dimension is reduced.

If the selected partition does not fulfill the stopping criterion, its dataset is the output of the current iteration and the input for the next iteration.

According to the stopping criterion, if the accuracy of the created dataset of the selected partition is better than the accuracy of the initial dataset (the input for the iteration), the new dataset is the output for this iteration and an additional iteration will be performed. If the accuracy of the new dataset is lower from or equal to the accuracy of the initial dataset, then the algorithm ends and the output is the initial dataset of the last performed iteration, S.

In addition, when the iteration is started, the number of attributes in the dataset is checked. If the attributes number in the initial dataset is equal to or lower than 3, the algorithm ends and the output is the initial dataset of this iteration.

9.5.5   *Time Complexity Analysis*

The discussion on the complexity of the suggested algorithm is divided into two parts: the complexity of the first iteration and the complexity of the rest of the iterations. Assuming that $G_I(m, n)$ represents the time complexity for building a classifier using inducer I, on a dataset with m rows and n attributes, the first iteration requires the following computations:

- The number of possible partitions of A when $b = 2$ is $0.5 \cdot n(n-1)$
- The time complexity for building all possible classifiers for a single partition, using I, where $d_{\max}^2$ is the maximal number of value combinations for a single partition is $O\left(d_{\max}^2 \cdot G_I(m,n)\right)$.
- The time complexity for the comparisons between classifiers, where $0.5 \cdot \left(d_{\max}^2(d_{\max}^2 - 1)\right)$ is the maximal number of comparisons between classifiers for a single partition and m is the time complexity of the Cross Inspection method, thus we obtain $O\left(d_{\max}^4 \cdot m\right)$.
- The time complexity for the graph coloring procedure, where $d_{\max}^2$ is the maximal number of vertices in the graph is $O\left(d_{\max}^2\right)$.
- The time complexity for creating the new dataset of a single partition is $O(m)$ so is the time complexity for finding the accuracy of the classifier built on the new dataset for a single partition.

Following the first iteration there is only one new attribute in comparison to the previous iterations. Therefore, the basic stage should be performed only for partitions with the new attribute in H. For the remaining partitions, the sample accuracy for the new generated dataset is still needs to be evaluated.

9.5.6 *Classifying New Instances*

After the IBAC preprocessing algorithm generates a new dataset, a classifier is built on this new dataset, using any classification algorithm in a data mining process. In order to classify new examples according to this classifier, the new examples, which most likely appear in the form of the original dataset, should be transformed into the form of the new dataset. This is done by applying the same transformation used in the training phase.

9.5.7 *Example*

This section demonstrates the IBAC on the Breast Cancer databases, obtained from UCI repository. This database contains 9 input attributes; each has 10 possible integer values, and a target attribute with 2 possible values. The attributes and their possible values are summarized in Table 9.1.

This Breast Cancer dataset contains 699 records, 629 of which are used

Table 9.1   Attribute Information of Wisconsin Cancer Database.

Attribute	Domain
a_1 - Clump Thickness	1-10
a_2 - Uniformity of Cell Size	1-10
a_3 - Uniformity of Cell Shape	1-10
a_4 - Marginal Adhesion	1-10
a_5 - Single Epithelial Cell Size	1-10
a_6 - Bare Nuclei	1-10
a_7 - Bland Chromatin	1-10
a_8 - Normal Nucleoli	1-10
a_9 - Mitoses	1-10
y - Class	2 for benign, 4 for malignant

to generate the classifier and the remaining 70 records are used as an external test set, in order to examine the results. The C4.5 is used as the internal classifier and $\overline{D} = 50$. The training set is divided into the internal training set (419 records) and the internal test (210 records). The initial accuracy of a classifier built on the internal training set and tested over the internal test set is 92.38%.

In the first iteration the basic stage is performed on each of the possible partitions (there are 36 possible partitions assuming $b = 2$). For example, the partitioning of the dataset into $H = \{a_4, a_6\}$ and $A - H = \{a_1, a_2, a_3, a_5, a_7, a_8, a_9\}$, has 100 possible different value combinations. A classifier is built on each subgroup corresponding to each of these value combinations and then the Cross Inspection method is used for comparing these classifiers. The accepted dissimilarity matrix for this partition contains 100 rows and 100 columns. The new attribute is obtained by coloring the dissimilarity graph.

According to the selection criterion, the partition with maximal accuracy should be selected. The results show that the maximal accuracy is 96.67% and there are 5 partitions with this accuracy. Therefore, the partition which produces a new attribute with a minimal number of values is selected. In this case the selected partition is $H = \{a_1, a_2\}$ and $A - H = \{a_3, a_4, a_5, a_6, a_7, a_8, a_9\}$ (with accuracy of 96.67% and 27 values to the new attribute). Because this accuracy is higher than the original one (92.38%), a second iteration is performed.

In the second iteration there are 28 possible partitions (in 7 of them H contains the new attribute created in the first iteration). The best partition is $H = \{a_6, new_1\}$ and $A - H = \{a_3, a_4, a_5, a_7, a_8, a_9\}$ having an accuracy of 98.57% and a new attribute with 40 possible values. The new accuracy

(98.57%) is higher than the initial accuracy of this iteration (96.67%), so the algorithm continues to the third iteration.

The best partition in the third iteration is $H = \{a_4, new_2\}$ and $A - H = \{a_3, a_5, a_7, a_8, a_9\}$. The accuracy of the new dataset is 99.05% and there are 49 possible values to the new attribute. The stopping criterion is not fulfilled yet and the algorithm continues to the fourth iteration.

The accuracy of the best partition in the fourth iteration, in which $H = \{a_5, a_9\} A - H = \{a_3, a_7, a_8, new_3\}$ is 99.05%. This accuracy is not better than the initial accuracy of the fourth iteration (99.05%). Therefore, according to the stopping criterion, the algorithm ends and the output is the initial dataset of the fourth iteration.

In order to evaluate the contribution of the proposed method, the C4.5 algorithm has been executed on the original training set and on the transformed training set (629 records). Each of these classifiers is examined over the external test set (70 records). The accuracy of the original classifier is 90% and the accuracy of the new classifier is 92.86%. Namely, there is an improvement of 2.86% in the accuracy using the suggested preprocessing algorithm.

9.6 Experimental Study

This section describes the experimental stages performed in order to evaluate the efficiency of this technique and presents the empirical results of the experiments. The results present the classification accuracy of some databases before and after using the suggested preprocessing algorithm.

9.6.1 *Databases Used*

Most of the datasets used in this experimental study were taken from the UCI Machine Learning Repository, including both artificial and real-world databases.

9.6.2 *Dataset Discretization*

Discretization is normally used to reduce the number of values for a given continuous attribute by dividing the range of the attribute into intervals. Interval labels can then be used to replace actual data values.

In order to use the IBAC algorithm, which only accepts attributes with nominal and finite number of values, discretization was performed on databases with numeric attributes. The result of the discretization is a finite (relatively small) number of values (labels) to each attribute which could originally contain a continuous or nonfinite number of values.

The discretization method that has been used here is the Equal Width Discretization. This is the simplest approach for discretization, in which the attribute values are partitioned into k equal-sized ranges. For each numerical attribute, a_i, with minimum value, $\min(v_{a_i})$, and maximum value, $\max(v_{a_i})$ the size of the interval, d, is calculated according to k:

$$d = \frac{\max(v_{a_i}) - \min(v_{a_i})}{k} \tag{9.5}$$

This yields the following cuts in the intervals:

$$\min(v_{a_i}) + d, \min(v_{a_i}) + 2d, \ldots, \min(v_{a_i}) + (k-1)d \tag{9.6}$$

In the presented experimental study the value of k was set to 10.

9.6.3   *Evaluating the Algorithm Performance*

In order to evaluate the proposed procedure, a leave-out approach has been employed. For this purpose each dataset was randomly partitioned into a training set (90% of the records) and a test set (10% of the records). The test set accuracy was measured twice: one time using the IBAC algorithm and one time using the original dataset. In order to evaluate the significance of the results, this procedure was repeated 10 times and the results have been compared using a statistical test. This statistical test determines whether one inducer performs better than the other in a particular dataset. The comparison in this work was performed using the Resample Paired t Test, which is considered one of the most popular method for comparing performance.

9.6.4   *Experimental Results*

Two induction algorithms have been examined in this experimental study: C4.5 and Naïve Bayes. Table 9.2 shows, for example, the accuracies achieved in all the experiments made on the database MONKS1. The first line contains the results of 10 experiments in which C4.5 was used for classification. The second line contains the results of experiments made on the same datasets as the first line (the same partition of the records to training set and test set), in which IBAC with C4.5 as an internal inducer was first activated and then C4.5 was used for classification. The third line contains the results of 10 experiments, in which Naïve Bayes was used for classification, and the fourth line contains the results of experiments made on the same datasets as the third line, in which IBAC with Naïve Bayes as an internal inducer was first activated and then Naïve Bayes was used for classification.

Table 9.2   Accuracies Achieved in the MONKS1 Dataset.

MONKS1	1	2	3	4	5	6	7	8	9	10
C4.5	0.91	0.95	0.94	0.91	0.98	0.94	0.89	0.95	0.95	0.93
IBAC (C4.5)	0.99	0.99	1.00	0.99	0.99	0.99	0.97	0.99	0.99	1.00
Naïve Bayes	0.84	0.71	0.80	0.74	0.68	0.72	0.72	0.75	0.79	0.64
IBAC (NB)	0.94	0.92	1.00	0.91	1.00	0.99	0.83	0.96	0.94	0.87

After completing the runs, the Paired t Test is employed. Two methods are compared based on the accuracy obtained by implementing the two methods on the same training set and examine the resulting classifiers on a certain test set. Tables 9.3 and 9.4 show the final accuracy results of all databases using all the examined methods. The tables present the average accuracy of each set of 10 runs and the results of the significance test. A '+' sign before a result represents a significant improvement in accuracy using the IBAC algorithm in comparison to the original state (not using the IBAC algorithm), A '-' represents a significant decrease in accuracy using the IBAC algorithm in comparison to the original state, and inexistence of any sign before a result represents an insignificant result. "(d)" denotes a discretization performed on the database.

The results show that there are databases for which by using the IBAC algorithm with a certain internal inducer results in a significant better accuracy than using that inducer only. There are also much fewer cases in which by using the IBAC algorithm with a certain internal inducer leads to an accuracy more unfavourable than by using that inducer by itself. IBAC with C4.5 results in a significant improvement in the accuracy in 6 databases, and to a significant decrease in the accuracy in one database only. IBAC with Naïve Bayes results in a significant improvement in the accuracy in 6 databases, and to a significant decrease in the accuracy in 3 databases. The results vary from one database to another and from one internal inducer to another, but in general it can be seen that the two different internal inducers significantly affect the same on the accuracy of the same database,

Table 9.3   Results of C4.5 and IBAC (C4.5).

Database	Number of records	Number of input attributes	C4.5	IBAC (C4.5)
DNF(3,3)	1024	12	0.94 ± 0.03	+ 0.99 ± 0.01
TTT	958	9	0.84 ± 0.04	+ 0.90 ± 0.06
AUST	690	14	0.87 ± 0.04	0.84 ± 0.05
BCAN	699	9	0.94 ± 0.03	0.95 ± 0.03
HOSPITAL	864	10	0.17 ± 0.02	0.15 ± 0.05
MONKS1	124	6	0.82 ± 0.13	+ 0.98 ± 0.05
MONKS2	169	6	0.59 ± 0.11	0.56 ± 0.09
MONKS3	122	6	0.95 ± 0.05	0.93 ± 0.06
NURSE	12960	8	0.97 ± 0.00	+ 1.00 ± 0.00
VOTE	290	16	0.97 ± 0.02	0.97 ± 0.05
HEART (d)	270	13	0.78 ± 0.07	0.79 ± 0.06
BALANCE	625	4	0.66 ± 0.05	+ 0.72 ± 0.07
CAR	1728	6	0.92 ± 0.02	+ 0.96 ± 0.02
ZOO	101	16	0.95 ± 0.05	0.95 ± 0.06
LED	220	24	0.65 ± 0.12	- 0.58 ± 0.08
ECOLI (d)	336	7	0.70 ± 0.06	0.66 ± 0.06
YEAST(d)	1484	8	0.51 ± 0.04	0.51 ± 0.03
GLASS(d)	214	9	0.61 ± 0.13	0.61 ± 0.12
CMC(d)	1473	9	0.49 ± 0.04	0.48 ± 0.04
DERMATOLOGY (d)	336	34	0.95 ± 0.04	0.97 ± 0.03

and therefore it is not important which internal inducer we choose. It is clearly seen that the algorithm performs well on artificial databases, such as Nursery. This is due to fact that these kinds of databases have an explicit hierarchical structure. It is also seen that the algorithm does not perform well on databases with numeric values, on which discretization was performed, such as Ecoli and glass. These are only preliminary conclusions regarding the performance of the algorithm on different kinds of databases. The next section further examines the relationship between the performance of the IBAC algorithm and the characteristics of the databases using a Meta learning approach.

9.7   Meta-Classifier

In the last section it was shown that the *a-priori* probability of IBAC to improve the accuracy performance is about 30%. Therefore, using this procedure is not always worthwhile. This section suggests a Meta learning

Table 9.4   Results of NB and IBAC (NB).

Database	Number of records	Number of attributes	Naïve Bayes	IBAC (NB) with NB
DNF(3,3)	1024	12	0.74 ± 0.06	+ 0.94 ± 0.06
TTT	958	9	0.69 ± 0.03	+ 0.75 ± 0.04
AUST	690	14	0.86 ± 0.05	0.85 ± 0.04
BCAN	699	9	0.97 ± 0.02	- 0.97 ± 0.02
HOSPITALS	864	10	0.16 ± 0.04	0.17 ± 0.03
MONKS1	124	6	0.78 ± 0.16	+ 0.98 ± 0.03
MONKS2	169	6	0.48 ± 0.10	+ 0.61 ± 0.14
MONKS3	122	6	0.95 ± 0.05	0.95 ± 0.05
NURSE	12960	8	0.91 ± 0.00	+ 0.95 ± 0.00
VOTE	290	16	0.89 ± 0.05	0.90 ± 0.05
HEART (d)	270	13	0.85 ± 0.04	- 0.81 ± 0.06
BALANCE	625	4	0.93 ± 0.03	0.93 ± 0.03
CAR	1728	6	0.87 ± 0.03	+ 0.93 ± 0.02
ZOO	101	16	0.94 ± 0.07	0.94 ± 0.07
LED	220	24	0.66 ± 0.10	0.64 ± 0.12
ECOLI (d)	336	7	0.83 ± 0.05	- 0.79 ± 0.06
YEAST (d)	1484	8	0.57 ± 0.04	0.57 ± 0.05
GLASS (d)	214	9	0.61 ± 0.11	0.59 ± 0.14
CMC (d)	1473	9	0.49 ± 0.03	0.49 ± 0.02
DERMATOLOGY (d)	336	34	0.99 ± 0.01	0.99 ± 0.01

approach, which supports the IBAC algorithm. This approach helps to estimate the performance of the IBAC algorithm on new datasets before activating the algorithm on these datasets. The estimation is based on the characteristics of the databases presented in the experimental stage and the performance of the algorithm on these databases.

9.7.1   *Building the Meta-Database*

In addition to the regular meta-features presented in previous chapters, we have added in this case another input attribute which characterizes the IBAC algorithm. More specifically this feature describes the type of internal inducer, which was used by the IBAC algorithm. This can be, in the case presented above, the C4.5 or Naïve Bayes. In fact, each dataset has two corresponding records in the Meta database — one for each of the internal inducers — where "1" represents C4.5 and "2" represents Naïve Bayes.

The aim of this process is to induce a mapping between data characteristics and the performance of the IBAC algorithm on different databases, and with different internal inducers. In order to do so, the target attribute of the

Meta database is chosen to be the categorized P value results, achieved in the experimental stage. The target attribute has two possible values: 1 — a significant improvement in the accuracy when using the IBAC algorithm and 2 — all other possibilities (an insignificant improvement, no change, a significant decrease in the accuracy using the IBAC algorithm and an insignificant decrease). Note that the accuracy using the IBAC algorithm with C4.5 as the internal inducer is examined in comparison to using C4.5 alone and the accuracy using the IBAC algorithm with Naïve Bayes as the internal inducer is examined in comparison to using Naïve Bayes alone.

9.7.2   *Inducing the Meta-Classifier*

A meta-classifier can be induced by activating any induction algorithm on the meta-dataset. In this case the C4.5 algorithm and the Naïve Bayes algorithm have been chosen for this task. By employing the meta-classifier on a new characterized dataset, it is possible to predict whether a significant improvement in the accuracy will be achieved on this database using the IBAC algorithm. If the meta-classifier predicts an insignificant improvement or even deterioration, it is advised against using the IBAC.

9.7.3   *Examining the Meta-Learning Approach*

In order to examine the contribution of the meta-learning approach two sets of experiments have been conducted:

(1) The first set is used to examine the general accuracy of the meta-classifier. For this purpose, the meta-dataset has been partitioned randomly into the Meta training set and the Meta test set. The Meta training set contained the records of 14 databases (28 records) and the Meta test set contained the records of 6 databases (12 records). This experiment has been repeated ten times. It should be noted that the partition of the meta-dataset to train set and test set was performed such that any two records of a certain database are assigned to the same set. This is important because these records are dependent.

(2) The second set of experiments employs the "leave-one-out" methodology. This set is used to evaluate the accumulative effect of IBAC together with the meta-classifier. For this purpose the meta training set contained the records of 19 databases (38 records) and the meta test set contained the records of one database (2 records). Twenty

experiments have been conducted, each of which has placed a different database in the Meta test set. The meta-classifier tried to predict the performance of the IBAC on the left-out dataset. According to this prediction the IBAC procedure was either activated or disabled. The obtained classifier was then compared to the classifier obtained without using this procedure. It should be noted that if the prediction of the meta-classifier indicates that the IBAC should be disabled then the two classifiers are identical.

9.7.4 Meta-Classifier Results

Table 9.5 presents the results obtained for the first experimental set using the C4.5 and Naïve Bayes as a meta-inducer. It can be seen that both Meta classifiers have achieved high accuracies rate (over 80%).

The Naïve Byes Meta classifier performs a little better than the C4.5 Meta classifier, probably because the meta-dataset contains a small number of records (40 records).

Table 9.5   The Accuracy of the Meta Classifier.

	Accuracy of C4.5 meta classifier	Accuracy of Naïve Bayes meta classifier
1	100.00%	83.33%
2	75.00%	91.66%
3	83.33%	83.33%
4	66.66%	83.33%
5	83.33%	100.00%
6	75.00%	75.00%
7	91.66%	58.33%
8	100.00%	100.00%
9	75.00%	91.66%
10	83.33%	83.33%
Average	**83.33%**	**85.00%**

In the second set of Meta learning experiments, the success of the classifier in predicting the performance of the IBAC algorithm on new databases has been examined. This was preformed using a leave-one-out procedure. Following this procedure *all but one* (19 databases) are used in the training set, while the remaining database is used for testing. The results for these experiments are given in Tables 9.6 and 9.7. Table 9.6 presents the decisions made by using the C4.5 Meta classifier and Naïve Bayes meta-classifier regarding the usage of the IBAC algorithm with C4.5 as an internal induction algorithm. Similarly, Table 9.7 presents the results for the IBAC algorithm with Naïve Bayes as an internal induction algorithm. The first column shows the real target of the Meta database. The second column shows the classification according to the C4.5 Meta classifier and the third column shows the classification according to the Naïve Bayes Meta classifier. As stated before, the value "1" stands for "use IBAC" and the value "2" stands for "don't use IBAC". The fourth and fifth columns show the accuracy according to classification of the C4.5 and Naïve Bayes classifiers respectively. As seen from the tables, the accuracy results achieved by using any of the meta classifiers in order to predict on which databases the IBAC preprocessing approach should be used, are better than the accuracy results achieved by using the IBAC approach on all databases and the accuracy results achieved by not using the IBAC approach at all. This justifies the use of Meta learning here.

Table 9.6   The Meta-Classifier's Results for IBAC Using C4.5 as the Internal Inducer.

Database	Real Target	C4.5	Naïve Bayes	C4.5 Accuracy	Naïve Bayes Accuracy
DNF(3,3)	1	1	2	0.99 ± 0.01	0.94 ± 0.03
TTT	1	1	1	0.90 ± 0.06	0.90 ± 0.06
AUST	2	2	2	0.87 ± 0.04	0.87 ± 0.04
BCAN	2	2	2	0.94 ± 0.03	0.94 ± 0.03
HOSPITALS	2	2	2	0.17 ± 0.02	0.17 ± 0.02
MONKS1	1	2	1	0.82 ± 0.13	0.98 ± 0.05
MONKS2	2	1	1	0.56 ± 0.09	0.56 ± 0.09
MONKS3	2	1	1	0.93 ± 0.06	0.93 ± 0.06
NURSE	1	1	1	1.00 ± 0.00	1.00 ± 0.00
VOTE	2	2	2	0.97 ± 0.02	0.97 ± 0.02
HEART	2	2	2	0.78 ± 0.07	0.78 ± 0.07
BALANCE	1	1	2	0.72 ± 0.07	0.66 ± 0.05
CAR	1	1	1	0.96 ± 0.02	0.96 ± 0.02
ZOO	2	2	2	0.95 ± 0.05	0.95 ± 0.05
LED	2	1	2	0.58 ± 0.08	0.65 ± 0.12
ECOLI	2	2	2	0.70 ± 0.06	0.70 ± 0.06
YEAST	2	2	2	0.51 ± 0.04	0.51 ± 0.04
GLASS	2	2	2	0.61 ± 0.13	0.61 ± 0.13
CMC	2	2	2	0.49 ± 0.04	0.49 ± 0.04
DERMATOLOGY	2	2	2	0.95 ± 0.04	0.95 ± 0.04

Table 9.7 The Meta-Classifier's Decisions for IBAC using Naïve Bayes as the Internal Inducer.

Database	Preferred	C4.5	Naïve Bayes	Accuracy of C4.5	Accuracy of Naïve Bayes
DNF(3,3)	1	1	2	0.94 ± 0.06	0.74 ± 0.06
TTT	1	1	1	0.75 ± 0.04	0.75 ± 0.04
AUST	2	2	2	0.86 ± 0.05	0.86 ± 0.05
BCAN	2	2	2	0.97 ± 0.02	0.97 ± 0.02
HOSPITALS	2	2	2	0.16 ± 0.04	0.16 ± 0.04
MONKS1	1	2	1	0.78 ± 0.16	0.98 ± 0.03
MONKS2	1	1	1	0.61 ± 0.14	0.61 ± 0.14
MONKS3	2	1	1	0.95 ± 0.05	0.95 ± 0.05
NURSE	1	1	1	0.95 ± 0.00	0.95 ± 0.00
VOTE	2	2	2	0.89 ± 0.05	0.89 ± 0.05
HEART	2	2	2	0.85 ± 0.04	0.85 ± 0.04
BALANCE	2	1	2	0.93 ± 0.03	0.93 ± 0.03
CAR	1	1	1	0.93 ± 0.02	0.93 ± 0.02
ZOO	2	2	2	0.94 ± 0.07	0.94 ± 0.07
LED	2	1	2	0.64 ± 0.12	0.66 ± 0.10
ECOLI	2	2	2	0.83 ± 0.05	0.83 ± 0.05
YEAST	2	2	2	0.57 ± 0.04	0.57 ± 0.04
GLASS	2	2	2	0.61 ± 0.11	0.61 ± 0.11
CMC	2	2	2	0.49 ± 0.03	0.49 ± 0.03
DERMATOLOGY	2	2	2	0.99 ± 0.01	0.99 ± 0.01

9.8 Conclusions

This chapter presented a new function decomposition method. This method uses an internal inducer to generate the function decomposition structure. It has been seen that this method can be used for improving accuracy, nevertheless it is not always useful. A meta-classification has been used to predict the cases in which this method is beneficial. The reliability of the meta-classifier has been validated in two experimental studies.

Chapter 10

Concept Aggregation

10.1 Overview

The main goal of a classification task is to assign new data instances into pre-defined classes. The classifiers aim is to predict the correct class as accurately as possible, according to the given class domain. This predefined domain is not necessarily the most beneficial to the end user, who may prefer greater accuracy to resolution (defined by the number of categories, referred to as concepts). This is therefore resolved as a multi criteria problem, for which a solution should consist of an efficient set of pareto-optimal points, rather than one optimal solution.

Given an inducer and a database, this chapter introduces 3 unique heuristic Concept Aggregation methods for creating this efficient frontier by reduction of resolution, according to a Similarity Based Aggregation (SBA) approach and an Error Based Aggregation (EBA) approach. Regarding the latter, this chapter offers optional optimal and greedy solutions, which proved to yield very similar results, and demonstrated distinctive predominance over the Similarity Based method solution. The problem is also considered from a different perspective. As opposed to the offered aggregation approaches, this chapter deals also with Concept de-aggregation method, namely increasing resolution, by extending the class domain.

Furthermore, this chapter discusses the existence of a phase transition within the efficient frontier curves, and a natural number of concepts (classes) for a given classification problem.

10.2   Motivation

As stated in Chapter 1, the main goal of the classification task is to assign new data instances into a set of classes. The set of classes or class domain is usually a predefined, integral part of the problem, and the classifier's aim is to predict the correct class as accurately as possible.

An important issue is whether this predefined class domain, as defined, is indeed the most appropriate one to represent reality. Will a different classification be more beneficial to the end user than the one initially proposed if it will yield better results? The end user may sometimes prefer greater accuracy to resolution.

In the case of numerical target attributes, the problem may be perceived as feature discretization of the target attribute. [Dougherty *et al.* (1995)] distinguished among supervised and unsupervised discretization methods. Supervised methods are capable of handling only discretization of input attributes, and unsupervised methods may result in a decrease in accuracy rate, since values which naturally differ from each other, and should be seen as different concepts, may be aggregated.

Given an inducer and a training set, this chapter introduces unique methods for creating an efficient frontier for the Classification problem. On the one hand, the accuracy of the classifier, and on the other hand, the number of categories, referred to as concepts. The problem is confronted by two means: Concept Aggregation, reducing resolution, and Concepts de-aggregation, enhancing the resolution level.

This chapter presents two different manners to solve the problem; the first enables the use of the inducer whenever needed. The second, uses the inducer only once.

The output of all suggested solutions is the greatest accuracy found by the method for each number of clusters ξ, along with its appropriate classifier. The final findings can be presented on a graph, enabling the end user to easily conclude which is the most efficient position that suits his problem domain.

One of the consequences of the statistical approach to the computational problem is the identification of situations where small changes in local behavior give especially large changes in global performance [Chizi *et al.* (2002)]. The origin of these phenomena stems from natural domains such as thermodynamics and kinetics.

For example, one of the important properties of materials is that they can change their properties suddenly when the temperature is changed by

a small amount. A transition of a solid to a liquid, or a liquid to a gas will
be considered as a phase transition . Each well defined state of the material
is considered a particular phase.

One of the goals of this chapter is to identify a phase transition within
the generated efficient set. Identifying such a phase transition may indicate
the existence of a natural number of concepts to the given classification
problem.

The presented methods may be applied to any learning algorithm (inducer), but this chapter presents experiments for decision trees, using the
C4.5 learning algorithm.

10.3   The Multi Criteria Problem

The desired resolution level (defined by the number of concepts) and its
applicable accuracy is something to be determined by the user. There is,
of course, a trade off between the two measures. Since there exists such a
trade off between two desired measures, the decision has to be made based
on multiple criteria. The result would be a set of efficient points, rather
than one optimal solution.

According to [Steuer (1986)], the idea of efficiency refers to points in
the decision space. A point is efficient if it is not possible to move feasibly so as to increase one of the objectives without necessarily decreasing
at least one of the others. In other disciplines, the term efficiency is also
known as Pareto-optimality, admissibility, or noninferiority. More specifically [Steuer (1986)] defines dominance, and efficiency as follows:

Definition 10.1
z^1 dominants z^2 iff $z^1 \geq z^2$ and $z^1 \neq z^2$ (i.e., $z_i^1 \geq z_i^2$ for all i and $z_i^1 > z_i^2$
for at least one i, where the criterion vector z is defined as: (objective
function vector, z-vector), $z - \text{vector} = \{z_1, \ldots, z_k\}$, and z_i is the criterion
value of the i-th objective.

As opposed to dominance, which refers to vectors in the criterion space,
efficiency refers to points in the decision space. In a MOLP (Multi objective
linear problem) it is defined by:

Definition 10.2   A point $\bar{x} \in S$ is efficient iff there does not exist another
point $x \in S$ such that $C_x \geq C_{\bar{x}}$ and $C_x \neq C_{\bar{x}}$. Otherwise $\bar{x}$ is inefficient,
where S is the feasible region in the decision space, and C is the criterion
matrix whose rows are the c^i gradients of the objectives.

That is, from an efficient point, it is not possible to move feasibly so as to increase one of the objectives without necessarily decreasing at least one of the others.

Such an efficient point or a pareto-optimal point in our case is a point from which it is not possible to move feasibly so that the resolution (i.e. the number of concepts) increases without necessarily decreasing the accuracy, or vice versa. The efficient frontier will be composed from this set of efficient points.

As mentioned above, it is reasonable to have a certain tradeoff between the two criteria, yet the pattern or behavior of this tradeoff is not known in advance. Figure 10.1 demonstrates several alternatives for the pattern of the efficient frontier curves.

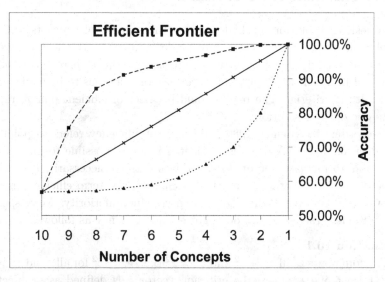

Fig. 10.1   Alternative Patterns for the Efficient Frontier Curves.

10.4   Problem Formulation

Recall from Chapter 5, the formal definition of Concept Aggregation problem is:

Given a learning method I and a training set S with input attribute set $A = \{a_1, a_2, \ldots, a_n\}$ and target attribute y from a distribution D over the labeled instance space, the goal is to find an optimal decomposition of the target values set into ζ subsets $Y_k \subseteq V_y$ $k = 1, \ldots, \zeta$ fulfilling $(\bigcup_{k=1}^{\zeta} Y_k) = V_y$ and $Y_i \cap Y_j = \emptyset$; $i, j = 1, \ldots, \zeta$; $i \neq j$ such that the generalization error of the two steps classification made first by the classifier $I(\{\langle x_i, k \rangle \, | \forall \langle x_i, y_i \rangle \in S; y_i \in Y_k\})$ and then by appropriate classifier $I_k(\{\langle x_i, y_i \rangle \, | \forall \langle x_i, y_i \rangle \in S; y_i \in Y_k\})$ will be minimized over the distribution D.

10.5 Basic Solution Approaches

In order to create a "real" or optimal efficient frontier, one has to investigate all possible aggregations of classes for each number of concepts ξ, finding or building a classifier for each possibility. This is, of course, a nonrealistic solution. Therefore, the problem should be solved with heuristic methods, attempting to find the greatest accuracy level for each given number of concepts ξ, along with the appropriate classifier $I(S)$.

The proposed solutions approach the specified problem from three different aspects:

Aggregation manner Will the new classes or concepts be generated by merging new existing classes of the original database (i.e. a certain class of the original database could belong to one concept only), or will new concepts be generated with no respect to the original classes?. As formulated above, the solution must be one merging existing classes.

Aggregation criteria Will the aggregation be based upon the behavior of the records within the training set (i.e. the attribute values), or based upon the error or misclassification of the original classifier, generated by the given learning algorithm for the original $d_y = |dom(y)|$ class problem?.

The inducer's usage Does the solution enable multiple use of the given inducer, or retain the basic structure of the original classifier, allowing one single employment of the algorithm?.

These various aspects will be discussed in the depiction of each of the suggested methods.

10.6 Concept Aggregation — Similarity Based Approach (SBA)

The motivation for this method comes from data behavior, namely the set of records belonging to each one of the classes is examined, while classes having records behaving "similarly" should be aggregated. The term "similarity" refers to the similarity between the values of the input attributes.

The procedure starts by a partition of the database into $d_y = |dom(y)|$ sample subsets S_k, each containing the records belonging to a specific class. A Meta-Data vector is created for each subset. This vector characterizes the behavior of the records in the subset using summary features.

The original classes are then merged into new concepts, based on a clustering procedure of the Meta-data vectors representing them. For each set of concepts found by the procedure, a new classifier is generated by repetitive use of the given inducer. Figure 10.2 illustrates the outline of this approach.

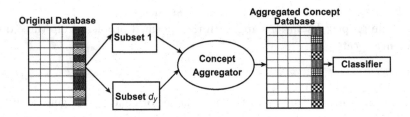

Fig. 10.2   General Outline of the SBA Method.

10.6.1 *SBA — Procedure*

(1) Partition the training set into S_k subsets according to the class labels, $k = 1, \ldots, d_y$
(2) For each S_k create a meta-data vector.
(3) For $\xi = 2, \ldots, d_y$:

    (a) Apply the K-means algorithm on Meta-data vector records with $K = \xi$

    (b) Aggregate classes with Meta-data vectors belonging to the same clusters

    (c) Generate a new classifier for aggregated concepts by applying the given inducer

10.6.2 *Meta-Data Vectors*

As mentioned above, the Meta-data vector characterizes the behavior of the records in the subset using summary features.

The meta-attributes are computed differently for nominal and continuous attributes. For each continuous attribute a_i and for each subset S_k the following meta-attributes are computed:

(1) The normalized average value:

$$b_{k,i,1} = \frac{avg_{k,i}}{\max\limits_{k=1}^{d_y}(avg_{k,i}) - \min\limits_{k=1}^{d_y}(avg_{k,i})} \tag{10.1}$$

where:

$$avg_{k,i} = \frac{\sum\limits_{\langle x_q,y_q \rangle \in S_k} x_{q,i}}{|S_k|} \tag{10.2}$$

(2) The normalized standard deviation:

$$b_{k,i,2} = \frac{dev_{k,i}}{\max\limits_{k=1}^{d_y}(dev_{k,i}) - \min\limits_{k=1}^{d_y}(dev_{k,i})} \tag{10.3}$$

where:

$$dev_{k,i} = \sqrt{\frac{\sum\limits_{\langle x_q,y_q \rangle \in S_k} (x_{q,i} - avg_{k,i})^2}{|S_k|}} \tag{10.4}$$

For each nominal attribute a_i the following meta-attributes are computed:

(1) The probability of value $v_{i,j}$ of attribute a_i in sample S_k:

$$b_{k,i,j+1} = p(a_i = v_{i,j} \,|\, S_k) \tag{10.5}$$

(2) The normalized entropy:

$$b_{k,i,1} = - \sum\limits_{j=1}^{|dom(a_i)|} p(v_{i,j} \,\Big|\, S_k) \cdot \log_{|dom(a_i)|} p(v_{i,j} \,|\, S_k) \tag{10.6}$$

Note that each continuous attribute is represented in each sub-sample by two new attributes in the metadata vector, whereas each nominal attribute is represented by $d_y + 1$ new attributes.

The above meta-vector assumes that the instances in each class are homogeneous. Obviously this assumption is not always true, resulting in potential loss of important information. Nevertheless, this is a simple way for prototyping a set of instances.

10.6.3 *SBA — Detailed Illustration*

Table 10.1 presents a small 30 records database, where 2/3 of the records are used as a training set and the rest as a test set. The database will serve as a basis for illustration of all suggested solution methods.

Table 10.1   Database for Detailed Illustration.

A1	A2	A3	A4	Target		A1	A2	A3	A4	Target
0	1	0	0	3		1	0	0	0	2
0	0	1	1	1		0	0	0	0	1
0	1	0	1	1		0	1	0	0	3
1	1	1	0	4		1	1	0	0	1
1	1	1	1	1		0	0	0	1	3
1	1	0	1	2		0	1	0	0	3 .
1	0	1	1	3		1	0	0	1	1
1	0	1	0	3 .		1	0	0	0	2
1	0	1	0	3		0	1	1	0	4
1	0	0	0	2		0	1	1	0	4
0	0	1	1	1		(b) Test Set				
1	1	0	1	2
1	1	1	0	4
0	0	1	0	2
1	0	1	1	3
0	1	1	1	3
1	1	0	0	1
0	0	1	0	2
0	0	0	0	1
1	0	0	1	1

(a) Training Set

(1) The procedure starts with partitioning the training set into 4 subsets, one for each target class, as illustrated in Table 10.2.
(2) The algorithm continues by building the metadata vectors for the four subsets. Computing Equation 10.5 and Equation 10.6 for each attribute a_i and for each subset S_k, will result in the Meta-Data vectors

Table 10.2 Partition of Training Set in Table 10.1 Into Subsets According to Attribute Class as a Basic Step of the Similarity Based Aggregation Method.

A1	A2	A3	A4	Target
0	0	1	1	1
0	1	0	1	1
1	1	1	1	1
0	0	1	1	1
1	1	0	0	1
0	0	0	0	1
1	0	0	1	1

(a) S1 - Subset of Class 1

A1	A2	A3	A4	Target
1	1	0	1	2
1	0	0	0	2
1	1	0	1	2
0	0	1	0	2
0	0	1	0	2

(b) S2 - Subset of Class 2

A1	A2	A3	A4	Target
0	1	0	0	3
1	0	1	1	3
1	0	1	0	3
1	0	1	0	3
1	0	1	1	3
0	1	1	1	3

(c) S3 - Subset of Class 3

A1	A2	A3	A4	Target
1	1	1	0	4
1	1	1	0	4

(d) S4 - Subset of Class 4

illustrated in Table 10.3. Note that in this case, the original database contains only nominal attributes.

Table 10.3 Metadata Vectors for Subsets in Table 10.2 as Generated in the Similarity Based Aggregation Method Process.

	b_{11}	b_{12}	b_{13}	b_{21}	b_{22}	b_{23}	b_{31}	b_{32}	b_{33}	b_{41}	b_{42}	b_{43}
S_1	0.99	0.43	0.57	0.99	0.43	0.57	0.70	0.86	0.29	0.99	0.43	0.57
S_2	0.97	0.4	0.6	0.97	0.6	0.4	0.97	0.4	0.6	0.97	0.4	0.6
S_3	0.91	0.33	0.67	0.91	0.67	0.33	0.66	0.17	0.83	1	0.5	0.5
S_4	0	0	1	0	0	1	0	0	1	0	1	0

(3) These 4 vectors are now clustered by implementing the K-means clustering algorithm with $K = 2$ and $K = 3$. Table 10.4 presents the results obtained for $K = 2$ (the same results were obtained for $K = 3$, i.e. the K-means algorithm found only two clusters, in spite of the value of the parameter K).

Table 10.4 Aggregation Pattern of 10.1 Database, as Aggregated by The Similarity Based Aggregation Method for $\xi = 2$.

Class	1	2	3	4
Concept	1'	0'	0'	0'

(4) A classifier is now built using C4.5 for $\xi = 2, 3, 4$. Figure 10.3 presents

the classifier obtained for $\xi = 4$ (with the original target classes). The classifier for $\xi = 2$ is presented in Figure 10.4.

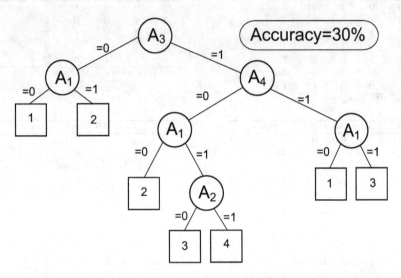

Fig. 10.3   C4.5 Decision Tree Classifier for Original Target Classes of Table 10.1 Database ($\xi = 4$).

10.7   Concept Aggregation — Error Based Approach (eBA)

The second approach confronts the problem from a different perspective. Here the motivation is to examine accuracy or error rate of the original problem classifier. The original classes are aggregated into ξ new concepts in such a way that the error rate of the given classifier will be minimized.

The main idea is to examine the confusion matrix of the classifier over the test set, ignoring errors between classes belonging to the same concept.

For this second approach, two optional solutions are proposed: optimal and greedy. As defined in the problem formulation, the aim of these two methods is to aggregate the existing classes by merging them into new concepts. The aggregation criterion is to minimize the error rate of the original problem classifier. Note that the offered solution enables a single usage of the given inducer.

The outline of the proposed procedure is presented in Figure 10.5, where

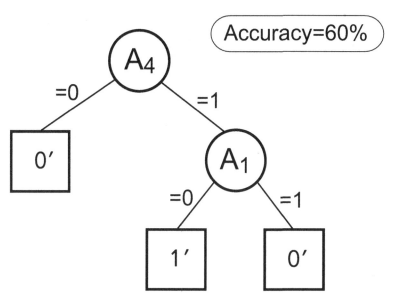

Fig. 10.4   C4.5 Decision Tree Classifier with new Aggregated Concepts for $\xi = 4$ — Similarity Based Method.

the Concept Aggregator is explicated below, as well as the form of updating the existing classifier model.

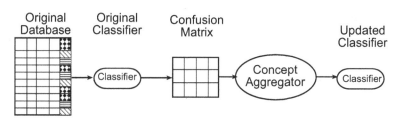

Fig. 10.5   General Outline of the EBA Methods.

10.7.1   *The Confusion Matrix*

The Confusion Matrix is a convenient tool for analyzing the performance of a classifier [Kohavi and Provost (1998)]. A confusion matrix is a square matrix that specifies the accuracy of the classifier to the classification problem. Given $d_y = |dom(y)|$ classes, a confusion matrix is a $d_y \times d_y$ matrix where the entry $c_{i,j}$ indicates the number of instances from the test set whose actual class is c_i but are assigned to class c_j. Obviously a good classifier should have a diagonal confusion matrix (all off-diagonal entries of are zero). Table 10.5 presents the confusion matrix of a C4.5 classifier for the GLASS database (taken from the UCI repository).

Table 10.5   Confusion Matrix of C4.5 Classifier for the GLASS Database.

1	2	3	4	5	6	← Classified As
52	13	4	0	0	1	1
14	49	7	2	2	2	2
6	7	4	0	0	0	3
0	1	0	11	0	1	4
1	1	0	0	7	0	5
4	2	0	0	0	23	6

10.7.2   EBA Method — Optimal Solution

Based on the confusion matrix, the main idea of this method is to aggregate the classes into $\xi = 2, \ldots, |dom(y)| - 1$ new concepts, in such a way that the error rate will be minimized (due to the aggregation, errors between classes belonging to the same concept can be ignored).

For instance, the user would like to find the optimal aggregation for $\xi = 5$ to the problem presented in Table 10.5, meaning that two of the original classes must be aggregated into one, and the rest remain as individual classes. The decrease in misclassified records caused by aggregating each pair of classes may be calculated, namely:

- If classes 1 and 2 are aggregated then 13+14=27 errors can be ignored;
- If classes 1 and 3 are aggregated then 4+6=10 errors can be ignored;
- If classes 1 and 4 are aggregated then 0+0=0 errors can be ignored;
- and so forth, aggregating the pair with the greatest decrease in error rate.

In order to find the optimal solution for each xi, the problem is formulated as an IP Linear programming problem. Thus, a separate linear programming problem is solved for each number of concepts. Figure 10.6 illustrates the outline of the optimal solution of the EBA method.

The ILP problem can be defined as:

Given:

- d_y — The original number of classes ($|dom(y)|$)

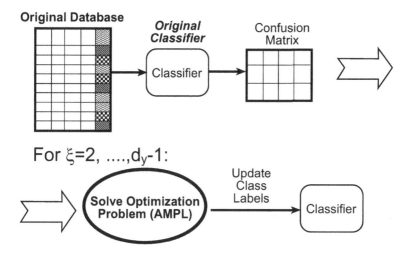

Fig. 10.6   General Outline of the EBA 0ptimal Solution Method.

- x_i — The desired number of classes
- $C_{i,j}$ — The decrease in misclassified instances when class i and class j are joined.

Decision Variables

- $X_{i,j,m}$ — A binary variable indicating whether class i and class j are joined into new class m.
- $X_{i,m}$ — A binary variable indicating whether class i belong to class m.

$$Z = \max\{\sum_{i=1}^{d_y-1} \sum_{j=i+1}^{d_y} \sum_{m=1}^{\xi} X_{i,j,m} \cdot C_{i,j}\}$$

Subject to:

$$Y_{i,m} + Y_{j,m} \leqslant 1 + X_{i,j,m} \forall i, j, m$$

$$\sum_{m=1}^{\xi} Y_{i,m} = 1 \forall i$$

$$\sum_{i=1}^{d_y} Y_{i,m} \geq 1 \forall m$$

The first constraint ensures that the variables $X_{i,j,m}$ gets the value 1 only if both class i and class j are assigned to the new class m. The second constraint verifies that each original class belongs to one new class exactly. The last constraint ensures that each new class consists of at least one original class. For aggregating numerical targets attributes while keeping continuity, an additional constraint should be added, so that only adjacent target values can be aggregated:

$$X_{i,j,m} \leq X_{i,k,m} \forall m, i > k > j$$

As mentioned previously, this problem is solved separately for each number of desired concepts, with the appropriate ξ.

The following illustration solves the same classification problem, with training and test sets depicted in Table 10.1. The procedure starts with the original Classifier in Figure 10.3, having the following confusion matrix, as presented in Table 10.6.

Table 10.6   Confusion Matrix of C4.5 Classifier Presented in Figure 10.3.

1	2	3	4	← Classified As
2	2	0	0	1
0	2	0	0	2
3	0	0	0	3
0	2	0	0	4

The linear programming problem is then solved for $\xi = 2, \ldots, d_y - 1$. For $\xi = 3$ the final values of the binary variables, found by using AMPL Plus with the CPLEX Solver, are presented in Table 10.7. The new classifier, which has an accuracy of 60%, is presented in Figure 10.7.

Similarly, solving for $\xi = 2$ will result in the solution presented in Table 10.8. The value of the target function is 5, and therefore the accuracy of the new classifier is 80%.

Table 10.7 Results of Linear Optimization Problem of Optimal EBA Detailed Illustration for $\xi = 3$.

$Y_{i,m}$:	1'	2'	3'	i
	0	0	1	1
	1	0	0	2
	0	0	1	3
	0	1	0	4

$X_{i,j,1}$:	1	2	3	4	j
	0	0	0	0	1
	0	0	0	0	2
	0	0	0	0	3
	0	0	0	0	4

$X_{i,j,2}$:	1	2	3	4	j
	0	0	0	0	1
	0	0	0	0	2
	0	0	0	0	3
	0	0	0	0	4

$X_{i,j,3}$:	1	2	3	4	j
	0	0	1	0	1
	0	0	0	0	2
	0	0	0	0	3
	0	0	0	0	4

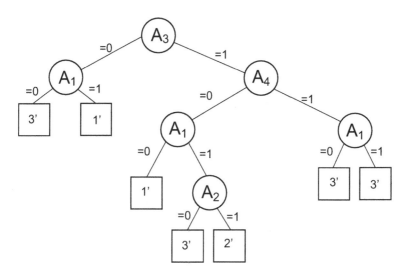

Fig. 10.7 Updated C4.5 Decision Tree Classifier for $\xi = 3$ - Optimal EBA Detailed Illustration.

10.7.3   *EBA Method — Heuristic Greedy Solution*

As with the optimal solution depicted above, this method starts with the original classifier, built by the given learning algorithm. Once again, the idea is to examine the classifier's confusion matrix, and aggregate the classes into new concepts, while trying to minimize the classifier error. Only here, the procedure starts from $k = d_y$ concepts, and in a greedy manner

Table 10.8   Results of Linear Optimization Problem of
Optimal EBA Detailed Illustration for $\xi = 2$.

$Y_{i,m}$:	m		i
	1'	2'	
	1	0	1
	0	1	2
	1	0	3
	0	1	4

aggregates the concepts one by one. Thus, this is an iterative process, where
each iteration is solved optimally. The general outline of the EBA method
is specified in Figure 10.8.

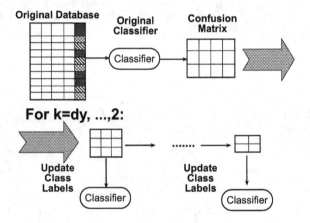

Fig. 10.8   General Outline of the Greedy EBA Method.

10.7.3.1   *Detailed Procedure*

Start from $\xi = d_y$ concepts, and in a greedy manner aggregate the concepts
one by one:

(1) For every iteration, aggregate the ξ existing concepts into $\xi-1$ concepts,
so that the number of misclassified records is minimized according to
the confusion matrix. Update classifier labels according to new found
concepts.
(2) If the number of concepts = 2 Then Stop Else Go to Step 3.
(3) Update the confusion matrix (See detailed illustration below).
(4) Return to Step 1.

In view of the fact that this is a myopic method, it will not necessarily result in an optimal solution. For aggregating numerical target attributes while keeping continuity, only adjacent classes or concept should be candidates for aggregation.

10.7.3.2 *Illustration*

Once again, the procedure starts with the confusion matrix in Table 10.6.

(1) The illustration begins with 4 original classes, and we would like to find 3 new concepts. Therefore, the decrease in instances misclassification for the aggregation of every possible couple of classes/concepts is computed as illustrated in Table 10.9.

Since the aggregation of Classes 1 and 3 will result in the greatest decrease in misclassified records, those are the ones to be aggregated. The obtained model and accuracy (60%) is identical to the optimal solution (where the concept labels may be different).

(2) $\xi = 3 \neq 2 \rightarrow$ Go to Step 3.

(3) The confusion matrix is then updated (where the new aggregated concept is labelled 1') as described in Table 10.10, and we return to Step 1.

(4) If all possible couples of concepts to be aggregated are examined, the greatest decrease in misclassified records will be achieved when concept 2 is aggregated with the new concept 1', or with the original concept 4, as aggregated by the optimal method. Both will result in the same accuracy (80%).

(5) Since $\xi = 2 \rightarrow$ Stop.

Table 10.9   Decrease in Error for All Possible Aggregations Based on Confusion Matrix Table 10.6 — Greedy EBA Detailed Illustration.

Aggregated Concepts	Error Decrease
1,2	2
1,3	3
1,4	0
2,3	0
2,4	2
1,4	0

Table 10.10   Updated Confusion Matrix — Greedy EBA Detailed Illustration.

2	4	1'	← Classified As
2	0	0	2
2	0	0	4
2	0	5	1'

By comparing the efficient frontier curves generated by each of the two suggested approaches, one can note that the EBA approach has a greater performance, namely the EBA approach results with a higher rate of accuracy for any given number of concepts.

10.8   Experimental Study

As mentioned previously, the offered methods of this chapter may be applied to any of the classification learning algorithms. Yet, in the experiments held for the purpose of this chapter and the examination of the hereby suggested methods, we have decided to make use of the C4.5 decision tree classification algorithm.

In order to examine the three methods described in this chapter, twelve different databases from the UCI repository have been chosen. Each dataset has been divided into a training set (2/3 of the instances) and a test set (1/3 of the instances).

10.8.1   *Solving the Optimization Problem of the EBA Optimal Method*

In order to solve the described optimization problem, the AMPL package with the CPLEX Solver has been used. For each solution we must create a model of the problem and a data file. A single model served all problems, and only a specific data file had to be created for each database, updated according to each number of concepts sought. Figure 10.9 presents the AMPL model used here and an illustration of a data file.

10.8.2   *Experiment Results*

The experimental study indicated that the Error Based Approach resulted in an obvious tradeoff between the two measures of resolution and accuracy. A decrease in resolution (number of concepts) enabled an increase in

```
set Class; set Concept;

param ed 'error_decrease'{Class,Class};

var X {Class,Class,Concept} binary ;

var Y{Class,Concept} binary;

maximize total_decrease:
  sum {i in Class,j in Class, k in Concept : j>i}
    ed[i,j]*X[i,j,k];

subject to S1 {i in Class, j in Class, k in Concept :j>i}:
  Y[i,k]+Y[j,k]<=1+X[i,j,k];

subject to S2 {i in Class}:
  sum {k in Concept} Y[i,k]=1;

subject to S3 {k in Concept}:
  sum {i in Class}Y[i,k]>=1;

subject to S4 {i in Class, j in Class, k in Concept: j>i}:
  Y[i,k]>= X[i,j,k];

subject to S5 {i in Class, j in Class, k in Concept: j>i}:
  Y[j,k]>= X[i,j,k];

set Class:= 1 2 3 4 5 6 7; set Concept:= m1 m2 ;

param ed: 1 2 3 4 5 6 7:=

1 0  0  4  4  5  0  0

2 0  0  1  0  0  0  0

3 0  0  0  4 33  0  0

4 0  0  0  0 11  2  1

5 0  0  0  0  0  0  0

6 0  0  0  0  0  0  1;
```

Fig. 10.9   AMPL Model for the Optimal EBA Method and the Data File for Image Segmentation Database.

accuracy and vice verse. The Similarity Based method, on the other hand, resulted in some unanticipated results, when a decrease in resolution did not necessarily result in a classifier having a greater rate of accuracy.

The suggested solutions for Concept Aggregation were all heuristic solutions, yet it is obvious that the presented results demonstrate a distinctive predominance to the Error Based Aggregation approach. Both the greedy and the optimal methods resulted in a higher rate of accuracy for any given number of concepts in all databases. This is most likely due to the fact that the Error Based methods are based on the classifier, taking into consideration the inducer along with it's strengths and weaknesses, whereas the Similarity Based Method refers to all inducers and classifiers equally. Moreover, the proposed meta-vector might be too simple. By using more complicated meta-attributes described in the literature, better results might be obtained.

It is obvious that the greedy method of the Error Based approach is a myopic method, and therefore may result in non optimal solutions for an optimization problem. Yet, in all experiments, both methods generated equal results, demonstrating empirically that the greedy method has reasonable performance.

A drawback of the Error Based Approach, with both in the greedy and the optimal methods, is found in the aggregation manner. When analyzing the manner in which the classes are aggregated into concepts, it may be perceived that in most cases there is a formation of one main concept, into which more and more classes are aggregated with every decrease in resolution. For every ξ, the outcome is therefore $\xi - 1$ concepts containing individual classes, and one concept containing all other $d_y - \xi + 1$ classes.

This phenomenon would seem more appropriate to the greedy method, but as noted before, in the experiments held on these twelve databases, the greedy and optimal methods both generated equal results. This phenomenon occurred in all databases except for DERMATOLOGY, LED17 and ECOLI, in which two larger concepts were formed, and were eventually aggregated into one.

This phenomenon can be explained by the fact that we used absolute numbers of errors as the aggregation criterion. If the relative error rates between any two classes are about the same level, the expected number of absolute numbers of errors is naturally higher for large classes. This phenomenon can be avoided by switching the criteria to a relative error which may result in more balanced classes, but with a higher overall error rate.

When analyzing the efficient frontier curves generated by the Error Based Approach methods, two main patterns may be identified. In the OPTDIGITS, PENDIGITS and LED17 databases the form of the efficient frontier curve generated is almost linear. Whereas in the other 9 databases the efficient frontier curves have an asymptotic logarithmical increasing pattern.

10.9 Concept De-Aggregation

Similarly to the Aggregation approaches suggested above, we approach the problem from a different perspective. Until now, we have explored the reduction of the target class domain and its effect on the classifier accuracy. We would now like to explore the possibility of increase of this domain. Namely to develop a method for increasing the number of concepts of the original problem, and generating a classifier for the new updated classification problem with the best accuracy possible.

Once again, we must face the fact that in order to create a "real" or optimal efficient frontier, one has to investigate all possible de-aggregations of classes for each number of desired concepts, finding or building a classifier for each possibility. This, of course, is also a nonrealistic solution. Therefore, we shall therefore approach the problem yet again with a heuristic method, attempting to find the greatest accuracy level for each given number of concepts $\xi > d_y$, along with the appropriate classifier $I(S)$.

As with the proposed solutions approaches for the Concept Aggregation problem, Concept De-Aggregation is also considered from the three different aspects specified above;

- As apposed to the aggregation manner of all Concept Aggregation suggested methods, from the nature of the de-aggregation problem itself, there will be no merging of classes into new concepts. Yet, the de-aggregation process will take place with respect to the original classes;
- The motivation for this approach, as with the SBA method detailed above, results from data behavior, therefore the aggregation criteria will be based on this specified behavior;
- Hence, the offered solution enables the multiple use of the given inducer.

For the Concept De-Aggregation problem one heuristic method is described in the following section.

10.9.1   *Concept De-Aggregation — Outline*

As stated above, the de-aggregation process takes place with respect to the original classes. As with the Greedy EBA method, the process is iterative. The objective is at each phase of the process to examine the de-aggregation or partitioning of each of the existing classes or concepts into two new concepts.

The procedure starts by a partition of the database into d_y sample subsets S_j, each containing the records belonging to a specific class or concept. In an iterative process, one of the existing concepts is then partitioned into two new concepts, based on a clustering procedure of the records within each subset.

For each set of concepts found by the procedure, a new classifier is generated by repetitive use of the given inducer. An illustration of the de-aggregation suggested method can be seen in Figure 10.10.

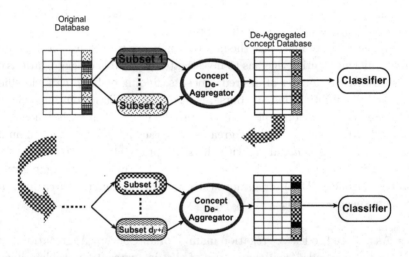

Fig. 10.10   Outline of De-Aggregation Suggested Method.

10.9.2   *Models Generation Procedure*

We begin with the original $\xi = d_y$ concept problem:

(1) If the Termination Condition is fulfilled then stop
(2) Partition the training set into S_j subsets according to concepts/class attribute

(3) Run the K-means algorithm on each subset with $K = 2$ (We consider de-aggregating each existing concept into two new concepts)

(4) Find optimal partition ($C_{\xi+1} = K$-means clustering model of the selected concept chosen for de-aggregation)

(5) Update training set according to the new de-aggregated concepts

(6) Build new classifier applying the given inducer: $I(S)_{\xi+1}$

(7) $\xi = \xi + 1$

(8) Return to (1)

10.9.3 Termination Condition

The termination condition could consist of several options:

- A given number of concepts (i.e. the maximum level of resolution one would like to reach or examine)
- Minimum accuracy level
- Minimum number of records in new partitioned concepts
- $\max(R/r) > \alpha$ (a predefined parameter)

Of course the procedure cannot continue at the point in which each of the records in the training set is a concept in itself, or where the K-means algorithm can no longer partition each of the subsets.

10.9.4 Finding the Optimal Partition

Similarly to the clustering criterion measures, we define inter-cluster and intra-cluster distances that will assist us in defining the optimal partition criteria. For each possible two cluster partition we define:

Intra-cluster distance (r) The maximum Euclidean Distance between any instance belonging to the cluster, and the cluster center.

Inter-cluster distance (R) The Euclidean Distance between the centers of the two clusters.

The optimal partition will be the one which maximizes the ratio R/r.

10.10 Conclusions

This chapter dealt with the issues of generating Efficient Frontiers for a multi criteria decision problem, due to the tradeoff between accuracy and resolution (number of concepts) of any given classification problem and in-ducer. The solutions incorporated the manner of discerning the appropriate concepts for each level of resolution, and the procedure of generating the appropriate classifiers for the new updated classification problem.

The problem was tackled from two different perspectives. One, reducing the resolution level of the classification problem, while aggregating the given classes into new concepts, and the other, enhancing the resolution level of the classification problem, while de-aggregating the given classes.

The Error Based Approach for Concept Aggregation proved predom-inant over the Similarity Based Approach, taking into consideration the strength and weakness of the inducer and classifier, rather than just the training data itself. This Error Based Approach is based on the non-polynomial optimization problem, yet the greedy solution method for the defined problem yielded equal results to the optimal one, thus enabling a simple solution, with lower computational costs.

The pattern of the generated Efficient Frontier curves observed in three out of the twelve databases was linear, whereas the other 9 databases re-sulted in asymptotic logarithmic curves.

The de-aggregation method presented is in its preliminary stages, yield-ing no large scale experimental results, enabling us to reach general conclu-sions. Yet, the detailed illustration resulted in a tradeoff between the two measures of resolution and accuracy.

We will hereby analyze the results of Concept Aggregation, referring only to the EBA approach, which has proved its predominance.

When analyzing the pattern of the Efficient Frontier curves we are look-ing for a phase transition, i.e., a point in which a small change in one pa-rameter causes a large change in another parameter: In this case, the effect of resolution (number of concepts) on the accuracy of the classifier. The number of phase transitions, if they exist, is not limited to one, and the derivative curve may have two or more.

These two basic patterns of the derivative curves are in correlation with patterns of the Efficient Frontier curves discussed previously. The asymp-totic logarithmic curves instigate these phase transitions, and the "linear" ones do not (if the Efficiency Frontier curves were in fact linear, we would have had flat curves with the same value for all number of concepts).

We call these points of phase transition a "natural number of concepts" to the classification problem. The basic assumption is that the original construction and partitioning of the target or class domain, which has been created by man, is not the best one to describe reality. Thus, a better one may be established.

As mentioned, in nine out of the twelve databases there was a clear existence of these phase transitions. The three databases in which no transitions can be found were ones describing synthetic domains, a very unsurprising result, since the phase change phenomenon is known to transpire in natural domains.

The SBA and EBA methods introduced can be used as a supervised Class Based Clustering method. A clustering method that partitions the database in such a way, in which records having a certain value of a defined attribute or class, belong to precisely one cluster.

The Greedy EBA method can be perceived as an agglomerative hierarchical method, since each class initially represents an individual concept, and the concepts are successively merged, and once two concepts are aggregated, they can no longer be separated. The greedy EBA and the SBA methods do not share that property, but neither can they be classified as relocation clustering methods, since no iterational relocation occurs for a specific number of clusters.

Note that the clustering can be based on any of the database attributes, by defining the desirable attribute as the "Class".

Chapter 11

A Meta-Classification for
Decomposition Methodology

11.1 Meta Classifier Schema

As stated in Chapter 5, our ultimate goal is to develop a mechanism that combines all decomposition methods such that given an unseen dataset; the most appropriate decomposition (if any) could be selected. There are two alternatives to achieve this automatic and systematic decomposition procedure:

The wrapper approach Given a certain dataset, use each elementary decomposition and select the one that appears to give the highest success rate. The main advantage of this approach is its ability to predict quite well the performance of each examined method. The main disadvantage of this method is it's prolonged processing time. For some inducers the induction times may be very long, particularly in large real-life datasets. [Schaffer (1993)] has implemented this method for selecting induction algorithms and showed that it produces classifiers that are superior to any individual inducers. [Kohavi and John (1998)] has implemented this methodology for dimension reduction.

The Meta-Classifier approach Based on datasets characteristics, the meta-classifier decides whether to decompose the problem or not and what elementary decomposition to use. The idea of the meta-classifier approach can be summarized as follows: If a certain decomposition method outperforms other decomposition methods in a particular dataset, then one should expect that this method will be preferable when other problems with similar characteristics are presented. Meta-learning focuses on explaining what causes a decomposition method to be successful or not in a particular problem. Thus, this approach attempts to understand the conditions under which a decomposition method is most appropriate. This goal can be accomplished by performing the following phases: In the first phase one should examine the performance of all investigated decomposition methods on various datasets. Upon examination of each dataset, the characteristics of the dataset are extracted. The dataset's characteristics, together with the indication of the most preferable decomposition method, (in this dataset) are stored in a meta-dataset. This meta-dataset reflects the experience accumulated across different datasets. In the second phase, an inducer can be applied to this meta-dataset to induce a meta-classifier that can map a dataset to the most appropriate decomposition method (based on the characteristics of the dataset). In the last phase, the meta-classifier is actually used to match a new unseen dataset to the most appropriate decomposition method.

This book adopts the second alternative and examines it on real world problems. Previous works have already considered this approach for selecting the most appropriate induction algorithm given dataset characteristics (see for instance [Brazdil *et al.* (1994); Giraud–Carrier *et al.* (2004); Michie *et al.* (1994); Pfahringer *et al.* (2000); Bensusan and Kalousis (2001)]) However, applying this methodology for selecting the most appropriate decomposition given a certain dataset, has not yet been considered. The main disadvantages of the meta-learning process concern the assumption that datasets with similar properties behave the same. Furthermore, in meta-learning, the amount of data available (dataset descriptions and different performances) is usually quite small, thus the Meta classifier is based on small Meta datasets. Nevertheless, the main advantage of this approach is that after the meta-learning phase is completed, it can be used to select the best decomposition in negligible processing time.

Figures 11.1 and 11.2 present the schematic framework of the meta-decomposer. Figure 11.1 presents the meta-data generation phase. Figure 11.2 presents (A) the meta-learning phase and (B) the usage of the meta-decomposer. As it can be seen in Figure 11.1, the Dataset Generator component is responsible to extend the original datasets repository into a much bigger repository by manipulating the original datasets.

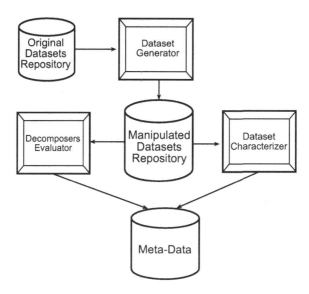

Fig. 11.1 Meta-Data Generation Phase.

11.2 Dataset Characterizer

It appears that datasets can be described using a vector of numeric values using certain features. [Brazdil *et al.* (1994)], divide the characteristic measures of a dataset into:

- Simple measures (e.g. number of attributes, number of classes, proportion of binary, categorical or ordinal attributes).
- Statistical measures (e.g. standard deviation ratio).
- Information based measures (e.g. mean entropy).

The Meta attributes used here are:

(1) Number of instances in the training dataset.
(2) Number of attributes.
(3) Ratio of number of instances to the number of attributes - Potential for overfitting. If this value is small, inducers may find a classifier that adapts too well to the specificities of the training data, which may be caused by noisy or irrelevant attributes, and thus result in poor generalization performance.
(4) Number of classes — The domain size of the target attribute.
(5) Proportion of the binary attributes.

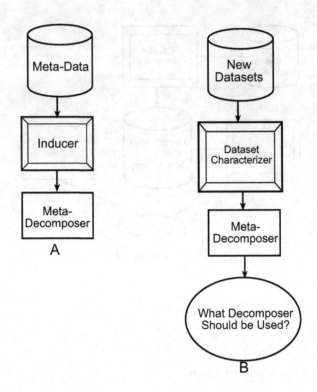

Fig. 11.2   (A) Meta Induction Phase Figure and (B) Meta-Decomposer Usage.

(6) Proportion of the categorical attributes.

(7) Proportion of the ordinal attributes.

(8) Default accuracy — accuracy obtained when using the most frequent class in the training set, without building any classifier.

(9) Mean of means — the mean of all numerical attributes means.

(10) Mean of standard deviation — the mean of all numerical attributes standard deviations. Standard deviation is the square root of the variance, which is a measure of how much the distribution is dispersed. For univariate data $Y_1, Y_2, \ldots, Y_N$, the formula for variance is:

$$Variance = s^2 = \frac{\sum\limits_{i=1}^{N} (Y_i - \bar{Y})^2}{(N-1)} \qquad (11.1)$$

where $\bar{Y}$ is the mean and N is the number of instances.

(11) Mean Kurtosis - The mean of all numerical attributes kurtosis measure.

Kurtosis is a measure of whether the data are peaked or flat relative to a normal distribution. That is, data sets with high kurtosis tend to have a distinct peak near the mean, decline rather rapidly, and have heavy tails (leptokurtic). Data sets with low kurtosis tend to have a flat top near the mean rather than a sharp peak and small tails. A uniform distribution would be the extreme case. For univariate data $Y_1, Y_2, \ldots, Y_N$, the formula for kurtosis is:

$$Kurtosis = \frac{\sum\limits_{i=1}^{N} (Y_i - \bar{Y})^4}{(N-1)s^4} - 3 \tag{11.2}$$

where $\bar{Y}$ is the mean, s is the standard deviation and N is the number of data points. The standard normal distribution has a kurtosis of zero. Positive kurtosis indicates a "peaked" distribution and negative kurtosis indicates a "flat" distribution.

Fig. 11.3   Kurtosis Illustration.

(12) Mean Skewness — The mean of all numerical attributes skewness measure. Skewness is a measure of symmetry, or more precisely, the lack of symmetry. A distribution, or data set, is symmetric if it looks the same to the left and right of the center point. For univariate data $Y_1, Y_2, \ldots, Y_N$, the formula for kurtosis is:

$$Skewness = \frac{\sum\limits_{i=1}^{N} (Y_i - \bar{Y})^3}{(N-1)s^3} \tag{11.3}$$

where $\bar{Y}$ is the mean, s is the standard deviation and N is the number of data points. The skewness for a normal distribution is zero, and any symmetric data should have skewness near zero. Negative values for the skewness indicate data that are skewed left and positive values for the skewness indicate data that are skewed right. By skewed left, we mean that the left tail is heavier than the right tail. Similarly, skewed right means that the right tail is heavier than the left tail. Some measurements have a lower bound and are skewed right. For example, in reliability studies, failure times cannot be negative.

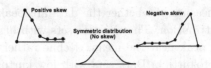

Fig. 11.4   Skewness Illustration.

(13) Mean of entropies — mean of all attributes simple entropy. Entropy measures the amount of uncertainty of a random variable. For a random variable x with K discrete values, each with probability p_k where $p = (p_1, p_2, \ldots, p_k)$ is a proper distribution, the entropy measure is:

$$H(x) = -\sum_k p_k \log p_k \qquad (11.4)$$

Notice that it is dependent only on the probability distribution of a random variable and not on its values.

(14) Average absolute correlation between numeric attributes: indicate robustness to irrelevant attributes.

(15) Proportion of numeric attributes with outliers: Indicate robustness to outlying values. A certain attribute is considered to have outliers if the ratio of the variances of mean value and the α-trimmed mean (where $\alpha = 0.05$) is smaller than 0.7.

(16) Average Gain Ratio — Average information gain ratio of the target attribute obtained by splitting the data according to each attribute. Useful as an indicative to the amount of relevant information embodied in the input attributes.

11.3   New Entropy Measure for Characterizing Mixed Datasets

The last section has shown that datasets can be characterized using classical statistical measures that are based on distribution's moments, namely: mean, standard deviation, skewness and kurtosis. However, these measures cannot be implemented directly on nominal variables. In order to overcome this problem, [Brazdil *et al.* (1994)] suggest converting a single nominal variable with K discrete values to $K - 1$ Bernuli variables, and then measures the mean, the standard deviation, etc. on each variable.

The Shanon entropy measure resembles in many ways to the classic variance measurement. Both of them are measures of quantifying uncertainty changes. However, entropy is different from variance by its metric-free nature: It is dependent only on the probability distribution of a random variable and not on its values. There is no universal relationship between the variance and entropy because the variance measures concentration of probabilities around the mean, whereas the entropy measures concentration of probabilities over subsets of the support of the distribution. Nevertheless, in certain cases, these measures behave in similar manners and entropy is considered as the "variance" equivalent for nominal attributes.

However,the entropy measure is not expressive as much as the cumulative effect of all statistical measures. For this purpose it is possible to use one of the generalized entropy measures available in the literature. [R'enyi (1970)] suggested generalizing the basic entropy measure in the following way:

$$H_\alpha^R(x) = \frac{1}{1-\alpha} \log \sum_k p_k^\alpha \qquad (11.5)$$

On the other hand [Tsallis (1988)] proposed a different generalized entropy measure, formulated as:

$$H_\alpha^T(x) = c\frac{\sum_k p_k^\alpha - 1}{1 - \alpha} \qquad (11.6)$$

R'enyi's measure and Tsallis's measure share some important properties. Both converge to Shannon's entropy measure when $\alpha \to 1$. Both indexes are concave for any arbitrary p. Both entropy measures are monotonically decreasing functions for any p. Both entropy measures are nonnegative for any arbitrary p. Both converge to zero when all probabilities but one equal zero. Both indexes reach a maximum value when all probabilities are equal. However, on the Bernoulli distribution the available generalized entropy measures and the classical statistical moment functions about the mean do not share the same shape. Figure 11.5 illustrates this observation.

This section suggests a new generalized entropy measure that is equivalent to the moment functions about the mean for the Bernoulli distribution. Thee goal of this new measure is to enable the definition of the skewness and kurtosis equivalence for nominal attributes.

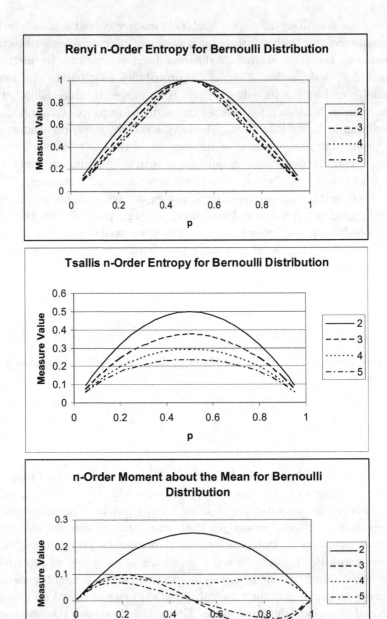

Fig. 11.5 Comparing R'enyi, Tsallis and Moment about the Mean for Bernoulli Distribution.

Definition 11.1

The α-order entropy of nominal variable x with K discrete values distributed according to $p = (p_1, \ldots, p_K)$ is defined as:

$$H_\alpha^*(x) = -\sum_{i=1}^{K} (-1)^{i*\alpha} p_i^{\alpha+1} \cdot \log p_i \qquad (11.7)$$

The above measure converges to Shannon's entropy for $\alpha = 0$. Furthermore, it is nonnegative for any arbitrary p and $\alpha \in \{0, 2, 4, 6, 8, \ldots\}$. However, due to the sign's rotation in the last formula for $\alpha \in \{1, 3, 5, 7, 9, \ldots\}$, the value of the proposed measure can be negative and depends on the order of p_i. Namely, two nominal variables with the same distribution structure might differ in their generalized entropy measure absolute values.

In order to avoid this inconvenience and keep the consistency, the measure should be calculated in such order which maximizes its absolute value and results in a positive value. Finding this order can be performed by converting this problem into an assignment problem (which is a particular class of classical graph matching and transportation linear programming problems). Given a bipartite graph and utility value for connecting nodes from one set to the other, the goal is to find an assignment that maximizes the total utility, such that each node in the first set is matched with exactly one node in the second set. This assignment problem is solvable in polynomial time, preferably by using the Hungarian algorithm developed by [Kuhn (1955)].

In this case, it is required to define two nodes for each possible value of the nominal variable, namely one node for each set. The utility value for matching one node to the other is defined as follows:

$$f^n(i, j) = -(-1)^{j*\alpha} p_i^{n+1} \log p_i \qquad (11.8)$$

For instance if $p = (0.24, 0.3, 0.15, 0.05, 0.26)$ then solving the appropriate assignment problem for $\alpha = 3$ indicates that the measure should be calculated $p = (0.24, 0.3, 0.15, 0.26, 0.05)$.

Definition 11.2 The Nominal Skewness Equivalence of nominal variable x with K discrete values distributed according to $p = (p_1, \ldots, p_K)$ is defined as:

$$S_1(x) = \frac{H_3(x)}{H_2(x) \cdot \sqrt{H_2(x)}} \qquad (11.9)$$

Definition 11.3

The Nominal Kurtosis Equivalence of nominal variable x with K discrete values distributed according to $p = (p_1, \ldots, p_K)$ is defined as:

$$S_2(x) = \frac{H_4(x)}{H_2(x)^2} \tag{11.10}$$

The following theorem discusses the relation of the proposed generalized entropy measure to the corresponding moment about the mean for the Bernoulli distribution. This distribution was selected because it can be referenced both as a nominal variable as well as an ordinary discrete variable.

Theorem 11.1   *Let $\mu_n^B(p)$ represent the $n -$ moment about the mean of the Bernoulli distribution with parameter p (n gets non-negative integer values) and $H_n^B(p)$ represents the corresponding n-order entropy, then the following statements are true:*

(1) μ_n and H_n get the same value when $p = \frac{1}{2}$.

(2) μ_n is positive if and only if H_n is positive.

(3) μ_n is decreasing (increasing) at p if and only if H_n is decreasing (increasing) at p.

(4) μ_n is concave (convex) at p if and only if H_n is concave (convex) at p.

(5) μ_n gets local minimum (maximum) at p if and only if H_n gets local minimum (maximum) at p

(6) μ_n has saddle point at p if and only if H_n saddle point at p.

The moment generating function of the Bernoulli distribution is:

$$M(t) = \sum^{e^{tn}} p^n (1-p)^{1-n} = e^0(1-p) + e^t p = 1 - p + e^t p \tag{11.11}$$

Consequently the n-order derivative of $M(t)$ is:

$$\frac{dM(t)}{dt^n} = pe^t \tag{11.12}$$

Namely the moment about 0 for any n is:

$$\frac{dM}{dt^n}(0) = p \tag{11.13}$$

Consequently the n-order moment about the mean is:

$$\mu_n^B(p) = p \cdot (1-p)^n + (-1)^n \cdot p^n \cdot (1-p) \qquad (11.14)$$

Furthermore, in the case of the Bernoulli distribution the n-order entropy measure can be expressed as:

$$H_n^B(p) = -(1-p)^{n+1} \cdot \log(1-p) - (-1)^n \cdot p^{n+1} \cdot \log(p) \qquad (11.15)$$

Due to the fact that $0 < p < 1$, the functions $H_n^B(p)$ and $\mu_n^B(p)$ have continuous derivatives up to any required order and the proof of sections 2 through 6 can be converted to the proof of the following inequalities:

$$H_n^B(p) \cdot \mu_n^B(p) \geq 0; \quad \frac{dH_n^B(p)}{dp} \cdot \frac{d\mu_n^B(p)}{dp}(p) \geq 0; \frac{dH_n^B(p)}{dp^2} \cdot \frac{d\mu_n^B(p)}{dp^2} \geq 0 \qquad (11.16)$$

The correctness of these inequalities can be validated by using the Taylor Series of the above products expanded about $1/2$ for $n \in \{1, 3, 5, 7, 9, \ldots\}$ and for $n \in \{2, 4, 6, 8, 10, \ldots\}$ separately. Figure illustrates Theorem 11.1.

Lemma 11.1 *Let $\gamma_1(p) = \frac{1-2p}{\sqrt{p(1-p)}}$ and $\gamma_2(p) = \frac{6p^2-6p+1}{p(1-p)}$ represent the Skewness and Kurtosis of the random variable distributed Bernoulli with parameter p respectively, and let $S_1^B(p)$ and $S_2^B(p)$ represent the Nominal Skewness Equivalence and the Nominal Kurtosis Equivalence of the same variable respectively, then the following statements are true:*

(1) $\gamma_i(p)$ and $S_i^B(p)$ get the same value when $p = 1/2$.

(2) $\gamma_i(p)$ is positive at p if and only if $S_i^B(p)$ is positive.

(3) $\gamma_i(p)$ is decreasing (increasing) at p if and only if $S_i^B(p)$ is decreasing (increasing) at p.

(4) $\gamma_i(p)$ is concave (convex) at p if and only if $S_i^B(p)$ is concave (convex) at p.

(5) $\gamma_i(p)$ gets local minimum (maximum) at p if and only if $S_i^B(p)$ gets local minimum (maximum) at p.

(6) $\gamma_i(p)$ has saddle point at p if and only if $S_i^B(p)$ has saddle point at p.

The proof of sections 1 and 2 can be obtained by using Theorem 11.1. Other sections can be verified by analyzing the functions explicitly.

The applicability of the proposed measure is verified by comparing the performance of the conventional meta-classifier described in the above and

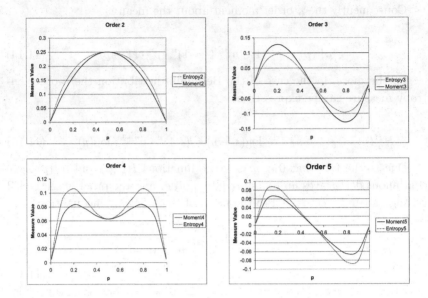

Fig. 11.6   Comparing the New Generalized Entropy Measure and Moment about the Mean for the Bernoulli Distribution.

the performance of the revised meta-classifier that utilizes the new measure. The above proofs are provided only for binomial distributions. Further research is required to verify whether the equivalence is kept in variables with more than two discrete values. Furthermore, it is required to investigate whether the proposed measure can be useful to recover the unknown probability distribution of nominal variables, namely is it possible to recover the distribution $p = (p_1, p_2, \ldots, p_k)$ of a random variable x with K, discrete values can be recovered by knowing the values of $H_1^*(x), H_2^*(x), \ldots, H_{k-1}^*(x)$

11.4   Dataset Manipulator

As stated above one of the main drawbacks of the meta-learning methodology is the necessity to induce from a very limited meta-dataset. The purpose of the Dataset Manipulator component is to extend the original repository of datasets into a much bigger repository and by that overcoming the limited meta-dataset problem.

Obviously the manipulation operators should efficiently affect the dataset characteristics in order to explore new options that are not represented in the original repository. The following simple operators can be suitable to this task:

Projection Randomly choose a subset of the original input attributes set and project the data according to it. This operation can have different levels of manipulation by setting a parameter that represents the subset size as a portion of the original attribute set. Note that this operation is disabled if the parameter is set to 100%.

Selection Randomly select a sub-sample of the original dataset. This operation can have different levels of manipulation by setting a parameter that represents the sub-sample size as a portion of the original dataset. Note that this operation is disabled if the parameter is set to 100%.

Distortion Changing the distribution of the target attribute by reassigning some of the instances to a different class. This operation can have different levels of manipulation by setting a parameter that represents the portion of instances that remain untouched. Note that this operation is disabled if the parameter is set to 100%.

Each manipulated dataset is obtained by performing these three operations. Note that there is no meaning to the order of manipulative operations. For each operation we have examined four different levels of manipulation: 100%, 90%, 75% and 50%. This results in 64 different combinations (manipulated datasets) for every dataset in the original repository. Because the original dataset repository contains 25 datasets, the manipulated repository consists of 1600 datasets.

11.5 Decomposer Evaluator

The aim of this component is to evaluate the performance of each decomposition method on each dataset in the manipulated repository using the C4.5 algorithm as the internal inducer. Furthermore, we checked the performance of C4.5 without performing any decomposition at all. Each manipulated dataset is represented in the meta-dataset as a single tuple, where its target value is chosen to be the method's name having the highest performance (from accuracy perspective) for this dataset. The performance is evaluated by averaging the results obtained by 10-fold-cross-validation procedure repeated 5 times. This book compares only three decomposition methods: Feature set decomposition using DOG algorithm,

Space Decomposition using K-Classifier algorithm and Sample Decomposition using Cluster Based Concurrent algorithm. All algorithms were executed using their default parameters. Obviously there are several limitations in the methodology presented above. First, the results could be altered if the algorithms' parameters are tuned differently. Second, there is no guarantee that these algorithms precisely represent the corresponded decomposition method, namely if different decomposition algorithms had been employed here the results could be different.

11.6   The Meta-Decomposer

Figure 11.7 presents the decision tree obtained by employing the C4.5 algorithm on meta-data (the tree has been slightly modified for legibility). It can be seen that space decomposition is useful when there are numeric attributes. This makes sense as the employed algorithm uses the K-Means algorithm which is more suitable to numeric instance space. The Instance-Attribute Ratio Meta attribute is used to differentiate between ATTRIBUTE (Attribute Decomposition) and NONE (not performing decomposition at all) in the second and third leaves. In this case, if the Instance-Attribute Ratio is below a 78.77 (namely there are many attributes relatively to the dataset size), then attribute decomposition should be applied. Another interesting observation is that both MeanEntropy2 (The new proposed entropy measure) and MeanTsallisEntropy2 (Tsallis' Entropy Measure) are found to be relevant. This indicates that the new proposed measure is not redundant.

11.7   Evaluating the Meta-Decomposer

To evaluate whether meta-decomposer brings some benefits, we have carried out the leave-one-out procedure. According to this procedure the meta-decomposer has been generated by learning from a partial meta-dataset obtained by removing one original dataset (and all its derived datasets). Then the obtained meta-decomposer has been evaluated on the dataset that has been left out. This procedure has been repeated 26 times, each time leaving out a different dataset. Table 7.1 presents the obtained results. The first column shows the dataset name. The second and third columns correspondingly present the actual best method and the method anticipated by the meta-decomposer to be the most suitable method. The

```
num prop <= 0
   MeanEntropy2 <= 0.03 ⟶ ATTRIBUTE (362.0/57.0)
   MeanEntropy2 > 0.03
      Cat prop <= 0.67
         MeanTsallisEntropy2 <= 0.57
            Instance-Attribute Ratio <= 78.77
                    ⟶ ATTRIBUTE (336.0/135.0)
            Instance-Attribute Ratio > 78.77
                    ⟶ NONE (213.0/56.0)
         MeanTsallisEntropy2 > 0.57
                    ⟶ SAMPLE (425.0/235.0)
      Cat prop > 0.67 ⟶ NONE (328.0)
num count > 0 ⟶ SPACE (280.0/151)
```

Fig. 11.7   Meta-Decomposer Decision Tree.

fourth, fifth and sixth columns present the accuracy obtained using C4.5, the actual best method and the anticipated method respectively. As it can be seen in almost two thirds of the datasets, the meta-decomposer was able to predict which decomposition method (if at all) outperforms other methods. In the remaining cases the performance of the anticipated method has been slightly less accurate than the actual best method with no statistical significance. Moreover, employing the meta-decomposer together with its corresponded decomposition method can improve on average the accuracy of C4.5 in 6.86% (while the best improvement that might be obtained by selecting the most suitable decomposition method is 7.07%).

Table 11.1   Performance Results of Meta-Decomposer Procedure.

Dataset Name	Actual Best Method	Anticipated Best Method	Accuracy C4.5	Accuracy Actual Best Method	Accuracy Anticipated Best Method
AUST	Attribute	None	85.36±5.1	86.52±2.5	85.36±5.1
AUDIOLOGY	Attribute	ATT	75±6.95	78.5±6.54	78.5±6.54
BCAN	Attribute	None	92.99±2.87	97.42±1.17	92.99±2.87
HEPATITIS	Attribute	Attribute	70.32±8.46	80±6.89	80±6.89
IRIS	None	None	96±3.33	95.33±5.05	96±3.33
KR-VS-KP	Space	None	99.44±0.55	99.62±0.43	99.44±0.55
LABOR	Attribute	Attribute	87.72±12.72	98.24±4.52	98.24±4.52
LED17	Attribute	Attribute	59.09±6.9	73.64±5.5	73.64±5.5
LETTER	Space	Space	74.96±0.8	77.46±0.64	77.46±0.64
LCAN	Attribute	Attribute	38.71±17.82	93.55±10.05	93.55±10.05
MONKS1	Attribute	Attribute	75.81±8.2	98.39± 2.3	98.39± 2.3
MONKS2	Sample	Sample	61.54±8.6	65.36 ±5.7	65.36 ±5.7
MONKS3	Attribute	None	93.44±3.7	93.442±3.3	93.44±3.7
MUSH	None	Attribute	100±0	100±0	100±0
NURSE	None	Space	97.45±0.4	90.65±0.6	90.65±0.6
OPTIC	Attribute	Attribute	62.42±2	91.73±1.4	91.73±1.4
SONAR	Attribute	Attribute	69.71±5.4	77.12±8.7	77.12±8.7
SOYBEAN	Space	Attribute	92.83±1.52	94.9±4.61	92.9±2.56
SPI	Attribute	Attribute	91.2±1.9	95.8±0.9	95.8±0.9
TTT	None	Space	85.7±1.65	79.33±4	79.33±4
VOTE	None	None	96.21±2.45	90.52±1.23	96.21±2.45
WINE	Attribute	Attribute	85.96±6.9	96.63±3.9	96.63±3.9
ZOO	Attribute	Attribute	93.07±5.8	98.02±3.02	98.02±3.02
ARCENE	Sample	None	75 ±9.2	79±8.1	75 ±9.2
DEXTER	Attribute	Attribute	78.33 ±3.6	89.33±2.7	89.33±2.7
MADELON	Attribute	Attribute	69.8±4.7	71.4 ±2.6	71.4 ±2.6

Bibliography

Aha, D. W.; Kibler, D.; and Albert, M. K., Instancebased learning algorithms. Machine Learning 6(1):37-66, 1991.

Al-Sultan K. S., A tabu search approach to the clustering problem, Pattern Recognition, 28:1443-1451,1995.

Al-Sultan K. S. , Khan M. M. : Computational experience on four algorithms for the hard clustering problem. Pattern Recognition Letters 17(3): 295-308, 1996.

Ali K. M., Pazzani M. J., Error Reduction through Learning Multiple Descriptions, Machine Learning, 24: 3, 173-202, 1996.

Almuallim H., An Efficient Algorithm for Optimal Pruning of Decision Trees. Artificial Intelligence 83(2): 347-362, 1996.

Almuallim H,. and Dietterich T.G., Learning Boolean concepts in the presence of many irrelevant features. Artificial Intelligence, 69: 1-2, 279-306, 1994.

Alsabti K., Ranka S. and Singh V., CLOUDS: A Decision Tree Classifier for Large Datasets, Conference on Knowledge Discovery and Data Mining (KDD-98), August 1998.

Anand R, Methrotra K, Mohan CK, Ranka S. Efficient classification for multiclass problems using modular neural networks. IEEE Trans Neural Networks, 6(1): 117-125, 1995.

Anderson, J.A. and Rosenfeld, E. Talking Nets: An Oral History of Neural Network Research. Cambridge, MA: MIT Press, 2000.

Ashenhurst, R. L., The decomposition of switching functions, Technical report, Bell Laboratories BL-1(11), pp. 541-602, 1952.

Attneave F., Applications of Information Theory to Psychology. Holt, Rinehart and Winston, 1959.

Avnimelech R. and Intrator N., Boosted Mixture of Experts: an ensemble learning scheme, Neural Computations, 11(2):483-497, 1999.

Baker E., and Jain A. K., On feature ordering in practice and some finite sample effects. In Proceedings of the Third International Joint Conference on Pattern Recognition, pages 45-49, San Diego, CA, 1976.

Banfield J. D. and Raftery A. E. . Model-based Gaussian and non-Gaussian clustering. Biometrics, 49:803-821, 1993.

Bartlett P. and Shawe-Taylor J., Generalization Performance of Support Vector Machines and Other Pattern Classifiers, In "Advances in Kernel Methods, Support Vector Learning", Bernhard Scholkopf, Christopher J. C. Burges, and Alexander J. Smola (eds.), MIT Press, Cambridge, USA, 1998.

Bauer, E. and Kohavi, R., "An Empirical Comparison of Voting Classification Algorithms: Bagging, Boosting, and Variants". Machine Learning, 35: 1-38, 1999.

Baxt, W. G., Use of an artificial neural network for data analysis in clinical decision making: The diagnosis of acute coronary occlusion. Neural Computation, 2(4):480-489, 1990.

Bay, S., Nearest neighbor classification from multiple feature subsets. Intelligent Data Analysis, 3(3): 191-209, 1999.

Bellman, R., Adaptive Control Processes: A Guided Tour, Princeton University Press, 1961.

BenBassat M., Myopic policies in sequential classification. IEEE Trans. on Computing, 27(2):170-174, February 1978.

Bennett X. and Mangasarian O.L., Multicategory discrimination via linear programming. Optimization Methods and Software, 3:29-39, 1994.

Bensusan H. and Kalousis A., Estimating the Predictive Accuracy of a Classifier, In Proc. Proceedings of the 12th European Conference on Machine Learning, pages 25-36, 2001.

Bentley J. L. and Friedman J. H., Fast algorithms for constructing minimal spanning trees in coordinate spaces. IEEE Transactions on Computers, C-27(2):97-105, February 1978. 275

Bernard M.E., Decision trees and diagrams. Computing Surveys, 14(4):593-623, 1982.

Berry M., and Linoff G., Mastering Data Mining, John Wiley & Sons, 2000.

Bhargava H. K., Data Mining by Decomposition: Adaptive Search for Hypothesis Generation, INFORMS Journal on Computing Vol. 11, Iss. 3, pp. 239-47, 1999.

Biermann, A. W., Faireld, J., and Beres, T. (1982). Signature table systems and learning. IEEE Trans. Syst. Man Cybern., 12(5):635-648.

Blum, A. L. and Langley, P., 1997, Selection of relevant features and examples in machine learning, Artificial Intelligence, 97, pp.245-271.

Blum A., and Mitchell T., Combining Labeled and Unlabeled Data with CoTraining. In Proc. of the 11th Annual Conference on Computational Learning Theory, pages 92-100, 1998.

Bonner, R., On Some Clustering Techniques. IBM journal of research and development, 8:22-32, 1964.

Booker L., Goldberg D. E., and Holland J. H., Classifier systems and genetic algorithms. Artificial Intelligence, 40(1-3):235-282, 1989.

Brachman, R. and Anand, T., 1994, The process of knowledge discovery in databases, in: Advances in Knowledge Discovery and Data Mining, AAAI/MIT Press, pp. 37-58.

Bratko I., and Bohanec M., Trading accuracy for simplicity in decision trees, Machine Learning 15: 223-250, 1994.

Brazdil P., Gama J., Henery R., Characterizing the Applicability of Classification Algorithms using Meta Level Learning, in Machine Learning: ECML-94, F.Bergadano e L. de Raedt (eds.), LNAI No. 784: pp. 83-102, Springer-Verlag, 1994.

Breiman L., Bagging predictors, Machine Learning, 24(2):123-140, 1996.

Breiman L., Friedman J., Olshen R., and Stone C.. Classification and Regression Trees. Wadsworth Int. Group, 1984.

Br Brodley, C. E., Automatic selection of split criterion during tree growing based on node selection. In Proceedings of the Twelfth International Conference on Machine Learning, 73-80 Taho City, Ca. Morgan Kaufmann, 1995.

Brodley C. E. and Utgoff. P. E., Multivariate decision trees. Machine Learning, 19:45-77, 1995.

Buchanan, B.G. and Shortliffe, E.H., Rule Based Expert Systems, 272-292, Addison-Wesley, 1984.

Buja, A. and Lee, Y.S., Data mining criteria for tree based regression and classification, Proceedings of the 7th International Conference on Knowledge Discovery and Data Mining, (pp 27-36), San Diego, USA, 2001.

Buntine, W., A Theory of Learning Classification Rules. Doctoral dissertation. School of Computing Science, University of Technology. Sydney. Australia, 1990.

Buntine, W., "Graphical Models for Discovering Knowledge", in U. Fayyad, G. Piatetsky-Shapiro, P. Smyth, and R. Uthurusamy, editors, Advances in Knowledge Discovery and Data Mining, pp 59-82. AAAI/MIT Press, 1996.

Buntine W., Niblett T., A Further Comparison of Splitting Rules for Decision-Tree Induction. Machine Learning, 8: 75-85, 1992.

Buczak A. L. and Ziarko W., "Neural and Rough Set Based Data Mining Methods in Engineering", Klosgen W. and Zytkow J. M. (Eds.), Handbook of Data Mining and Knowledge Discovery, pages 788-797. Oxford University Press, 2002.

Can F. , Incremental clustering for dynamic information processing, in ACM Transactions on Information Systems, no. 11, pp 143-164, 1993.

Catlett J., Mega induction: Machine Learning on Vary Large Databases, PhD, University of Sydney, 1991.

Chan P. K. and Stolfo, S. J., Toward parallel and distributed learning by meta-learning, In AAAI Workshop in Knowledge Discovery in Databases, pp. 227-240, 1993.

Chan P.K. and Stolfo, S.J., A Comparative Evaluation of Voting and Meta-learning on Partitioned Data, Proc. 12th Intl. Conf. On Machine Learning ICML-95, 1995.

Chan P.K. and Stolfo S.J, On the Accuracy of Meta-learning for Scalable Data Mining, J. Intelligent Information Systems, 8:5-28, 1997.

Charnes, A., Cooper, W. W., and Rhodes, E., Measuring the efficiency of decision making units, European Journal of Operational Research, 2(6):429-444, 1978.

Chen K., Wang L. and Chi H., Methods of Combining Multiple Classifiers with Different Features and Their Applications to Text-Independent Speaker

Identification, International Journal of Pattern Recognition and Artificial Intelligence, 11(3): 417-445, 1997.

Cheeseman P., Stutz J.: Bayesian Classification (AutoClass): Theory and Results. Advances in Knowledge Discovery and Data Mining 1996: 153-180

Cherkauer, K.J., Human Expert-Level Performance on a Scientific Image Analysis Task by a System Using Combined Artificial Neural Networks. In Working Notes, Integrating Multiple Learned Models for Improving and Scaling Machine Learning Algorithms Workshop, Thirteenth National Conference on Artificial Intelligence. Portland, OR: AAAI Press, 1996.

Chizi, B., Maimon, O. and Smilovici A. On Dimensionality Reduction of High Dimensional Data Sets, Frontiers in Artificial Intelligence and Applications, IOS press, pp. 230-236, 2002.

Clark P., and Niblett T., The CN2 rule induction algorithm. Machine Learning, 3:261-284, 1989.

Clark, P. and Boswell, R., "Rule induction with CN2: Some recent improvements." In Proceedings of the European Working Session on Learning, pp. 151-163, Pitman, 1991.

Clearwater, S., T. Cheng, H. Hirsh, and B. Buchanan. Incremental batch learning. In Proceedings of the Sixth International Workshop on Machine Learning, San Mateo CA:, pp. 366-370. Morgan Kaufmann, 1989.

Crawford S. L., Extensions to the CART algorithm. Int. J. of ManMachine Studies, 31(2):197-217, August 1989.

Curtis, H. A., A New Approach to the Design of Switching Functions, Van Nostrand, Princeton, 1962.

Dhillon I. and Modha D., Concept Decomposition for Large Sparse Text Data Using Clustering. Machine Learning. 42, pp.143-175. (2001).

Dempster A.P., Laird N.M., and Rubin D.B., Maximum likelihood from incomplete data using the EM algorithm. Journal of the Royal Statistical Society, 39(B), 1977.

Dietterich, T. G., "Approximate statistical tests for comparing supervised classification learning algorithms". Neural Computation, 10(7): 1895-1924, 1998.

Dietterich, T. G., An Experimental Comparison of Three Methods for Constructing Ensembles of Decision Trees: Bagging, Boosting and Randomization. 40(2):139-157, 2000.

Dietterich T., Ensemble methods in machine learning. In J. Kittler and F. Roll, editors, First International Workshop on Multiple Classifier Systems, Lecture Notes in Computer Science, pages 1-15. Springer-Verlag, 2000

Dietterich, T. G., and Ghulum Bakiri. Solving multiclass learning problems via error-correcting output codes. Journal of Artificial Intelligence Research, 2:263-286, 1995.

Dietterich, T. G., and Kong, E. B., Machine learning bias, statistical bias, and statistical variance of decision tree algorithms. Tech. rep., Oregon State University, 1995.

Dietterich, T. G., and Michalski, R. S., A comparative review of selected methods for learning from examples, Machine Learning, an Artificial Intelligence approach, 1: 41-81, 1983.

Dietterich, T. G., Kearns, M., and Mansour, Y., Applying the weak learning framework to understand and improve C4.5. Proceedings of the Thirteenth International Conference on Machine Learning, pp. 96-104, San Francisco: Morgan Kaufmann, 1996.

Domingos, P., Using Partitioning to Speed Up Specific-to-General Rule Induction. In Proceedings of the AAAI-96 Workshop on Integrating Multiple Learned Models, pp. 29-34, AAAI Press, 1996.

Domingos, P., & Pazzani, M., On the Optimality of the Naive Bayes Classifier under Zero-One Loss, Machine Learning, 29: 2, 103-130, 1997.

Dougherty, J., Kohavi, R, Sahami, M., Supervised and unsupervised discretization of continuous attributes. Machine Learning: Proceedings of the twelfth International Conference, Morgan Kaufman pp. 194-202, 1995.

Duda, R., and Hart, P., Pattern Classification and Scene Analysis, New-York, Wiley, 1973.

Duda, P. E. Hart and D. G. Stork, Pattern Classification, Wiley, New York, 2001.

Dunteman, G.H., Principal Components Analysis, Sage Publications, 1989.

Elder I. and Pregibon, D., "A Statistical Perspective on Knowledge Discovery in Databases", In U. Fayyad, G. Piatetsky-Shapiro, P. Smyth, and R. Uthurusamy editors., Advances in Knowledge Discovery and Data Mining, pp. 83-113, AAAI/MIT Press, 1996.

Esposito F., Malerba D. and Semeraro G., A Comparative Analysis of Methods for Pruning Decision Trees. EEE Transactions on Pattern Analysis and Machine Intelligence, 19(5):476-492, 1997.

Ester M., Kriegel H.P., Sander S., and Xu X., A density-based algorithm for discovering clusters in large spatial databases with noise. In E. Simoudis, J. Han, and U. Fayyad, editors, Proceedings of the 2nd International Conference on Knowledge Discovery and Data Mining (KDD-96), pages 226-231, Menlo Park, CA, 1996. AAAI, AAAI Press.

Estivill-Castro, V. and Yang, J. A Fast and robust general purpose clustering algorithm. Pacific Rim International Conference on Artificial Intelligence, pp. 208-218, 2000.

Fraley C. and Raftery A.E., "How Many Clusters? Which Clustering Method? Answers Via Model-Based Cluster Analysis", Technical Report No. 329. Department of Statistics University of Washington, 1998.

Fayyad, U., Piatesky-Shapiro, G. & Smyth P., From Data Mining to Knowledge Discovery: An Overview. In U. Fayyad, G. Piatetsky-Shapiro, P. Smyth, & R. Uthurusamy (Eds), Advances in Knowledge Discovery and Data Mining, pp 1-30, AAAI/MIT Press, 1996.

Fayyad, U., Grinstein, G. and Wierse, A., Information Visualization in Data Mining and Knowledge Discovery, Morgan Kaufmann, 2001.

Fayyad U., and Irani K. B., The attribute selection problem in decision tree generation. In proceedings of Tenth National Conference on Artificial Intelligence, pp. 104–110, Cambridge, MA: AAAI Press/MIT Press, 1992.

Ferri C., Flach P., and Hernández-Orallo J., Learning Decision Trees Using the Area Under the ROC Curve. In Claude Sammut and Achim Hoffmann, editors, Proceedings of the 19th International Conference on Machine Learning, pp. 139-146. Morgan Kaufmann, July 2002

Fifield D. J., Distributed Tree Construction From Large Datasets, Bachelor's Honor Thesis, Australian National University, 1992.

Fisher, D., 1987, Knowledge acquisition via incremental conceptual clustering, in machine learning 2, pp. 139-172.

Fischer, B., "Decomposition of Time Series - Comparing Different Methods in Theory and Practice", Eurostat Working Paper, 1995.

Fix, E., and Hodges, J.L., Discriminatory analysis. Nonparametric discrimination. Consistency properties. Technical Report 4, US Air Force School of Aviation Medicine. Randolph Field, TX, 1957.

Fortier, J.J. and Solomon, H. 1996. Clustering procedures. In proceedings of the Multivariate Analysis, '66, P.R. Krishnaiah (Ed.), pp. 493-506.

Fountain, T. Dietterich T., Sudyka B., "Mining IC Test Data to Optimize VLSI Testing", ACM SIGKDD Conference, 2000, pp. 18-25, 2000.

Frawley W. J., Piatetsky-Shapiro G., and Matheus C. J., "Knowledge Discovery in Databases: An Overview," G. Piatetsky-Shapiro and W. J. Frawley, editors, Knowledge Discovery in Databases, 1-27, AAAI Press, Menlo Park, California, 1991.

Freitas X., and Lavington S. H., Mining Very Large Databases With Parallel Processing, Kluwer Academic Publishers, 1998.

Freund Y. and Schapire R. E., Experiments with a new boosting algorithm. In Machine Learning: Proceedings of the Thirteenth International Conference, pages 325-332, 1996.

Friedman J. H., A recursive partitioning decision rule for nonparametric classifiers. IEEE Trans. on Comp., C26:404-408, 1977.

Friedman, J. H., "Multivariate Adaptive Regression Splines", The Annual Of Statistics, 19, 1-141, 1991.

Friedman, J.H. (1997a). Data Mining and Statistics: What is the connection? 1997.

Friedman, J.H. (1997b). On bias, variance, 0/1 - loss and the curse of dimensionality, Data Mining and Knowledge Discovery, 1: 1, 55-77, 1997.

Friedman, J.H. & Tukey, J.W., A Projection Pursuit Algorithm for Exploratory Data Analysis, IEEE Transactions on Computers, 23: 9, 881-889, 1973.

Friedman N., Geiger D., and Goldszmidt M., Bayesian Network Classifiers, Machine Learning 29: 2-3, 131-163, 1997.

Fukunaga, K., Introduction to Statistical Pattern Recognition. San Diego, CA: Academic, 1990.

Fürnkranz, J., More efficient windowing, In Proceeding of The 14th national Conference on Artificial Intelegence (AAAI-97), pp. 509-514, Providence, RI. AAAI Press, 1997.

Gallinari, P., Modular Neural Net Systems, Training of. In (Ed.) M.A. Arbib. The Handbook of Brain Theory and Neural Networks, Bradford Books/MIT Press, 1995.

Gama J., A Linear-Bayes Classifier. In C. Monard, editor, Advances on Artificial Intelligence – SBIA2000. LNAI 1952, pp 269-279, Springer Verlag, 2000

Gams, M., New Measurements Highlight the Importance of Redundant Knowledge. In European Working Session on Learning, Montpeiller, France, Pitman, 1989.

Gardner M., Bieker, J., Data mining solves tough semiconductor manufacturing problems. KDD 2000: pp. 376-383, 2000.

Gehrke J., Ganti V., Ramakrishnan R., Loh W., BOAT-Optimistic Decision Tree Construction. SIGMOD Conference 1999: pp. 169-180, 1999.

Gehrke J., Ramakrishnan R., Ganti V., RainForest - A Framework for Fast Decision Tree Construction of Large Datasets,Data Mining and Knowledge Discovery, 4 (2/3) 127-162, 2000.

Gelfand S. B., Ravishankar C. S., and Delp E. J., An iterative growing and pruning algorithm for classification tree design. IEEE Transaction on Pattern Analysis and Machine Intelligence, 13(2):163-174, 1991.

Geman S., Bienenstock, E., and Doursat, R., Neural networks and the bias/variance dilemma. Neural Computation, 4:1-58, 1995.

Gillo M. W., MAID: A Honeywell 600 program for an automatised survey analysis. Behavioral Science 17: 251-252, 1972.

Giraud–Carrier Ch., Vilalta R., Brazdil R., Introduction to the Special Issue of on Meta-Learning, Machine Learning, 54 (3), 197-194, 2004.

Gluck, M. and Corter, J. (1985). Information, uncertainty, and the utility of categories. Proceedings of the Seventh Annual Conference of the Cognitive Science Society (pp. 283-287). Irvine, California: Lawrence Erlbaum Associates.

Grossman R., Kasif S., Moore R., Rocke D., and Ullman J., Data mining research: Opportunities and challenges. Report of three NSF workshops on mining large, massive, and distributed data, 1999.

Grumbach S., Milo T., Towards Tractable Algebras for Bags. Journal of Computer and System Sciences 52(3): 570-588, 1996.

Guo Y. and Sutiwaraphun J., Knowledge probing in distributed data mining, in Proc. 4h Int. Conf. Knowledge Discovery Data Mining, pp 61-69, 1998.

Guha, S., Rastogi, R. and Shim, K. CURE: An efficient clustering algorithm for large databases. In Proceedings of ACM SIGMOD International Conference on Management of Data, pages 73-84, New York, 1998.

Han, J. and Kamber, M. Data Mining: Concepts and Techniques. Morgan Kaufmann Publishers, 2001.

Hancock T. R., Jiang T., Li M., Tromp J., Lower Bounds on Learning Decision Lists and Trees. Information and Computation 126(2): 114-122, 1996.

Hand, D., Data Mining – reaching beyond statistics, Research in Official Stat. 1(2):5-17, 1998.

Hampshire, J. B., and Waibel, A. The meta-Pi network - building distributed knowledge representations for robust multisource pattern-recognition. Pattern Analyses and Machine Intelligence 14(7): 751-769, 1992.

Hansen J., Combining Predictors. Meta Machine Learning Methods and Bias/Variance & Ambiguity Decompositions. PhD dissertation. Aurhus University. 2000.

Hansen, L. K., and Salamon, P., Neural network ensembles. IEEE Transactions on Pattern Analysis and Machine Intelligence, 12(10), 993–1001, 1990.

Hartigan, J. A. Clustering algorithms. John Wiley and Sons., 1975.

Huang, Z., Extensions to the k-means algorithm for clustering large data sets with categorical values. Data Mining and Knowledge Discovery, 2(3), 1998.

He D. W., Strege B., Tolle H., and Kusiak A., Decomposition in Automatic Generation of Petri Nets for Manufacturing System Control and Scheduling, International Journal of Production Research, 38(6): 1437-1457, 2000.

Holmstrom, L., Koistinen, P., Laaksonen, J., and Oja, E., Neural and statistical classifiers - taxonomy and a case study. IEEE Trans. on Neural Networks, 8,:5–17, 1997.

Holte R. C., Very simple classification rules perform well on most commonly used datasets. Machine Learning, 11:63-90, 1993.

Holte, R. C.; Acker, L. E.; and Porter, B. W., Concept learning and the problem of small disjuncts. In Proceedings of the 11th International Joint Conference on Artificial Intelligence, pp. 813-818, 1989.

Hoppner F. , Klawonn F., Kruse R., Runkler T., Fuzzy Cluster Analysis, Wiley, 2000.

Hrycej T., Modular Learning in Neural Networks. New York: Wiley, 1992.

Hu, X., Using Rough Sets Theory and Database Operations to Construct a Good Ensemble of Classifiers for Data Mining Applications. ICDM01. pp 233-240, 2001.

Hubert, L. and Arabie, P. (1985) Comparing partitions. Journal of Classification, 5. 193-218.

Hunter L., Klein T. E., Finding Relevant Biomolecular Features. ISMB 1993, pp. 190-197, 1993.

Hwang J., Lay S., and Lippman A., Nonparametric multivariate density estimation: A comparative study, IEEE Transaction on Signal Processing, 42(10): 2795-2810, 1994.

Hyafil L. and Rivest R.L., Constructing optimal binary decision trees is NP-complete. Information Processing Letters, 5(1):15-17, 1976

Jacobs, R. A., Jordan, M. I., Nowlan, S. J., and Hinton, G. E. Adaptive mixtures of local experts. Neural Computation 3(1):79-87, 1991.

Jain, A.K. Murty, M.N. and Flynn, P.J. Data Clustering: A Survey. ACM Computing Surveys, Vol. 31, No. 3, September 1999.

Jenkins R. and Yuhas, B. P. A simplified neural network solution through problem decomposition: The case of Truck backer-upper, IEEE Transactions on Neural Networks 4(4):718-722, 1993.

Jimenez, L. O., & Landgrebe D. A., Supervised Classification in High- Dimensional Space: Geometrical, Statistical, and Asymptotical Properties of Multivariate Data. IEEE Transaction on Systems Man, and Cybernetics — Part C: Applications and Reviews, 28:39-54, 1998.

Johansen T. A. and Foss B. A., A narmax model representation for adaptive control based on local model -Modeling, Identification and Control, 13(1):25-39, 1992.

John G. H., Robust linear discriminant trees. In D. Fisher and H. Lenz, editors, Learning From Data: Artificial Intelligence and Statistics V, Lecture Notes in Statistics, Chapter 36, pp. 375-385. Springer-Verlag, New York, 1996.

John G. H., Kohavi R., and Pfleger P., Irrelevant features and the subset selection problem. In Machine Learning: Proceedings of the Eleventh International Conference. Morgan Kaufmann, 1994.

John G. H., and Langley P., Estimating Continuous Distributions in Bayesian Classifiers. Proceedings of the Eleventh Conference on Uncertainty in Artificial Intelligence. pp. 338-345. Morgan Kaufmann, San Mateo, 1995.

Jordan, M. I., and Jacobs, R. A., Hierarchical mixtures of experts and the EM algorithm. Neural Computation, 6, 181-214, 1994.

Jordan, M. I., and Jacobs, R. A. Hierarchies of adaptive experts. In Advances in Neural Information Processing Systems, J. E. Moody, S. J. Hanson, and R. P. Lippmann, Eds., vol. 4, Morgan Kaufmann Publishers, Inc., pp. 985-992, 1992.

Joshi, V. M., "On Evaluating Performance of Classifiers for Rare Classes", Second IEEE International Conference on Data Mining, IEEE Computer Society Press, pp. 641-644, 2002.

Kanal, L. N., "Patterns in Pattern Recognition: 1968-1974". IEEE Transactions on Information Theory IT-20, 6: 697-722, 1974.

Kargupta, H. and Chan P., eds, Advances in Distributed and Parallel Knowledge Discovery , pp. 185-210, AAAI/MIT Press, 2000.

Kaufman, L. and Rousseeuw, P.J., 1987, Clustering by Means of Medoids, In Y. Dodge, editor, Statistical Data Analysis, based on the L1 Norm, pp. 405-416, Elsevier/North Holland, Amsterdam.

Kaufmann, L. and Rousseeuw, P.J. Finding groups in data. New-York: Wiley, 1990.

Kass G. V., An exploratory technique for investigating large quantities of categorical data. Applied Statistics, 29(2):119-127, 1980.

Kearns M. and Mansour Y., A fast, bottom-up decision tree pruning algorithm with near-optimal generalization, in J. Shavlik, ed., 'Machine Learning: Proceedings of the Fifteenth International Conference', Morgan Kaufmann Publishers, Inc., pp. 269-277, 1998.

Kearns M. and Mansour Y., On the boosting ability of top-down decision tree learning algorithms. Journal of Computer and Systems Sciences, 58(1): 109-128, 1999.

Kenney, J. F. and Keeping, E. S. "Moment-Generating and Characteristic Functions," "Some Examples of Moment-Generating Functions," and "Uniqueness Theorem for Characteristic Functions." §4.6-4.8 in Mathematics of Statistics, Pt. 2, 2nd ed. Princeton, NJ: Van Nostrand, pp. 72-77, 1951.

Kerber, R., 1992, ChiMerge: Descretization of numeric attributes, in AAAI-92, Proceedings Ninth National Conference on Artificial Intelligence, pp. 123-128, AAAI Press/MIT Press.

Kim J.O. & Mueller C.W., Factor Analysis: Statistical Methods and Practical Issues. Sage Publications, 1978.

Kim, D.J., Park, Y.W. and Park,. A novel validity index for determination of the optimal number of clusters. IEICE Trans. Inf., Vol. E84-D, no.2 (2001), 281-285.

King, B. Step-wise Clustering Procedures, J. Am. Stat. Assoc. 69, pp. 86-101,

1967.

Klosgen W. and Zytkow J. M., "KDD: The Purpose, Necessity and Chalanges", Klosgen W. and Zytkow J. M. (Eds.), Handbook of Data Mining and Knowledge Discovery, pp. 1-9. Oxford University Press, 2002.

Kohavi, R., Bottom-up induction of oblivious read-once decision graphs, in F. Bergadano and L. De Raedt, editors, Proc. European Conference on Machine Learning, pp. 154-169, Springer-Verlag, 1994.

Kohavi R., Scaling up the accuracy of naive-bayes classifiers: a decision-tree hybrid. In Proceedings of the Second International Conference on Knowledge Discovery and Data Mining, pages 114–119, 1996.

Kohavi R., Becker B., and Sommerfield D., Improving simple Bayes. In Proceedings of the European Conference on Machine Learning, 1997.

Kohavi R. and John G., The Wrapper Approach, In Feature Extraction, Construction and Selection: A Data Mining Perspective, H. Liu and H. Motoda (eds.), Kluwer Academic Publishers, 1998.

Kohavi R., and Provost F., Glossary of Terms, Machine Learning 30(2/3): 271-274, 1998.

Kohavi R. and Quinlan J. R., Decision-tree discovery. In Klosgen W. and Zytkow J. M., editors, Handbook of Data Mining and Knowledge Discovery, chapter 16.1.3, pages 267-276. Oxford University Press, 2002.

Kohavi R. and Sommerfield D., Targeting business users with decision table classifiers, in R. Agrawal, P. Stolorz & G. Piatetsky-Shapiro, eds, 'Proceedings of the Fourth International Conference on Knowledge Discovery and Data Mining', AAAI Press, pp. 249-253, 1998.

Kohavi R. and Wolpert, D. H., Bias Plus Variance Decomposition for Zero-One Loss Functions, Machine Learning: Proceedings of the 13th International Conference. Morgan Kaufman, 1996.

Kolen, J. F., and Pollack, J. B., Back propagation is sesitive to initial conditions. In Advances in Neural Information Processing Systems, Vol. 3, pp. 860-867 San Francisco, CA. Morgan Kaufmann, 1991.

Kononenko, I., Comparison of inductive and Naive Bayes learning approaches to automatic knowledge acquisition. In B. Wielinga (Ed.), Current Trends in Knowledge Acquisition, Amsterdam, The Netherlands IOS Press, 1990.

Kononenko, I., SemiNaive Bayes classifier, Proceedings of the Sixth European Working Session on Learning, pp. 206-219, Porto, Portugal: SpringerVerlag, 1991.

Krogh, A., and Vedelsby, J., Neural network ensembles, cross validation and active learning. In Advances in Neural Information Processing Systems 7, pp. 231-238 1995.

Kuhn H. W., The Hungarian method for the assignment problem. Naval Research Logistics Quarterly, 2:83–97, 1955.

Kuncheva, L., & Whitaker, C., Measures of diversity in classifier ensembles and their relationship with ensemble accuracy. Machine Learning, pp. 181–207, 2003.

Kusiak, A., Decomposition in Data Mining: An Industrial Case Study, IEEE Transactions on Electronics Packaging Manufacturing, Vol. 23, No. 4, pp.

345-353, 2000.

Kusiak, A., Rough Set Theory: A Data Mining Tool for Semiconductor Manufacturing, IEEE Transactions on Electronics Packaging Manufacturing, 24(1): 44-50, 2001A.

Kusiak, A., 2001, Feature Transformation Methods in Data Mining, IEEE Transactions on Elctronics Packaging Manufacturing, Vol. 24, No. 3, pp. 214–221, 2001B.

Kusiak A., Kurasek C., Data Mining of Printed-Circuit Board Defects, IEEE Transactions on Robotics and Automation, 17(2): 191-196, 2001.

Kusiak, E. Szczerbicki, and K. Park, A Novel Approach to Decomposition of Design Specifications and Search for Solutions, International Journal of Production Research, 29(7): 1391-1406, 1991.

Langley, P., Selection of relevant features in machine learning, in Proceedings of the AAAI Fall Symposium on Relevance, pp. 140-144, AAAI Press, 1994.

Langley, P. and Sage, S., Oblivious decision trees and abstract cases. in Working Notes of the AAAI-94 Workshop on Case-Based Reasoning, pp. 113-117, Seattle, WA: AAAI Press, 1994.

Langley, P. and Sage, S., Induction of selective Bayesian classifiers. in Proceedings of the Tenth Conference on Uncertainty in Artificial Intelligence, pp. 399-406. Seattle, WA: Morgan Kaufmann, 1994.

Larsen, B. and Aone, C. 1999. Fast and effective text mining using linear-time document clustering. In Proceedings of the 5th ACM SIGKDD, 16-22, San Diego, CA.

Last, M., Maimon, O. and Minkov, E., Improving Stability of Decision Trees, International Journal of Pattern Recognition and Artificial Intelligence, 16: 2,145-159, 2002.

Last M., Kandel A., Data Mining for Process and Quality Control in the Semiconductor Industry, in Data Mining for Design and Manufacturing: Methods and Applications, D. Braha (ed.), Kluwer Academic Publishers, pp. 207-234, 2001.

Lewis D., and Catlett J., Heterogeneous uncertainty sampling for supervised learning. In Machine Learning: Proceedings of the Eleventh Annual Conference, pp. 148-156 , New Brunswick, New Jersey, Morgan Kaufmann, 1994.

Lewis, D., and Gale, W., Training text classifiers by uncertainty sampling, In seventeenth annual international ACM SIGIR conference on research and development in information retrieval, pp. 3-12, 1994.

Li X. and Dubes R. C., Tree classifier design with a Permutation statistic, Pattern Recognition 19:229-235, 1986.

Liao Y., and Moody J., Constructing Heterogeneous Committees via Input Feature Grouping, in Advances in Neural Information Processing Systems, Vol.12, S.A. Solla, T.K. Leen and K.-R. Muller (eds.),MIT Press, 2000.

Lim X., Loh W.Y., and Shih X., A comparison of prediction accuracy, complexity, and training time of thirty-three old and new classification algorithms . Machine Learning 40:203-228, 2000.

Lin Y. K. and Fu K., Automatic classification of cervical cells using a binary tree classifier. Pattern Recognition, 16(1):69-80, 1983.

Liu H. & Motoda H., Feature Selection for Knowledge Discovery and Data Mining, Kluwer Academic Publishers, 1998.

Loh W.Y.,and Shih X., Split selection methods for classification trees. Statistica Sinica, 7: 815-840, 1997.

Loh W.Y. and Shih X., Families of splitting criteria for classification trees. Statistics and Computing 9:309-315, 1999.

Loh W.Y. and Vanichsetakul N., Tree-structured classification via generalized discriminant Analysis. Journal of the American Statistical Association, 83:715-728, 1988.

Long C., Bi-Decomposition of Function Sets Using Multi-Valued Logic, Eng.Doc. Dissertation, Technischen Universitat Bergakademie Freiberg 2003.

Lopez de Mantras R., A distance-based attribute selection measure for decision tree induction, Machine Learning 6:81-92, 1991.

Lu B.L., Ito M., Task Decomposition and Module Combination Based on Class Relations: A Modular Neural Network for Pattern Classification, IEEE Trans. on Neural Networks, 10(5):1244-1256, 1999.

Lu H., Setiono R., and Liu H., Effective Data Mining Using Neural Networks. IEEE Transactions on Knowledge and Data Engineering, 8 (6): 957-961, 1996.

Luba, T., Decomposition of multiple-valued functions, in Intl. Symposium on Multiple-Valued Logic', Bloomigton, Indiana, pp. 256-261, 1995.

Lubinsky D., Algorithmic speedups in growing classification trees by using an additive split criterion. Proc. AI&Statistics93, pp. 435-444, 1993.

Maimon O. and Last M., Knowledge Discovery and Data Mining: The Info-Fuzzy network (IFN) methodology, Kluwer Academic Publishers, 2000.

Maimon O., and Rokach, L. Data Mining by Attribute Decomposition with semiconductors manufacturing case study, in Data Mining for Design and Manufacturing: Methods and Applications, D. Braha (ed.), Kluwer Academic Publishers, pp. 311-336, 2001.

Maimon O. and Rokach L., "Improving supervised learning by feature decomposition", Proceedings of the Second International Symposium on Foundations of Information and Knowledge Systems, Lecture Notes in Computer Science, Springer, pp. 178-196, 2002.

Maimon, O., Rokach, L. and Cohen, S., 2002, Comparing Classification Models Using Expert Knowledge, Proceeding of the 6th World Multiconference on Systemics, Cybernetics and Informatics (SCI 2002).

Mansour, Y. and McAllester, D., Generalization Bounds for Decision Trees, in Proceedings of the 13th Annual Conference on Computer Learning Theory, pp. 69-80, San Francisco, Morgan Kaufmann, 2000.

Marcotorchino, J.F. and Michaud, P. Optimisation en Analyse Ordinale des Donns. Masson, Paris.

Margineantu D. and Dietterich T., Pruning adaptive boosting. In Proc. Fourteenth Intl. Conf. Machine Learning, pages 211–218, 1997.

Martin J. K., An exact probability metric for decision tree splitting and stopping. An Exact Probability Metric for Decision Tree Splitting and Stopping, Machine Learning, 28 (2-3):257-291, 1997.

Mehta M., Rissanen J., Agrawal R., MDL-Based Decision Tree Pruning. KDD 1995: pp. 216-221, 1995.

Mehta M., Agrawal R. and Rissanen J., SLIQ: A fast scalable classifier for data mining: In Proc. If the fifth Int'l Conference on Extending Database Technology (EDBT), Avignon, France, March 1996.

Meretakis, D. and Wthrich, B., Extending Nave Bayes Classifiers Using Long Itemsets, in Proceedings of the Fifth International Conference on Knowledge Discovery and Data Mining, pp. 165-174, San Diego, USA, 1999.

Merz, C. J. and Murphy. P.M., UCI Repository of machine learning databases. Irvine, CA: University of California, Department of Information and Computer Science, 1998.

Michalski R. S., A theory and methodology of inductive learning. Artificial Intelligence, 20:111- 161, 1983.

Michalski R. S., Understanding the nature of learning: issues and research directions, in R. Michalski, J. Carbonnel and T. Mitchell,eds, Machine Learning: An Artificial Intelligence Approach, Kaufmann, Paolo Alto, CA, pp. 3–25, 1986.

Michalski R. S., and Tecuci G.. Machine Learning, A Multistrategy Approach, Vol. J. Morgan Kaufmann, 1994.

Michie, D., Problem decomposition and the learning of skills, in Proceedings of the European Conference on Machine Learning, pp. 17-31, Springer-Verlag, 1995.

Michie D., Spiegelhalter D.J., Taylor C .C., Machine Learning, Neural and Statistical Classification, Prentice Hall, 1994.

Mingers J., An empirical comparison of pruning methods for decision tree induction. Machine Learning, 4(2):227-243, 1989.

Minsky M., Logical vs. Analogical or Symbolic vs. Connectionist or Neat vs. Scruffy, in Artificial Intelligence at MIT., Expanding Frontiers, Patrick H. Winston (Ed.), Vol 1, MIT Press, 1990. Reprinted in AI Magazine, 1991.

Mishra, S. K. and Raghavan, V. V., An empirical study of the performance of heuristic methods for clustering. In Pattern Recognition in Practice, E. S. Gelsema and L. N. Kanal, Eds. 425436, 1994.

Mitchell, T., Machine Learning, McGraw-Hill, 1997.

Mitchell, T., The need for biases in learning generalizations. Technical Report CBM-TR-117, Rutgers University, Department of Computer Science, New Brunswick, NJ, 1980.

Moody, J. and Darken, C., Fast learning in networks of locally tuned units. Neural Computations, 1(2):281-294, 1989.

Morgan J. N. and Messenger R. C., THAID: a sequential search program for the analysis of nominal scale dependent variables. Technical report, Institute for Social Research, Univ. of Michigan, Ann Arbor, MI, 1973.

Muller W., and Wysotzki F., Automatic construction of decision trees for classification. Annals of Operations Research, 52:231-247, 1994.

Murtagh, F. A survey of recent advances in hierarchical clustering algorithms which use cluster centers. Comput. J. 26 354-359, 1984.

Murthy S. K., Automatic Construction of Decision Trees from Data: A Multi-Disciplinary Survey. Data Mining and Knowledge Discovery, 2(4):345-389, 1998.

Murthy S. K., Kasif S., and Salzberg S.. A system for induction of oblique decision trees. Journal of Artificial Intelligence Research, 2:1-33, August 1994.

Naumov G.E., NP-completeness of problems of construction of optimal decision trees. Soviet Physics: Doklady, 36(4):270-271, 1991.

Neal R., Probabilistic inference using Markov Chain Monte Carlo methods. Tech. Rep. CRG-TR-93-1, Department of Computer Science, University of Toronto, Toronto, CA, 1993.

Ng, R. and Han, J. 1994. Very large data bases. In Proceedings of the 20th International Conference on Very Large Data Bases (VLDB94, Santiago, Chile, Sept.), VLDB Endowment, Berkeley, CA, 144155.

Niblett T., Constructing decision trees in noisy domains. In Proceedings of the Second European Working Session on Learning, pages 67-78, 1987.

Niblett T. and Bratko I., Learning Decision Rules in Noisy Domains, Proc. Expert Systems 86, Cambridge: Cambridge University Press, 1986.

Nowlan S. J., and Hinton G. E. Evaluation of adaptive mixtures of competing experts. In Advances in Neural Information Processing Systems, R. P. Lippmann, J. E. Moody, and D. S. Touretzky, Eds., vol. 3, pp. 774-780, Morgan Kaufmann Publishers Inc., 1991.

Oates, T., Jensen D., 1998, Large Datasets Lead to Overly Complex Models: An Explanation and a Solution, KDD 1998, pp. 294-298.

Ohno-Machado, L., and Musen, M. A. Modular neural networks for medical prognosis: Quantifying the benefits of combining neural networks for survival prediction. Connection Science 9, 1 (1997), 71-86.

Opitz, D. and Maclin, R., Popular Ensemble Methods: An Empirical Study, Journal of Artificial Research, 11: 169-198, 1999.

Pagallo, G. and Huassler, D., Boolean feature discovery in empirical learning, Machine Learning, 5(1): 71-99, 1990.

Parmanto, B., Munro, P. W., and Doyle, H. R., Improving committee diagnosis with resampling techinques. In Touretzky, D. S., Mozer, M. C., and Hesselmo, M. E. (Eds). Advances in Neural Information Processing Systems, Vol. 8, pp. 882-888 Cambridge, MA. MIT Press, 1996.

Pearl, J., Probabilistic Reasoning in Intelligent Systems: Networks of Plausible Inference. Morgan-Kaufmann, 1988.

Peng, F. and Jacobs R. A., and Tanner M. A., Bayesian Inference in Mixtures-of-Experts and Hierarchical Mixtures-of-Experts Models With an Application to Speech Recognition, Journal of the American Statistical Association, 1995.

Perkowski, M. A., A survey of literature on function decomposition, Technical report, GSRP Wright Laboratories, Ohio OH, 1995.

Perkowski, M.A., Luba, T., Grygiel, S., Kolsteren, M., Lisanke, R., Iliev, N., Burkey, P., Burns, M., Malvi, R., Stanley, C., Wang, Z., Wu, H., Yang, F., Zhou, S. and Zhang, J. S., Unified approach to functional decompositions of switching functions, Technical report, Warsaw University of Technology and Eindhoven University of Technology, 1995.

Perkowski, M., Jozwiak, L. and Mohamed, S., New approach to learning noisy Boolean functions, Proceedings of the Second International Conference on Computational Intelligence and Multimedia Applications, pp. 693–706, World Scientific, Australia, 1998.

Pfahringer, B., Controlling constructive induction in CiPF, In Bergadano, F. and De Raedt, L. (Eds.), Proceedings of the seventh European Conference on Machine Learning, pp. 242-256, Springer-Verlag, 1994.

Pfahringer, B., Bensusan H., and Giraud-Carrier C., Tell Me Who Can Learn You and I Can Tell You Who You are: Landmarking Various Learning Algorithms, In Proc. of the Seventeenth International Conference on Machine Learning (ICML2000), pages 743-750, 2000.

Poggio T., Girosi, F., Networks for Approximation and Learning, Proc. IEER, Vol 78(9): 1481-1496, Sept. 1990.

Pratt, L. Y., Mostow, J., and Kamm C. A., Direct Transfer of Learned Information Among Neural Networks, in: Proceedings of the Ninth National Conference on Artificial Intelligence, Anaheim, CA, 584-589, 1991.

Prodromidis, A. L., Stolfo, S. J. and Chan, P. K., Effective and efficient pruning of metaclassifiers in a distributed data mining system. Technical report CUCS-017-99, Columbia Univ., 1999.

Provost, F.J. and Kolluri, V., A Survey of Methods for Scaling Up Inductive Learning Algorithms, Proc. 3rd International Conference on Knowledge Discovery and Data Mining, 1997.

Provost, F., Jensen, D. and Oates, T., 1999, Efficient Progressive Sampling, In Proceedings of the Fifth International Conference on Knowledge Discovery and Data Mining, pp.23-32.

Quinlan, J.R. *Learning efficient classification procedures and their application to chess endgames.* R. Michalski, J. Carbonell, T. Mitchel. Machine learning: an AI approach. Los Altos, CA. Morgan Kaufman , 1983.

Quinlan, J.R., Induction of decision trees, Machine Learning 1, 81-106, 1986.

Quinlan, J.R., Simplifying decision trees, International Journal of Man-Machine Studies, 27, 221-234, 1987.

Quinlan, J.R., Decision Trees and Multivalued Attributes, J. Richards, ed., Machine Intelligence, V. 11, Oxford, England, Oxford Univ. Press, pp. 305-318, 1988.

Quinlan, J. R., Unknown attribute values in induction. In Segre, A. (Ed.), Proceedings of the Sixth International Machine Learning Workshop Cornell, New York. Morgan Kaufmann, 1989.

Quinlan, J. R., Unknown attribute values in induction. In Segre, A. (Ed.), Proceedings of the Sixth International Machine Learning Workshop Cornell, New York. Morgan Kaufmann, 1989.

Quinlan, J. R., C4.5: Programs for Machine Learning, Morgan Kaufmann, Los Altos, 1993.

Quinlan, J. R., Bagging, Boosting, and C4.5. In Proceedings of the Thirteenth National Conference on Artificial Intelligence, pages 725-730, 1996.

Quinlan, J. R. and Rivest, R. L., Inferring Decision Trees Using The Minimum

Description Length Principle. Information and Computation, 80:227-248, 1989.

Ragavan, H. and Rendell, L., Look ahead feature construction for learning hard concepts. In Proceedings of the Tenth International Machine Learning Conference: pp. 252-259, Morgan Kaufman, 1993.

Rahman, A. F. R., and Fairhurst, M. C. A new hybrid approach in combining multiple experts to recognize handwritten numerals. Pattern Recognition Letters, 18: 781-790,1997.

Rastogi, R., and Shim, K., PUBLIC: A Decision Tree Classifier that Integrates Building and Pruning,Data Mining and Knowledge Discovery, 4(4):315-344, 2000.

Ramamurti, V., and Ghosh, J., Structurally Adaptive Modular Networks for Non-Stationary Environments, IEEE Transactions on Neural Networks, 10 (1):152-160, 1999.

Rand, W. M., Objective criteria for the evaluation of clustering methods. Journal of the American Statistical Association, 66: 846–850, 1971.

Rao, R., Gordon, D., and Spears, W., For every generalization action, is there really an equal or opposite reaction? Analysis of conservation law. In Proc. of the Twelveth International Conference on Machine Learning, pp. 471-479. Morgan Kaufmann, 1995.

Ray, S., and Turi, R.H. Determination of Number of Clusters in K-Means Clustering and Application in Color Image Segmentation. Monash university, 1999.

R'enyi A., Probability Theory, North-Holland, Amsterdam, 1970

Buczak A. L. and Ziarko W., "Stages of The Discovery Process", Klosgen W. and Zytkow J. M. (Eds.), Handbook of Data Mining and Knowledge Discovery, pages 185-192. Oxford University Press, 2002.

Ridgeway, G., Madigan, D., Richardson, T. and O'Kane, J. (1998), "Interpretable Boosted Naive Bayes Classification", Proceedings of the Fourth International Conference on Knowledge Discovery and Data Mining, pp 101-104.

Rissanen, J., Stochastic complexity and statistical inquiry. World Scientific, 1989.

Rokach L. and Maimon O., "Theory and Application of Attribute Decomposition", Proceedings of the First IEEE International Conference on Data Mining, IEEE Computer Society Press, pp. 473-480, 2001

Ronco, E., Gollee, H., and Gawthrop, P. J., Modular neural network and self-decomposition. CSC Research Report CSC-96012, Centre for Systems and Control, University of Glasgow, 1996.

Rounds, E., A combined non-parametric approach to feature selection and binary decision tree design, Pattern Recognition 12, 313-317, 1980.

Rumelhart, D., G. Hinton and R. Williams, Learning internal representations through error propagation. In Parallel Distributed Processing: Explorations in the Microstructure of Cognition, Volume 1: Foundations, D. Rumelhart and J. McClelland (eds.) Cambridge, MA: MIT Press., pp 2540, 1986.

Saaty, X., The analytic hierarchy process: A 1993 overview. Central European Journal for Operations Research and Economics, Vol. 2, No. 2, p. 119-137, 1993.

Safavin S. R. and Landgrebe, D., A survey of decision tree classifier methodology. IEEE Trans. on Systems, Man and Cybernetics, 21(3):660-674, 1991.

Salzberg. S. L., On Comparing Classifiers: Pitfalls to Avoid and a Recommended Approach. Data Mining and Knowledge Discovery, 1: 312-327, Kluwer Academic Publishers, Bosto, 1997.

Samuel, A., Some studies in machine learning using the game of checkers II: Recent progress. IBM J. Res. Develop., 11:601-617, 1967.

Schaffer, C., Selecting a classification method by cross-validation. Machine Learning 13(1):135-143, 1993.

Schaffer J., A Conservation Law for Generalization Performance. In Proceedings of the 11th International Conference on Machine Learning: pp. 259-265, 1993.

Schapire, R.E., *The strength of week learnability*. In Machine learning 5(2), 197-227, 1990.

Schmitt , M., On the complexity of computing and learning with multiplicative neural networks, Neural Computation 14: 2, 241-301, 2002.

Schlimmer, J. C. , Efficiently inducing determinations: A complete and systematic search algorithm that uses optimal pruning. In Proceedings of the 1993 International Conference on Machine Learning: pp 284-290, San Mateo, CA, Morgan Kaufmann, 1993.

Seewald, A.K. and Fürnkranz, J., Grading classifiers, Austrian research institute for Artificial intelligence, 2001.

Selim, S.Z., and Ismail, M.A. K-means-type algorithms: a generalized convergence theorem and characterization of local optimality. In IEEE transactions on pattern analysis and machine learning, vol. PAMI-6, no. 1, January, 1984.

Selim, S. Z. AND Al-Sultan, K. 1991. A simulated annealing algorithm for the clustering problem. Pattern Recogn. 24, 10 (1991), 10031008.

Selfridge, O. G. Pandemonium: a paradigm for learning. In Mechanization of Thought Processes: Proceedings of a Symposium Held at the National Physical Laboratory, November, 1958, 513-526. London: H.M.S.O., 1958.

Servedio, R., On Learning Monotone DNF under Product Distributions. Information and Computation 193, pp. 57-74, 2004.

Sethi, K., and Yoo, J. H., Design of multicategory, multifeature split decision trees using perceptron learning. Pattern Recognition, 27(7):939-947, 1994.

Shapiro, A. D. and Niblett, T., Automatic induction of classification rules for a chess endgame, in M. R. B. Clarke, ed., Advances in Computer Chess 3, Pergamon, Oxford, pp. 73-92, 1982.

Shapiro, A. D., Structured induction in expert systems, Turing Institute Press in association with Addison-Wesley Publishing Company, 1987.

Sharkey, A., On combining artificial neural nets, Connection Science, Vol. 8, pp.299-313, 1996.

Sharkey, A., Multi-Net Iystems, In Sharkey A. (Ed.) Combining Artificial Neural Networks: Ensemble and Modular Multi-Net Systems. pp. 1-30, Springer-Verlag, 1999.

Shafer, J. C., Agrawal, R. and Mehta, M. , SPRINT: A Scalable Parallel Classifier for Data Mining, Proc. 22nd Int. Conf. Very Large Databases, T. M. Vijayaraman and Alejandro P. Buchmann and C. Mohan and Nandlal L. Sarda (eds), 544-555, Morgan Kaufmann, 1996.

Shilen, S., Multiple binary tree classifiers. Pattern Recognition 23(7): 757-763, 1990.

Shilen, S., Nonparametric classification using matched binary decision trees. Pattern Recognition Letters 13: 83-87, 1992.

Sklansky, J. and Wassel, G. N., Pattern classifiers and trainable machines. SpringerVerlag, New York, 1981.

Sneath, P., and Sokal, R. Numerical Taxonomy. W.H. Freeman Co., San Francisco, CA, 1973.

Sohn S. Y., Choi, H., Ensemble based on Data Envelopment Analysis, ECML Meta Learning workshop, Sep. 4, 2001.

Sonquist, J. A., Baker E. L., and Morgan, J. N., Searching for Structure. Institute for Social Research, Univ. of Michigan, Ann Arbor, MI, 1971.

Spirtes, P., Glymour C., and Scheines, R., Causation, Prediction, and Search. Springer Verlag, 1993.

Steuer R.E.,Multiple Criteria Optimization: Theory, Computation and Application. John Wiley, New York, 1986.

Strehl A. and Ghosh J., Clustering Guidance and Quality Evaluation Using Relationship-based Visualization, Proceedings of Intelligent Engineering Systems Through Artificial Neural Networks, 5-8 November 2000, St. Louis, Missouri, USA, pp 483-488.

Strehl, A., Ghosh, J., Mooney, R.: Impact of similarity measures on web-page clustering. In Proc. AAAI Workshop on AI for Web Search, pp 58–64, 2000.

Tadepalli, P. and Russell, S., Learning from examples and membership queries with structured determinations, Machine Learning, 32(3), pp. 245-295, 1998.

Taylor P. C., and Silverman, B. W., Block diagrams and splitting criteria for classification trees. Statistics and Computing, 3(4):147-161, 1993.

Tibshirani, R., Walther, G. and Hastie, T. (2000). Estimating the number of clusters in a dataset via the gap statistic. Tech. Rep. 208, Dept. of Statistics, Stanford University.

Towell, G. Shavlik, J., Knowledge-based artificial neural networks, Artificial Intelligence, 70: 119-165, 1994.

Tresp, V. and Taniguchi, M. Combining estimators using non-constant weighting functions. In Tesauro, G., Touretzky, D., & Leen, T. (Eds.), Advances in Neural Information Processing Systems, volume 7: pp. 419-426, The MIT Press, 1995.

Tsallis C., Possible Generalization of Boltzmann-Gibbs Statistics, J. Stat.Phys., 52, 479-487, 1988.

Tumer, K. and Ghosh J., Error Correlation and Error Reduction in Ensemble Classifiers, Connection Science, Special issue on combining artificial neural networks: ensemble approaches, 8 (3-4): 385-404, 1996.

Tumer, K., and Ghosh J., Linear and Order Statistics Combiners for Pattern Classification, in Combining Articial Neural Nets, A. Sharkey (Ed.), pp.

127-162, Springer-Verlag, 1999.

Tumer, K., and Ghosh J., Robust Order Statistics based Ensembles for Distributed Data Mining. In Kargupta, H. and Chan P., eds, Advances in Distributed and Parallel Knowledge Discovery , pp. 185-210, AAAI/MIT Press, 2000.

Tyron R. C. and Bailey D.E. Cluster Analysis. McGraw-Hill, 1970.

Urquhart, R. Graph-theoretical clustering, based on limited neighborhood sets. Pattern recognition, vol. 15, pp. 173-187, 1982.

Utgoff, P. E., Perceptron trees: A case study in hybrid concept representations. Connection Science, 1(4):377-391, 1989.

Utgoff, P. E., Incremental induction of decision trees. Machine Learning, 4:161-186, 1989.

Utgoff, P. E., Decision tree induction based on efficient tree restructuring, Machine Learning 29 (1):5-44, 1997.

Utgoff, P. E., and Clouse, J. A., A Kolmogorov-Smirnoff Metric for Decision Tree Induction, Technical Report 96-3, University of Massachusetts, Department of Computer Science, Amherst, MA, 1996.

Valiant, L. G. (1984). A theory of the learnable. Communications of the ACM 1984, pp. 1134-1142.

Van Rijsbergen, C. J., Information Retrieval. Butterworth, ISBN 0-408-70929-4, 1979.

Van Zant, P., Microchip fabrication: a practical guide to semiconductor processing, New York: McGraw-Hill, 1997.

Vapnik, V.N., The Nature of Statistical Learning Theory. Springer-Verlag, New York, 1995.

Veyssieres, M.P. and Plant, R.E. Identification of vegetation state-and-transition domains in California's hardwood rangelands. University of California, 1998.

Wallace, C. S., MML Inference of Predictive Trees, Graphs and Nets. In A. Gammerman (ed), Computational Learning and Probabilistic Reasoning, pp 43-66, Wiley, 1996.

Wallace, C. S., and Patrick J., Coding decision trees, Machine Learning 11: 7-22, 1993.

Wallace C. S. and Dowe D. L., Intrinsic classification by mml – the snob program. In Proceedings of the 7th Australian Joint Conference on Artificial Intelligence, pages 37-44, 1994.

Wan, W. and Perkowski, M. A., A new approach to the decomposition of incompletely specified functions based on graph-coloring and local transformations and its application to FPGAmapping, In Proc. of the IEEE EURO-DAC '92, pp. 230-235, 1992.

Wang, X. and Yu, Q. Estimate the number of clusters in web documents via gap statistic. May 2001.

Ward, J. H. Hierarchical grouping to optimize an objective function. Journal of the American Statistical Association, 58:236-244, 1963.

Weigend, A. S., Mangeas, M., and Srivastava, A. N. Nonlinear gated experts for time-series - discovering regimes and avoiding overfitting. International

Journal of Neural Systems 6(5):373-399, 1995.

Wolpert, D.H., Stacked Generalization, Neural Networks, Vol. 5, pp. 241-259, Pergamon Press, 1992.

Wolpert, D. H., The relationship between PAC, the statistical physics framework, the Bayesian framework, and the VC framework. In D. H. Wolpert, editor, The Mathematics of Generalization, The SFI Studies in the Sciences of Complexity, pages 117-214. AddisonWesley, 1995.

Wolpert, D. H., "The lack of a priori distinctions between learning algorithms," Neural Computation 8: 1341–1390, 1996.

Wyse, N., Dubes, R. and Jain, A.K., A critical evaluation of intrinsic dimensionality algorithms, Pattern Recognition in Practice, E.S. Gelsema and L.N. Kanal (eds.), North-Holland, pp. 415–425, 1980.

Zahn, C. T., Graph-theoretical methods for detecting and describing gestalt clusters. IEEE trans. Comput. C-20 (Apr.), 68-86, 1971.

Zaki, M. J., Ho C. T., and Agrawal, R., Scalable parallel classification for data mining on shared- memory multiprocessors, in Proc. IEEE Int. Conf. Data Eng., Sydney, Australia, WKDD99, pp. 198– 205, 1999.

Zaki, M. J., Ho C. T., Eds., Large- Scale Parallel Data Mining. New York: Springer- Verlag, 2000.

Zantema, H., and Bodlaender H. L., Finding Small Equivalent Decision Trees is Hard, International Journal of Foundations of Computer Science, 11(2):343-354, 2000.

Zeira, G., Maimon, O., Last, M. and Rokach, L,, Change detection in classification models of data mining, Data Mining in Time Series Databases. World Scientific Publishing, 2003.

Zenobi, G., and Cunningham, P. Using diversity in preparing ensembles of classifiers based on different feature subsets to minimize generalization error. In Proceedings of the European Conference on Machine Learning, 2001.

Zhou, Z. H., and Tang, W., Selective Ensemble of Decision Trees, in Guoyin Wang, Qing Liu, Yiyu Yao, Andrzej Skowron (Eds.): Rough Sets, Fuzzy Sets, Data Mining, and Granular Computing, 9th International Conference, RSFDGrC, Chongqing, China, Proceedings. Lecture Notes in Computer Science 2639, pp.476-483, 2003.

Zhou, Z. H., Wu J., Tang W., Ensembling neural networks: many could be better than all. Artificial Intelligence 137: 239-263, 2002.

Zupan, B., Bohanec, M., Demsar J., and Bratko, I., Feature transformation by function decomposition, IEEE intelligent systems & their applications, 13: 38-43, 1998.

Zupan, B., Bratko, I., Bohanec, M. and Demsar, J., 2000, Induction of concept hierarchies from noisy data, in Proceedings of the Seventeenth International Conference on Machine Learning (ICML-2000), San Francisco, CA, pp. 1199-1206.

Index